For Instruction in Righteousness

A Topical Reference Guide for Biblical Child-Training

by

Pam Forster

Doorposts

Doorposts
5905 SW Lookingglass Dr., Gaston, OR 97119

Table of Contents

How to Use This Book 1

Sins of a Proud Heart

Pride 19

Self-Righteousness 32

Shifting Blame/Making Excuses 37

Hypocrisy 40

Stubbornness/Self-Will 46

Disobedience 49

Defiance 57

Scoffer/Scorner 62

Arguing/Contention 68

Complaining/Ingratitude 77

Brawling Woman 83

Vanity/Overconcern for Beauty 89

Judging Others 93

Sins of Discontent

Selfishness/Greed 98

Confidence in Riches 106

Envy/Jealousy 111

Covetousness 116

Theft 120

Rules for Borrowers 124

Sins of Unbelief

Easily Swayed/Double-minded 127

Fainthearted/Easily Discouraged 136

Depression 143

Fear 150

Worry/Anxiety 155

Sins of an Undisciplined Life

Laziness 161

Unfaithful Employee 171

Haste 176

Impatience 181

Anger 185

Gluttony/Pleasure-Seeking 191

Immorality 194

Sinful Thought Life 201

Immodesty 206

Wastefulness/Carelessness 210

Drunkenness 214

Sins of the Tongue
    Lying/Deceit/Dishonesty 217
    False Witness 224
    Gossip/Slander/Tattletale 227
    Meddling/Busybody 233
    Foolish, Unclean Speech 236
    Flattery 239
Sins of an Unloving Heart
    Hatred 243
    Bitterness 247
    Hitting/Biting/Kicking 251
    Revenge 255
    Cruelty/Bullying 259
    Unkind Speech 266
    Insensitivity/Lack of Compassion 272
Sins in Relationships
    Bad Friendships 278
    Poor Manners 286
    Teasing/Troublemaking 291
Comparisons of the Obedient and the Disobedient
    Foolishness vs. Wisdom 293
    Wickedness vs. Righteousness 296

    Comparison Worksheet 301
    Comparison Worksheet Sample 302
    Resources 303
    Doorposts Products 309
    Order Form 313

And that from a child thou hast known the holy scriptures, which are able to make thee wise unto salvation through faith which is in Christ Jesus.

All scripture is given by inspiration of God, and is profitable for doctrine, for reproof, for correction, for instruction in righteousness:

That the man of God may be perfect, thoroughly furnished unto all good works. (II Timothy 3:15-17)

This book is dedicated to the Hobby Brooks family, who have always provided the friendly push to keep us going in the right direction (even when I pushed back a little). ☺

Introduction

This book is the result of ignorance, not expertise. Our children are not perfect. On the contrary, they have very clearly inherited their parents' sinful natures. That's why we needed this book! Raising children is a humbling experience; each new baby exposes more of my weaknesses, more of my inadequacies, more of my need to rely on my sovereign Lord for strength and guidance.

We put this book together so that we could use it in our own family. It is the result of our prayer for God's wisdom, "Give therefore Thy servant an understanding heart to judge Thy people, that I may discern between good and bad." (I Kgs. 3:9)

I am not a family counselor; I am just a mother. I am not a Bible scholar; I am just a believer, studying the Bible as the guidebook for my life. The content of this book is simply a record of some of that study.

God's Word has the answers to our questions. Dr. Spock doesn't. Psychologists don't. Politicians don't. A brief glance at our society is proof enough that man's answers, divorced from God's law, are merely roads toward confusion, destruction, and hell.

My generation is the Dr. Spock generation; many of our parents were deceived into believing that man, reason, science, psychology, anything but a faithful interpretation of God's Word, would help them raise their families. Many of us, now parents ourselves, are left floundering with no real examples of how to be a godly father, how to love our husbands and children, how to train a god-fearing generation of young men and women.

We must turn back to the Bible, the source of all wisdom. In it we will find all that we need to know to be godly fathers and mothers.

In a conversation on the way to the grocery store one morning, my 9-year-old son was astonished to discover that most people don't know how to plant a garden anymore! I described my early gardening experiences -- standing in the middle of a freshly tilled thistle patch, with a how-to-garden book in one hand, and a shovel in the other. He thought that was pretty funny.

There is a lot of lost territory to reclaim, one step at a time -- skills, knowledge, and basic morals have been lost as men and women succumb to Satan's lie, believing that we can live life apart from God's commands and instructions.

Most of us don't know how to "grow" a family anymore.

We are training our children with the Bible, our how-to book, in one hand, and the rod in the other. This book is a compilation, *far* from exhaustive, of principles we have gleaned from Scripture as we have prayed and searched for answers.

The Bible is the authority. We have simply done some topical arranging, and we offer some ideas for practical application of Biblical principles in everyday life. I'm sure you will be able to add plenty of your own insights as you study the Scriptures given here.

It is our prayer that <u>For Instruction in Righteousness</u> will be a tool to help parents like us reclaim a little more territory for our King as we raise up our sons and daughters for His glory.

How To Use This Book

This book is a topical Bible for parents. It is divided into 53 chapters. Each chapter deals with one specific area of misbehavior or child training, listing verses that tell us about that topic. These verses can help us as parents to more effectively teach and discipline our children.

Scripture Is Our Authority

God's Word needs to be at the center of all our training. Moses outlined the perfect curriculum for parents.

> *And thou shalt love the Lord thy God with all thine*
> *heart, and with all thy soul, and with all thy might...*

First, if we are to serve God in training up godly men and women, we must be godly men and women ourselves. We must love our Lord and King with all our heart, soul, and might.

> *And these words which I command you this day shall*
> *be in thine heart...*

Second, God's Word must be in our hearts. Scripture should be such an integral part of our being that it becomes the very warp into which all the rest of the fabric of life is woven. We must acknowledge His Word as the final authority in all areas of life.

> *And thou shalt teach them diligently unto thy children,*
> *and shall talk of them when thou sittest in thine house, and*
> *when thou walkest by the way, and when thou liest down,*
> *and when thou risest up.*
> *And thou shalt bind them for a sign upon thine hand,*
> *and they shall be as frontlets between thine eyes.*
> *And thou shalt write them upon the post of thy house,*
> *and on thy gates. Deuteronomy 6:6-9*

Third, we should see and apply Scriptural principles during the everyday occurrences of life, and we should teach them to our children, both by our words and by our example.

What does God say about the sins that we, as parents, must constantly face in our own hearts, and in day-to-day life with our children? A child needs to know what God says about his misbehavior, what He specifically says about hitting a little brother, taking away a toy, "borrowing" sister's blouse without permission, making fun of the next-door neighbor, telling a Mommy a lie, disobeying Daddy's instruction. He needs to understand the consequences of sin in his life.

He needs to understand that the authority that we, as parents, exercise over him is delegated to us by God. When we discipline a child for wrongdoing we do so because God says his action is wrong, not because of some arbitrary standard we have fabricated.

God's Word should always be our standard, our pattern, our authority -- as we judge our children's actions and as we discipline them for sinful actions and attitudes.

II Timothy 3:16 says:

"All Scripture is given by inspiration of God, and is profitable for doctrine, for reproof, for correction, for instruction in righteousness."

Psalm 119:130 says,

"The entrance of thy words giveth light; it giveth understanding unto the simple."

Hebrews 4:12 tells us that,

"The Word of God is quick, and powerful, and sharper than any two-edged sword, piercing even to the dividing asunder of soul and spirit, and of the joints and marrow, and is a discerner of the thoughts and intents of the heart."

Psalm 119:105 says,

"Thy Word is a lamp unto my feet, and a light unto my path."

Psalm 19:8 reminds us that,

"The commandment of the Lord is pure, enlightening the eyes."

Psalm 119:9 declares the Bible and obedience to it as the means of cleansing our hearts of their sinful ways,

"Wherewithal shall a young man cleanse his way? by taking heed thereto according to Thy word."

And Psalm 119:11 tells us that God's Word can help us overcome temptation,

"Thy Word have I hid in my heart, that I might not sin against Thee."

God's Word, the Bible, is the authoritative how-to book on raising children.

Scripture Is Our Instruction Manual

Scripture gives us, as God's delegated authorities in the family, many principles to guide us in our responsibilities.

I Peter 2:14 says that the authorities God places over us are sent by Him *"for the punishment of evildoers, and for the praise of them that do well."*

Hebrews 3:13 says that we should,

"exhort one another daily, while it is called Today; lest there be in any of you an evil heart of unbelief, in departing from the living God."

Galatians 6:1 tells us,

"If a man be overtaken in a fault, ye which are spiritual, restore such an one in the spirit of meekness; considering thyself, lest thou also be tempted."

I Thessalonians 5:14 exhorts us to *"warn them that are unruly..."*

Isaiah 38:19 tells us that *"the father to the children shall make known Thy truth."*

In Acts 20:32, Paul says, as we should be able to say to our children,

"And now, brethren, I commend you to God, and to the word of His grace, which is able to build you up, and to give you an inheritance among all them which are sanctified."

In Ecclesiastes 8:11, the wisest man on earth tells us that,

"because sentence against an evil work is not executed speedily, therefore the heart of the sons of men is fully set in them to do evil."

II Samuel 23:3 says,

"He that ruleth over men must be just, ruling in the fear of God."

And Ephesians 6:4 exhorts,

"Ye fathers, provoke not your children to wrath: but bring them up in the nurture and admonition of the Lord."

From these verses we can surmise that among our many responsibilities are the following:

1. Punish a child when he transgresses God's law. (I Pet. 2:14)
2. Praise and encourage a child when he obeys God's law. (I Pet. 2:14)
3. Protect our children from hardened hearts by daily exhorting and restoring a child with a meek and loving spirit. (Heb. 3:13. Gal.6:1)
4. Warn the unruly child of the inevitable consequences of his disobedience. (I Thess. 5:14)
5. Constantly direct the child to God's Word for guidance, and teach him its truth. (Isa. 38:19, Acts 20:32)
6. Punish the child promptly and consistently so that sin does not become a habit in his life. (Eccles. 8:11)
7. Be an example of God's justice as we rule over our children.

(II Sam. 23:3, Eph. 6:4)

In this book we have categorized Scripture in a way that will help you to better serve God and your family in these duties:

To help you punish the wrongdoer and praise the righteous, each chapter offers a list of Bible verses that *describe the cursings that result from disobedience and the blessings that come from obedience. We also offer ideas for discipline and rewards* that are directly patterned after these Scriptures.

To help you in daily exhorting and encouraging your children with a humble spirit, *Scripture is listed topically for easy access.* If you make it a project to carefully study and meditate on the Scriptures in each of these chapters, many verses, truths, and illustrations will come to mind as you go through the day with your family. I am amazed at the "renewing" of my mind as I have studied and organized and prayed over these Scriptures during the past two or three years.

It is also much easier to maintain a proper spirit while reproving a child if Scripture is established as the authority. Our children are much more open to correction when God's standard, not ours, is held up before them.

To help you warn the unruly child, you can refer to an appropriate chapter, and then go through, verse by verse, showing him *exactly what God says will happen to the person who continues to sin in this way.* This is sobering information!

The *topical listing of Scripture* makes it much easier to *counsel your child from God's Word.* Study through the verses together as a family or in a special study time with one son or daughter. Or teach the child basic Bible study methods and let him study on his own through a listing of Scripture on a particular area.

Your own personal study of these passages will also enable you to more naturally instruct your children throughout the day. You will be able to truly *exhort him from Scripture,* teaching him in God's ways instead of scolding and nagging.

I can think of two main factors that influence how consistently and quickly I discipline a wayward child -- how lazy I'm feeling, and how ignorant I'm feeling. Sometimes it's just too much work to figure out *how* to discipline him. I don't know what to do with him! That makes it awfully tempting to ignore him, which in turn tempts him to repeat the offense, setting a pattern which can only be broken by a faithful, diligent parent under the Holy Spirit's direction.

Scripture categorized by topic makes it much easier to turn to God's Word for guidance in disciplining our children. We can quickly look to see what God says should happen to this child, and the suggestions we offer for discipline can stimulate your own imagination as you seek to apply God's Word in training your children.

Finally, we can picture God's just character before our children when we claim His Word as the authority in our "Household Law." If the Bible is our authority, our children will grow to understand that "right" and "wrong" are based on God's standards, not our own personal standards. These standards will not change when our children grow up and leave the authority of our home.

Our goal is to pattern the discipline of our children after God's method of disciplining His children -- working within the framework of covenants, outlining cursings that will result from disobedience and the blessings that reward obedience.

This creates a righteous family "judicial system," imparting peace and justice among family members. It also exhibits, within the home, God's righteous pattern for judicial law and order in government.

Scripture Is Our Example

The Bible also has plenty to teach us about teaching! It is a teaching book. It supplies the pattern we need to be effective teachers and counselors to our children.

There are four main principles that we have tried to facilitate in the listings we have included in each chapter:
1. Arouse the listener's curiosity and attention.
2. Involve the listener emotionally.
3. Help the listener remember.
4. Establish covenants.

Over and over in the Biblical accounts prophets and teachers *arouse the curiosity and attention* of their listeners. They draw them into their message with *object lessons, parables, and proverbs*.

Object Lessons:

The Old Testament prophets put on some amazing "performances" that graphically illustrated God's truth, and certainly attracted attention! Isaiah, Jeremiah, and Ezekiel offer great inspiration for object lessons! Bare feet, sashes, yokes, wine bottles, sighs, and sticks left spectators begging for answers! *"Won't you tell us what these things are to us, that thou doest so?"* (Ezek. 24:19) *"Why are you sighing?"* (Ezek. 21:7) *"Won't you show us what you mean by these?"* (Ezek. 37:18)

Scripture gives us many pictures to think about. In each chapter of this book we list verses that tell what the Bible compares man to when he indulges in sin. These comparisons are good material for object lessons. A quick little object lesson or an elaborate experiment can gain your child's attention and lead him into a frame of mind that leaves him much more teachable and open to your instruction. Use these ideas to heighten your child's interest in what you have to say to him. Object lessons also help a child to remember what you have taught him.

Parables:

Jesus constantly taught with memorable stories and parables that caught people's attention and curiosity. He spoke of everyday happenings and occupations that people could readily understand and relate to -- building houses, sowing seeds, attending weddings, caring for grapevines, searching for lost sheep and coins.

The stories were interesting, and left people open and waiting for their interpretations. Even those who scoffed at Jesus' teachings understood the meaning of many of his stories, whether they wanted to or not.

We have listed appropriate parables in each chapter of this book, which can be used as effective teaching tools with our children, just as they have effectively convicted sinners like us throughout the centuries.

Proverbs:

The wisest man in history knew how to teach! When he wanted to teach his son important truths, he taught them in the form of *proverbs*.

Look at the book of Proverbs -- short, pithy, straight-to-the-point distillations of truth, that leave us with plenty to think about. We have to ask ourselves, "What does that mean?" We have to think; we have to study the pictures that Proverbs bring to mind, and discern their subtle meaning.

We can read the book of Proverbs over and over and the Holy Spirit can always reveal new truths to us. We need to draw from the Proverbs when training up our children. They arouse curiosity, paint powerful mental images, and help us remember the important spiritual truths that they are teaching us.

Read the Proverbs together each day as a family. Quote an appropriate Proverb when situations arise throughout the day. Read one Proverb and have your children illustrate it with their felt pens or crayons, or you do the drawing and let the family identify the Proverb.

The Bible also shows us the *importance of drawing the listener emotionally into our message.*

Stories:

Look at the outcome of Nathan's confrontation with David after his adultery and murder. Nathan told David a story about sheep, a topic of interest to him. David became emotionally involved with the story, and quickly pronounced a just sentence for the pitiless man who had stolen and killed the pet lamb. He, in essence, pronounced his own judgment before Nathan even confronted him. His heart was prepared for reproof, and he quickly repented.

In each section, this book lists Bible stories that illustrate the consequences of sin and the blessings of resisting temptation to sin. In the margins of the pages, write down notes that will help you recall *stories from your own life* that also illustrate these truths.

Also, write down references to good, illustrative stories from *books and history*. If you're the creative type, make up some teaching stories to tell your children.

Everyone loves a story; stories can help our children remember a truth in a way that nothing else can.

Songs:

Songs are another effective way to involve your child emotionally while you instruct him in God's Word. The Psalms are full of truth and comfort for our souls.

Colossians 3:16 says,

> *"Let the word of Christ dwell in you richly in all wisdom; teaching and admonishing one another in psalms and hymns and spiritual songs, singing with grace in your hearts to the Lord."*

Sing the Psalms and hymns with your family, play recordings of the Psalms and other edifying music in your home, compose Scripture songs together, sing good, uplifting songs as you work throughout the day.

In the margins of the pages in this book, jot down recordings and hymns and songs with lyrics that relate to the sins discussed in each chapter. (For example, "Great Is Thy Faithfulness" is a wonderful song for those of us who are prone to worry or fear.)

Use these songs as another way to train your children in the way they should go.

History:

We can also help our children *remember* what they have learned by teaching them from *man's experience in the past.* History study can be a dry collection of facts and dates, or it can be a very exciting encounter with men and women from bygone years. Read *stories*, reenact *stories*; discuss the choices man has made throughout history, and the resultant judgment or blessing that those decisions have consistently brought.

God, in His Word, teaches us from history:

I Corinthians 10:1-13 offers a concise summary of Israel's rebellious decisions. Verse 6 tells us,

> *"Now these things were our <u>examples</u>, to the intent we should not lust after evil things, as they also lusted."*

Verses 11-13 also tell us,

> *"Now all these things happened unto them for <u>ensamples</u>: and they are written for our <u>admonition</u>, upon whom the ends of the world are come. Wherefore let him that thinketh he standeth take heed lest he fall. There hath no temptation taken you but such as is common to man..."*

History is given to us as examples, and for our instruction. We can learn from the mistakes of others.

History can also provide heroes for our children -- men and women they can admire and respect, men and women who have demonstrated faithfulness to our Lord.

Hebrews 11 and 12 gives us a tour through a Hall of Fame unlike any other that our modern-day sports world could provide. Contemporary heroes the world sets before our children are largely ungodly, but talented, people who are misusing the abilities God has given them.

These chapters in Hebrews recall the "great cloud of witnesses" who have stood firm and faithful to God's Word throughout history, Noah, Abraham, Sarah, Joseph, Moses and his parents, Rahab, Gideon, David, men and women who chose to suffer, who believed God's promises,

> *"who through faith subdued kingdoms, wrought righteousness, obtained promises, stopped the mouths of lions, quenched the violence of fire, escaped the edge of the sword, out of weakness were made strong, waxed valiant in fight, turned to flight the armies of the aliens.*
>
> *"Women received their dead raised to life again: and others were tortured, not accepting deliverance; that they might obtain a better resurrection: and others had trial of cruel mockings and scourgings, yea, moreover of bonds and imprisonment: they were stoned, they were sawn asunder, were tempted, were slain with the sword: they wandered about in sheepskins and goatskins; being destitute, afflicted, tormented; (Of whom the world was not worthy:) they wandered in deserts, and in mountains, and in dens and caves of the earth."*

What encouragement these flesh-and-blood heroes can provide! They are testimony of God's grace and strength that are provided for those who are willing to obey Him! They witness to us and our children that we can follow our Lord anywhere, just as these men and women did.

The Psalms give us some wonderful recountings of God's faithfulness throughout history.

In Psalm 89:1, David says,

> *"I will sing of the mercies of the Lord for ever: with my mouth will I make known thy faithfulness to all generations."*

Psalms 83, 105, 106, 107, 135, and 136 are all examples of these songs that, in great detail, review God's mercy throughout history. Take time to study these Psalms with your children. Almost every verse refers to a story from the Bible, historical events full of lessons for us, testimony after testimony of God's great faithfulness and mercy.

These Psalms are in the Bible for our instruction and encouragement. Psalm 78:2-8 reminds us of history's role in the training of our children,

> *"I will open my mouth in a parable: I will utter dark sayings of old: which we have heard and known, and our fathers have told us. We will not hide them from their children, shewing to the generation to come the praises of the Lord, and his strength, and his wonderful works that he hath done. For he established a testimony in Jacob, and appointed a law in Israel, which he commanded our fathers that they should make them known to their children: that the generation to come might know them, even the children which should be born: who should arise and declare them to their children: that they might set their hope in God, and not forget the works of God, but keep his commandments: and might not be as their fathers, a stubborn and rebellious generation; a generation that set not their heart aright, and whose spirit was not steadfast with God."*

The rest of the chapter then goes on to relate the story of God's wrath against the disobedient.

We do not want our children to be "as their fathers, a stubborn and rebellious generation." We do not want them to experience the fearful discipline that comes from disobedience, just as it has always come to the disobedient throughout history.

History proves out the truth of Proverbs 13:13,

> *"Whoso despiseth the word shall be destroyed: but he that feareth the commandment shall be rewarded."*

Let's use history, throughout the ages, and our own personal history, to teach our children of God's justice. Study history through the "eyeglasses" of Scripture -- always looking for demonstrations of God's truth in man's actions and choices. Study American history from a godly perspective. Go back to copies of original documents -- journals, letters, etc. -- that give the true story. Use the many good books that aren't afraid to tell us of the providential hand of God in our nation's history. (The Light and the Glory and From Sea to Shining Sea are good starting points. Also the little book The Bulletproof George Washington impressed upon my heart, like nothing else ever has, the truth that God will not allow anything to end my life until *He* is finished with me here on earth.)

Give witness to God's faithfulness in your own life. Tell your children stories of God's hand in your life, and gather up the rich stories of your ancestors to tell them. Write down your stories, so they can be passed on to your children, *"showing to the generation to come the praises of the Lord, and His strength, and His wonderful works that He hath done."* (Ps. 78:4)

Memorials and Celebrations:

Another effective way to teach our children is in the form of *memorials and celebrations*. I write these words on the day our country celebrates as "Memorial Day," a day set aside to remember the bravery and sacrifice of the men who have helped protect our freedoms throughout history. We use this day to remember those men. We read stories of Congressional Medal of Honor winners. The boys wear their camouflage and set up obstacle courses and have "bivouac" (a meal of individual canned and packaged foods) and a campout in the living room. We visit a national cemetery. Other years we have watched videos of Sergeant York and The Red Badge of Courage.

We want our children to understand that our freedoms have been dearly purchased. We want them to see that selfishness, cowardice, and covetousness will cost us our freedom.

Memorial Day is also a good day to remember our ancestors. Look at old pictures, retell old stories. Visit gravesites, and remember with thanksgiving the lives that have made ours possible.

Memorial Day can be a teaching day.

God established memorials. Why did He tell the Israelites to observe the Passover each year?

> *"And thou shalt show thy son in that day, saying, 'This is done because of that which the Lord did unto me when I came forth out of Egypt." (Ex. 13:8)*

When, in the future, Jewish boys asked,"What is this?" the fathers were to answer, *"By strength of hand the Lord brought us out from Egypt, from the house of bondage..."* (Ex. 13:14)

The Passover was a memorial, an opportunity to teach children about God's deliverance of the Israelites from Egypt.

There were other feasts -- the "Feast of First Fruits" (Deut. 16:9-12) and the "Feast of Booths" (from which our Pilgrim fathers derived their Thanksgiving feast.) (Deut. 16:13-15) These were days of remembrance, days of thanksgiving, days of important lessons for children.

Communion, the Lord's Supper, is a memorial. "This do in remembrance of me," Jesus told His disciples,

> *"For as often as ye eat this bread, and drink this cup, ye do shew the Lord's death till he come." (I Cor. 11:26)*

Communion reminds us of Christ's death for us; it can be a powerful teaching tool for children.

There were other memorials established in the Bible. An omer of manna was *"kept for your generations; that they may see the bread wherewith I have fed you in the wilderness, when I brought you forth from the land of Egypt."* (Ex. 16:32)

The priest wore two stones on the shoulder of his ephod, *"for a memorial."* (Ex. 28:12) He wore the 12 stones on the breastplate, *"for a memorial."* (Ex. 28:29)

God gave Joshua specific instructions for erecting a monument of 12 stones at the Jordan River so that when children later asked their fathers, "What mean ye by these stones?" the fathers could answer,

"That the waters of Jordan were cut off before the ark of the covenant of the Lord; when it passed over Jordan, the waters of Jordan were cut off: and these stones shall be for a memorial unto the children of Israel for ever." (Josh. 4:7)

After defeat of the Philistines, Samuel set up the stone, "Ebenezer", a stone that proclaimed, "Hitherto hath the Lord helped us."

These monuments and memorials were teaching opportunities for Israelite parents.

Holidays are memorials. Christmas and Easter celebrate the greatest events in history. Independence Day commemorates the beginnings of our nation. Thanksgiving helps us remember the Pilgrims and God's care for them.

Establish your own family memorials. Has God delivered members of your family from death? Celebrate that event each year. We annually remember the day of our Benjamin's appendectomy, when we discovered that our little 2-1/2 year-old toddler had miraculously survived for over a week with an undiagnosed ruptured appendix. We talk about God's guidance, our church family's prayers and support, the miraculous way that God caused his body to seal off the infection from the rest of his body. It is a reminder to our entire family that God is our faithful protector; we can trust in Him.

Has God provided for you at a crucial time? Have an annual day of thanksgiving to remember His special provision. Can you pinpoint a specific day of conversion? Have a Re-Birthday Party each year on that day. These can be special times of family fun, togetherness, and learning.

Create "monuments." Fill baby books and journals with stories of memorable events and milestones. Keep picture albums, or at least a *box* of photos to review occasionally. Write up a special commemorative plaque to display on the wall.

The memorials and monuments that we establish will help our children remember over and over again God's grace in their lives.

Covenants:

Finally, working within the framework of *covenants* can be a tremendous aid in our families. It is beyond the scope of this book (and this author☺) to thoroughly study the whole concept of covenants. Examine covenants in the Bible -- God's covenants with Adam, Noah, Abraham, Jacob, the Israelites, David.

Basically, a covenant is an agreement between two or more persons. Write up agreements in your family. (Our "If-Then" and "Blessing" charts are designed for this purpose. See information at back of this book.)

What will happen, the way of "cursing," when a child disobeys? When he injures another child? When he complains?

What sort of blessings might come a child's way when he is faithful in his work? When he makes peace instead of perpetuating an argument?

The Scripture verses listed in the rest of this book can help you formulate these agreements. Base your cursings and blessings on Scriptural principles, and explain them when disciplining or rewarding your children.

Doing Your Homework

To help accomplish these goals -- establishing Scripture as the authority in our home; punishing and praising our children; exhorting, warning and restoring our children in the spirit of meekness; disciplining promptly, consistently, and justly; following Scripture's example by teaching with parables, proverbs, object lessons, stories, songs, history, memorials and covenants -- most chapters of this book are divided into 6 sections:

1. General information and commandments about the sin.
2. What happens, or should happen, to the person who engages in the sin.
3. What the sin is likened to in Scripture.
4. The blessings to those who resist the sin and practice righteousness.
5. Bible stories that illustrate the consequences of practicing the sin and the blessings of resisting the sin.
6. Memory verses to help combat temptation to sin.

Let's consider some examples of how to use all this material with your children.

Quick Reference

This book can be used as a quick reference tool when individual problems arise throughout the day. While your child is waiting for you in his room (where you sent him to stay until you are ready to discipline him), open to the chapter that covers the appropriate misbehavior. Quickly scan through the verses and suggested disciplines, object lessons, and stories.

Using the book as your reference, take your Bible with you to speak to your child. Read through verses that apply best to your situation. Read a Bible story together, or relate a personal story.

Perhaps you could do a quick, related object lesson together. Demonstrate the object lesson before explaining it to the child, and then ask him how he thinks it might relate to the problem you are talking about. Explain how the lesson relates to what Scripture teaches about his sin.

Read the verses that tell what will happen to the person who habitually practices this sin, and explain the discipline you are going to give, as it relates to these verses.

For example, if you are going to take away a toy from the child because he has been selfish and contentious with it, read him Proverbs 13:25, which tells us that a selfish man will come to want. Explain to the child, "This is why I am disciplining you in this way. The Bible says that a wicked man comes to want. I want you to understand that now, so that you will learn to not be greedy. I don't want you to be a poor man someday because you have been greedy."

You could also take a minute or two to read verses that tell what happens to the person who does not practice this sin. How does God bless that person? Would the child rather be disciplined or blessed?

Pray with your child, giving him opportunity to confess his sin to God, and praying for strength to obey God in the future.

Then discipline him.

This is one way to use this book. It can help you in dealing with daily misbehaviors and problems.

Study Material For Long-Term Problems

Another way to use the book is a little more long-range oriented. Use it to deal with offenses that are often repeated by a child, to discipline chronic weaknesses out of his life.

Let's say that Johnny has been having some problems lately. We need to examine what is wrong and take the proper steps to train and correct him.

1. Identify the discipline problem:

Make a list of the things Johnny is or isn't doing that, with God's help, need to change. Try to make as thorough a list as possible.

For example:

He does not accept "no" for an answer.

He argues with you when you confront him about something he has done wrong.

He justifies his actions.

He blames others for what he has done wrong.

He argues with his brothers and sisters over toys.

He teases siblings into fights.

He insists that he is always right.

He insists on everybody doing things his way.

Looking over the list as a whole, it seems that Johnny has problems with pride, shifting blame, and arguing. (Pray for God's guidance in this process. Are you, as parents, sinning in ways that could be contributing to these problems? Note those sins, as well, for your own personal study and repentance.)

2. Study the chapters in this book on pride, shifting blame and arguing. You might want to start working with Johnny in the area of pride first since it is really the root problem behind blame-shifting and arguing. Study through that section.

Read through the Scriptures listed under "pride"; don't just read the notes next to the references, but *really study each verse*. Mark verses that you think would be especially good to read with Johnny later. Pray that God will give you wisdom as you look for creative and Biblical ways to encourage your son towards godliness.

Using a sheet of paper, or writing in a notebook, write down notes for use when talking with Johnny. Make a list of verses that you want to read with him, or verses that would be good for him to copy as a writing assignment.

Jot down notes of discipline ideas that you think would be appropriate and effective with Johnny. If you have chosen the "loss of privilege" as a possible discipline, make a list of privileges that Johnny would not like to lose. Write down the Scripture references that explain the reasoning for each discipline idea.

Write down ideas for object lessons that you could use with Johnny, by himself, or that you could use in family worship time. Make a list of materials you will need, if any, to do these object lessons. Be sure to write down the Bible references that go with the object lessons so that you can read the Scripture along with the lesson.

Choose one or two Bible stories to read that illustrate the consequences of pride. Think about your own life. Are there stories that you could share with Johnny that would help him to understand the bad effects of pride in his life? Can you think of fictional or historical stories that would also help illustrate this? Write down a few notes about those stories, or note page numbers in books that contain stories you would like to read to Johnny.

Can you think of some songs that would be helpful in strengthening Johnny in this area? Write down their titles.

Read through the blessings that God says come to those who do not sin against Him in pride. How does God bless the humble person? Choose at least one of these blessings as a potential example that you can use to encourage Johnny in his efforts to conquer his problem of pride. How could you "reward" him, or encourage him, in a way that would parallel that blessing that God promises? Write down some ideas.

Choose at least one memory verse that you think would be especially good for Johnny to memorize.

You should now have a page with notes that will help you in calmly and constructively confronting Johnny about the problem of pride that you have observed in his life.

We keep pages of notes about each child in our notebook, at the back of the appropriate chapters. We also keep our own "Table of Contents," which lists each child, their unique problems, and the pages to refer to in our book for our notes and "plan of action." (For instance, we would put our list of notes regarding Johnny's pride problem at the end of the "Pride" section and list it in our "Table of Contents" as page 30A.)

3. Now -- PRAY!

Pray for Johnny's responsive heart. Remember, God changes hearts; we can't. Ezek. 11:19 says, *"Then I will give them one heart, and I will put a new spirit within them, and take the stony heart out of their flesh, and give them a heart of flesh."*

Pray that Johnny will have an open, teachable spirit.

Johnny can't change by himself either. *"Can the Ethiopian change his skin or the leopard its spots?"* (Jer. 13:23) Johnny can only change as he allows the Holy Spirit to help him. *Pray* for his willing heart.

Pray for your own spirit. Pray that you will not provoke Johnny to anger (Eph. 6:4), that you will be clothed with humility (I Pet. 5:5). Truth is much less palatable when it is clothed in harshness, anger, and pride.

Beware of a spirit that rejoices in evil, that takes pleasure in finding fault in your child. (I Cor. 13:6)

Confess your sin to God, and be willing and ready to confess related sins to Johnny. Pray for the humility to ask Johnny's forgiveness for offenses you have committed against him, as they relate to the sins he is committing. (i.e. anger towards him, mocking him, laziness in disciplining him, setting an example of pride and rebellion as you work under God's delegated authorities in your life)

Pray for the right time to talk to Johnny. Do not shame him in front of the rest of the family. Confront him when emotions are not high, and when you can calmly look at the problem.

Ecclesiastes 3:7 reminds us that there is a "time to keep silence, and a time to speak."

Ecclesiastes 8:5 says, " He who keeps his command will experience nothing harmful; and a wise man's heart discerns both time and judgment."

Instructing the Child

Plan a time when you can talk with Johnny. Maybe you could go out to breakfast together. Go for a walk together. Set up a special Bible study time together in the evenings. Plan on a time by yourselves, without other children in the family overhearing the conversation.

Pray together.

Read through Scriptures together. (Read the actual verses out of the Bible.)

Give an object lesson, tell a story, discuss a Proverb. Get his attention.

Confess and ask Johnny's forgiveness for your offenses against him.

Explain to him in a gentle way that you have observed a particular sin in his life, and that you are concerned about it, and have the responsibility to correct him and train him.

Read verses to him that explain the consequences he can expect in his life if he continues in this sin. Explain that you are going to discipline him in ways that will give him a taste of God's greater discipline in his life.

Outline to him the ways in which he will be disciplined in the future when he sins in this way. Write down the disciplines that you intend to enforce, and perhaps you could write out the appropriate verses next to each discipline.

Then explain the ways in which he will be rewarded when you see true evidence of growth and progress in overcoming this sin. Explain how God will be able to exalt him if he truly learns to humble himself before God and others. Explain that you will be able to honor him with more privilege and blessing when his heart is not proud.

Perhaps there is a special privilege that your child has been desiring. Could you set some type of goal in the area of humility or peacemaking, and when it is reached, grant Johnny this privilege?

Matt. 11:29 tells us that when we take the meek and lowly yoke of Jesus upon ourselves, He will give rest to our souls. ' How about planning a special overnight trip away with Johnny when you see that he is learning to humble himself before others?

Don't use this as a bribe. God doesn't bribe us to obey Him. But He does promise that He will bless us for our obedience. Look for a real *pattern of growth* in the child's life, not just an outward action that is done merely with the hope of selfish gain. Pray for discernment in this area.

Write down the way in which you would like to "bless" Johnny for his progress in overcoming pride.

You have now written down the "cursings" and "blessings" that you intend to give when Johnny obeys or disobeys you in this area. If both parties agree to this, you have formed a covenant between the three of you. (Both parents and the child.) You know what to do when he transgresses; he knows what to expect when he transgresses.

Start working on a memory verse together. A young man will "cleanse His way" by taking heed to God's Word, and hiding it in his heart. This is part of the armor that he will need to combat Satan and the temptation that he will experience in this battle against his old sin nature.

Pray with Johnny again. I John 1:9 is a tremendous promise to each of us as we struggle to conform to Christ's image. Remind him that God is always faithful to forgive us when we confess our sins. Read Hebrews 4:15-16 together,

> *"For we do not have a High Priest who cannot sympathize with our weaknesses, but was in all points tempted as we are, yet without sin. Let us therefore come boldly to the throne of grace, that we may obtain mercy and find grace to help in time of need."*

Pray for God's strength. Rejoice together in the knowledge that He knows our temptation and weakness, and will grant us grace and help when we call on Him.

The Benefits of Disciplining in This Way

This approach requires some time, effort, study, and creativity. But the results are certainly worth the effort.

Basing our discipline on Scripture has encouraged me to examine my own life more prayerfully in the light of God's Word, and to obey His Word more faithfully. (*"Thou shalt love the Lord thy God with all thine heart..."*)

It has encouraged me to study the Bible more seriously, and has made God's Word a more real and practical part of my everyday life. (*"And these words which I command you this day, shall be in thine heart..."*)

It has helped us apply God's Word more naturally to our everyday life. We are more familiar with His Word and more sensitive to opportunities to discuss and apply it. (*"And thou shalt teach them diligently..."*)

It has established God's Word as the authority in our home, and in our lives.

"All Scripture is profitable for doctrine, for reproof, for correction, for instruction in righteousness; that the man of God may be perfect, thoroughly furnished unto all good works."

The Bible has all that we need to raise up men and women of God!

Additional notes:

The material in this book also fits in well with unit studies. For instance, if you have designed your own unit study based on a particular character quality, or if you are working with unit study curriculums such as KONOS or Weaver, use this book to furnish you with additional Bible study material, ideas for object lessons, etc.

Many references are made throughout this book to paying children for chores. This is one of those controversial areas! We have seen *many* advantages in paying our children for a *portion* of the work they do in our household. We want them to learn the very basic connection between work and material reward. Beyond that they learn how to handle money, how to save, how to budget, how to plan for the future, how to shop wisely. They are more motivated to learn new skills, they gain experience in employer/employee relationships, they put their math skills to practical use.

Other than an occasional gift or reward, our children receive no other money from us. They are required to budget their earnings into 7 different categories. Only 20% of this is available for their own personal spending. The rest is used to help purchase items we would have otherwise bought them (clothing, birthday gifts for others, etc.), to give as tithe to the church, to invest in their own business ventures, and to save for their own futures.

The existence of hard-earned spending money, long-term savings, etc. also opens up new avenues for disciplining a child. A fine hurts a lot more if it comes out of spending money the child has worked to earn. Laziness can be disciplined with the very natural consequence of withheld pay, etc.

(For a more detailed explanation of this system, see our little book, Stewardship Street. Ordering information is at the back of this book.)

Pride
(See also Self-Righteousness)

We start with "pride" as the first category in this book, since our sinful tendency to put our trust in ourselves and our abilities, rather than in God, is at the root of so many other destructive sins in our lives.

General information and commandments about this sin:

Pr. 28:25 A proud person is contrasted with one who puts his trust in God.

Pr. 25:27 To seek one's own glory is not glory.
Do not allow or unwittingly encourage a child's boasting.

Pr. 27:2 Let another praise. Do not praise yourself.

Pr. 27:21 Praise from others is test, refining pot.
Be judicious in use of praise. Praise can be helpful and encouraging but can also prove to be a stumbling-block if not used carefully. Don't flatter a child, and be especially careful not to tempt to pride a gifted child who may already have a problem with pride. "We cannot do our brother a greater injury, than by supplying fuel for pride by irregulated praise."[1]

Deu. 8:11-14,17-20 Forgets God and His grace.

Ps. 10:2 Wicked in pride persecutes poor.
Cruelty indicates pride. When disciplining for cruelty deal carefully with pride as well.

Ps 10:4,11 Doesn't seek God, God not in thoughts, thinks God will not see or punish.

Ps. 49:11 Think their name will continue forever.
Study verses on brevity of man.

Ps. 101:5 God will not tolerate high look and proud heart.
We must not either. A proud look calls for firm discipline.

Ps. 138:6 God knows the proud afar off.

Pr. 6:16-17, Pr. 8:13 God hates the proud look.

Pr. 13:10 Only by pride comes contention.
If there is a problem with constant contention in your household, look for pride at its roots, and discipline with the goal of bringing all members of the household to a place of humility. Pray for God's humbling discipline.

Pr.15:12 Doesn't love a reprover.
Exercise care when reproving a proud person. Reprove lovingly, humbly, with Scripture, and then leave the results to God.
Be careful to avoid your own pride when confronting a proud person.

I Cor. 4:6,7 We've received all that we have.
Make a list of what the child is proud of. Where did it come from?

Pr. 30:32 Foolish to exalt oneself.
Teach to give glory to God and to others. Praise and thank God in prayer. Have your children write thank you letters to those who have helped them, and publicly acknowledge thankfulness to others for their work and their influence in their lives.

Pr. 6:17 God hates.

Pr 21:4 Haughty look is sin.
Discipline the look, not just the action. Don't wait for the action that will naturally follow a haughty look; discipline at the first appearance of pride, especially when directed at those in authority.

Pr. 25:6,7 Don't exalt self before King/great men.

Pr 28:25 Stirs up strife.

Pr 28:26 Trusts in own heart, is fool.
Teach habit of prayer, seeking counsel, Bible study.

Pr. 26:12 More hope for a fool.
How much hope is there for a fool?

Pr. 28:11 Rich are wise in own conceit.

Matt. 23:6-8 Love chief seats in synagogue, uppermost rooms in feasts, greetings at markets, called Rabbi/Masters. Greatest shall be servant.
Teach to be servant when desirous of glory, being first.
Give servant's duties, have proud child serve especially those that he lords his supposed superiority over (like Haman ended up serving Mordecai as he led him through the city in the king's chariot.)

Rom. 12:16 Don't set mind on high things, not wise in own opinion.

I Tim. 6:3,4,17 Doesn't consent to wholesome words. Rich tempted to be high-minded.

Rom. 12:3 Don't think more highly of self than ought to. Think soberly.

James 4:13,14 Don't know tomorrow.
Teach this principle. Study brevity of man.

Jer. 9:23 Not glory in wisdom, might, riches.

I Cor 8:1 Knowledge puffs up, love edifies.
Help child devise projects and actions that demonstrate love and that will build another up, rather than tearing down as prideful actions tend to do.

Jer. 45:5 Don't seek great things for self.

Gal 5:26 Not desire vain glory.
Give glory to God. Teach child to offer public testimony of God's faithfulness and enabling. Have him write down in a journal or essay an account of "his" success that acknowledges and brings glory to God rather than to himself. (How did God equip and enable him for the task? How did He provide? How did He cause details to work out?)

Pr. 12:15 Fool is righteous in own eyes. Doesn't listen to counsel.
"The knowledge of the most intelligent is as nothing compared with his ignorance, and yet how strangely does the smallest quantum 'puff up' and fill a man full of himself...There is more hope of the fool, who knows himself to be one. The natural fool has only one hindrance -- his own ignorance. The conceited fool has two -- ignorance and self-delusion."[2]
Teach your children constantly of God's perfection and man's utter depravity, save for the grace of Christ's death. Study God's character; study man's character.

Jg. 21:25 Every man did what was right in his own eyes.

Ps. 10:6 Thinks he will never be in adversity.

What happens, or should happen, to the proud person:

II Tim. 3:13 Gets worse. Deceives and is deceived.

Deut. 8:19-20 Leads to worship of idols, destruction, disobedience.
Help the child see evidences of this in his own life.

I Sam. 2:3-5 God will humble.
Pray for God's obvious discipline in the child's life, and discuss it when it comes.

Dan. 5:20 Mind becomes hardened.
Withdraw your counsel.

Ps. 12:3-4 Tongue cut off.
Silence the proud child.
When he is voicing his pride, don't allow him to talk any more.

Isolate him.

Ps. 18:27 Bring down high looks.
Discipline pride in eyes. Humble the child by giving him service to perform, denying privileges, removing his "rank" and responsibilities

Jer. 49:16 Self-deception will be brought down.
Remove privileges and "rank."

Pr. 29:23 Brings low.

Is. 2:11,17 Brings him low.

Is. 24:4,21 Laid low, to ground, dust.

Pr. 25:6-7 Put lower.
Bring the proud low. Abase him, remove his source of pride (i.e. money, activities, privileges). Allow him to fall without bailing him out. Isolate. Require confession to those offended. Have proud child plan or participate in honoring the person he has treated as lower than himself. Place in position of servanthood. Deny the child the praise and honor that he would normally receive for a particular accomplishment if he is exhibiting sinful pride.

Ps. 52:5-7 Will uproot, destroy, pluck.

Pr. 15:25 Will destroy the house of the proud.

Pr. 16:18 Pride comes before destruction.

Pr. 18:12 The heart is haughty before destruction.

Ps. 119:78, Pr. 11:2 Pride is followed by shame.

Js. 5:16 Should confess faults.
Teach child to confess faults to and ask forgiveness of God and of those he has offended.

Matt. 5:16 We should let our light shine so that others can see our good works and glorify God.
Teach child to give glory to God, not to call attention and glory to self.

Pr. 31:31 Let works bring praise.
Keep journal in which you record works of kindness and service, and evidences of growth in the child's life. Read this to him occasionally.

Jer. 9:24 We should glory in understanding and knowledge of God.
Study the Bible, its practical application, God's character, our sinfulness.

Pr. 30:32 If you have acted proudly, lay hand upon your mouth.

Silence the proud tongue. Don't allow boasting about sinful, prideful actions.

Pr. 11:14 Where there is no counsel the people fall.
Teach your child to seek counsel from God's Word and from other believers, and not to lean solely on his own wisdom.

Pr. 15:22 Plans of the proud go awry.
Limit the proud child's activities. Deny privileges.

Pr. 16:5 No proud man will go unpunished.
We must not overlook the sin of pride; it needs to be disciplined.

Pr. 16:25 The way that seems right to a man leads to death.

Is. 10:5-16 God gathers up riches as eggs from a nest.
Deny wages for work. Deny in area of pride (i.e. sports, music, appearance, etc.). Limit participation in these areas if they have become a source of pride.

Matt. 23:6-8,11,12 He who exalts himself will be abased.
Our children quote this verse now when they see its truth demonstrated over and over in real life and in our reading.

Lk. 1:51-52 Proud are scattered in the imagination of their hearts, the mighty are put down from their seats.
Demote the proud child. Take away his "rank"/position, along with its attendant privileges.

Js. 4:6 God resists the proud.
We should resist, not encourage or aid the proud child. Do not make his prideful path an easy one.

I Cor. 10:12 Let him who thinks he stands take heed lest he falls.

Jer. 50:31-32 The proud will stumble and fall and no one will raise him up.
Do not bail the proud child out of the painful, humbling natural consequences of his pride. Allow him to suffer shame and abasement.

Pr. 28:13 He who covers his sins will not prosper.
A child needs to learn early to confess his sin. This has been one of the major initial battles of wills with each of our children. I very clearly remember our first "round" with our oldest son Daniel, when he was very young, but old enough to understand and resist our authority. He had committed some offense that we had disciplined, and we were then asking him to verbally confess, "I was wrong for hurting you. Will you please forgive me?" He was too proud and stubborn to submit to this, but it was very obvious that he understood. With much prayer, we persisted, clearly explaining to

him what he needed to do. When he resisted we spanked him and carefully explained again. This continued through many spankings, and many prayers, until Daniel finally humbled himself, submitted to our instruction, and confessed his wrong. It was important to us to humble this little boy, and to teach him to submit to authority at a young age.

Phil. 2:3 We should esteem others better than ourselves.
Teach the child to do something for the other person, instead of expecting everyone else to serve him and his desires. How could he show that he thinks the other person is more important than himself?

Rom. 12:16 Should associate with the humble.
Do not allow close friendships with proud children.

Rom. 1:28 + Turned over to a debased mind.

I Tim. 6:4-5 Withdraw from the proud.
Limit child's association with others who are proud.
Isolate him when he demonstrates pride, boasts, shows off for company, etc.

Mk. 9:35 Desire to be first will lead to being last and servant of all.
Make child last, serve last at mealtime, give last turn, etc.
Put child in the position of service to others.

This sin of pride is likened to:

Ps. 73:6 Pride wraps around like a chain.
Wrap chains around the child. How easy is it to move? To accomplish anything?

Ps. 119:69-70 The proud heart is as fat as grease.

Pr. 18:11 A high wall.
How easy is it to get to the other side of a high wall?
A high wall isolates, protects from intrusion.

Is. 10:5-16 An ax, a saw, a rod, a staff -- all boasting against the one who uses it, the person who gives it "life."
How useful are these tools if no one is operating them? How useful are we to God if we think we can function without Him?

Ob. 3-4 Exalting self as an eagle, building nest among the stars. Will be brought down.

Rom. 11:16-21 Grafted wild olive branch boasting against other branches. If God didn't spare natural branches, He won't spare the grafted branches either.
Study the art of grafting, and try it! Who is responsible for the grafted branch's position -- the branch or the gardener?
Purchase and plant a grafted fruit tree or rose bush. Did the grafted branch decide where it would be?

Js. 1:10 Pass away as flower of the grass.
Pick a bouquet of flowers. Enjoy its beauty, and notice how briefly it lasts.
Choose a specific flower to observe in your yard, or on a houseplant. Look at it each day and observe how long its beauty lasts.

Pr. 25:27 Searching for one's own glory is like eating too much honey.
Makes one sick. Recall incidents when someone has indulged in too many sweet treats, and ended up sick.

Stories that illustrate the consequences of pride:

Goliath, I Sam. 17 Shame, destruction, laid low to ground, fell.

Benhadad, I Kgs. 20:10 Food, tongue "cut out" (shame), brought low, destruction of army.

Sennacherib, II Kgs. 18:19-19:37 Destruction, put down mighty from seats, despises neighbor, shame.

Nebuchadnezzar, Dan. 4:30-34, 5:20 Was struck in area of pride, brought low, mind hardened, mighty brought down from seat, isolated, shamed.

Haman, Est. 6:6-13, 5:11, 7:10 and his sons, Est. 9:10 Seeking own glory led to death, contention, exalted himself and then was brought low and shamed, plans went awry, house was destroyed.
Haman offers us a good example of a proud person doing for the victim of his prideful contention what he would like to have had done for himself. This can be a good discipline action for a proud person.

Adonijah, I Kgs. 1 and 2:13-25 Seeking own glory, exalting self led to shame and destruction.

Naaman, II Kgs. 5:11-13 Angry at Elisha's instruction, proud heart, seeking great things. But he <u>did</u> listen to counsel, which led to his humbling and healing.

Lucifer, Is. 14:12-16 Exalted self and was abased.

Tower of Babel, Gen. 11:1-9 Seeking glory led to humbling and
scattering.
*This story could suggest the principle of separating a group
of proud children, rather than allowing them to associate with
each other, feeding each other's pride and causing even more
contention as a group.*

Korah, Dathan and Abiram, Num. 16 Exalted self, led to contention,
rebellion, and then to death for themselves, their families, and
their associates.

Peter, Mk. 14:29-30 Pride before fall, shame, humbled.

Disciples, Lk. 22:24-27 Strife, seeking glory and exaltation.

Parable of Pharisee and tax collector, Lk. 18:10-14 Forgot
God and His grace, puffed up with knowledge, haughty look,
trusting own heart, exalting self which led to abasement.
The humble tax collector received grace.

Miriam, Num. 12:2, 10-15 Exalted self, haughty, led to shame,
humility and isolation.

Herod, Acts 12:22-23 Proud heart, mighty brought down from seat,
death.

Uzziah, II Chr. 26:1-21, esp. vs. 16 Haughty heart, trusted
in self, thought God wouldn't punish, lost throne, brought to
shame, was leper until death.

Ephraimites, Jg. 8:1-3 and Jg. 12:1-6 Contentious and proud.
Note the different responses of Gideon and Jephthah, and the
different results.
*We are not to answer a fool according to his folly. Beware
of allowing your own pride or impatience to interfere with
your response to and reproof of a proud child.*

David, II Sam. 24:1-15 Taking of census led to nationwide
pestilence. David was struck in the area of his pride -- the
great number of people in his kingdom. David acknowledged
and repented of this sin.

Hezekiah, II Kgs. 20:12-18 Pride in possessions led to the
gathering up of his riches and the destruction of his
household.

Blessings of Humility:

Js. 4:10, Ps. 147:6 Lifted up.
Exalt the humble child with greater privileges and honor.

Ps. 22:26 Eat and be satisfied.
Have a special feast to honor humble person.
Take out to eat with Mom and/or Dad.
Allow child to choose menu for special meal.

Ps. 25:9 Will teach his way, guide his judgment.
Offer counsel and guidance; it will be more readily accepted by
the humble person.

Ps. 37:11 Will inherit the earth, abundant peace.

Ps. 25:13 Dwell in prosperity, descendants will inherit the earth.
Establish a special long-term savings fund into which the child
regularly budgets his earnings, and make a special contribution to
this fund in honor of noteworthy humility or progress in conquering
a proud heart.
Start a hope chest for a young girl and make an annual
"contribution," (perhaps on her birthday?) conditional on evidence
of a humble, quiet spirit throughout the year.
Establish a similar tradition with a son -- perhaps a carpenter's
tool set, mechanics tools, etc.
I think it is very appropriate to communicate to every child in
your family that inheritance of the family's wealth is conditional on
their spiritual faithfulness. If they live in sin and defiance of God,
good stewardship of God's blessings would require that they be
excluded from inheritance.

Ps. 131:1-2 Like a weaned child.
Any nursing mother can describe the difference between a nursing
baby and a weaned child! The weaned child is not anxious and
striving against his mother's breast; he is satisfied and relaxed.

Pr. 3:34 Receives grace.

Pr. 11:2 Receives wisdom.

Pr. 15:33, 18:12, 29:22 Receives honor.
"Indeed, without humility, honor would be our temptation, rather
than our glory."[3]
A humble person is more capable of receiving honor.

Pr. 22:4 Riches, honor and life.

Is. 29:19 Increased joy.

Plan a special activity that will bring special joy to the child.

Matt. 11:29 Rest.
Plan a special retreat, vacation, pay for a week at a special camp.

Matt. 18:2-4 Greatest in kingdom.
Give child increased responsibilities and attendant privileges.

Lk. 1:52, 14:11, 18:13,14 Exalted.
Honor the child in other ways previously mentioned.
Have a special family parade in honor of the child.
Fly a special "Name Flag" from the porch to honor the child.
(Note: See ordering information in back of book for a description of
 our pattern set that includes instructions for making "name flags.")
Make the child "Prince-for-the-Day." Allow him to choose menus
 for the day's meals, select the day's activities, choose what kind
 of cookies to bake, which stories to read at storytime, where to go
 for a special outing or meal out.
Let the child wear a special crown at dinnertime, and have other
 family members serve him.
Perform a special family program to entertain the honored person.

Ps. 10:17 God will hear their desire.
Grant a special request or provide for a special desire for the
 child.

I Pet. 5:6 Humble self under God's mighty hand. He will exalt you.

Stories that illustrate the blessings of humility:

Daniel, Daniel 2:30 Did not seek glory for himself, but gave
 glory to God. This led to his promotion.

Shadrach, Meshach and Abednego, Dan. 3:30 Were given more
 responsibility after their deliverance from the fiery furnace.

Moses, Ex. 3:1-12 Recognized his limitations and God's holiness.
 Num. 12:3 Most humble man on earth! Led to his leadership, was
 guided in judgment, descendants inherited the land.

Solomon, I Kgs. 3:11-14 Recognized his limitations, didn't seek his
 own glory. Led to riches, honor and life.

Centurion, Matt. 8:5-10 Recognized his unworthiness. Led to God's
 grace and mercy in his life.

Canaanite woman, Matt. 15:21-28 Didn't think of herself more highly than she should, received grace and increased joy.

Penitent woman, Lk. 7:37-48 Recognized her sinfulness. Led to grace, exaltation, and forgiveness.

Prodigal son, Lk. 15:17-21 Recognized unworthiness. Led to grace and forgiveness.

Publican and the Pharisee, Lk. 18:13-14 Recognized sinfulness. Was forgiven.

Stories that illustrate humility before honor:

Joseph, Gen. 41:14-44 Slavery and imprisonment. Gave God glory rather than himself. Was given great understanding, honored and made ruler.

David, Ps. 78:70-72 From shepherd to king.

Ruth, Ruth 2:10-16, 4:13-22, Matt. 1:5 Willing to serve mother-in-law, dwelled safely, received grace, ate and was satisfied, increased joy, Jesus born from her offspring.

Abigail, I Sam. 25:41-42 Humbled herself as servant to David, and was honored with marriage.

Verses to memorize:

1 Cor. 10:12 Therefore let him who thinks he stands take heed lest he fall. (NKJV)

Matt. 20:26-28 Yet it shall not be so among you; but whoever desires to become great among you, let him be your servant. And whoever desires to be first among you, let him be your slave; just as the Son of Man did not come to be served, but to serve, and to give His life a ransom for many. (NKJV)

Rom. 12:16 Be of the same mind toward one another. Do not set your mind on high things, but associate with the humble. Do not be wise in your own opinion. (NKJV)

1 Cor. 3:21 Therefore let no man glory in men. For all things are yours.

Pr. 22:4 By humility and the fear of the LORD are riches, and honour, and life.

2 Cor. 3:5 Not that we are sufficient of ourselves to think any thing as of ourselves; but our sufficiency is of God;

Lk. 17:10 So likewise ye, when ye shall have done all those things which are commanded you, say, We are unprofitable servants: we have done that which was our duty to do.

Lk. 18:14 ...for every one that exalteth himself shall be abased; and he that humbleth himself shall be exalted.

Jn. 13:15 For I have given you an example, that ye should do as I have done to you.

Gal. 5:26 Let us not be desirous of vain glory, provoking one another, envying one another.

Gal. 6:14 But God forbid that I should glory, save in the cross of our Lord Jesus Christ, by whom the world is crucified unto me, and I unto the world.

Phil. 2:3 Let nothing be done through strife or vainglory; but in lowliness of mind let each esteem other better than themselves.

Rom. 7:18 For I know that in me (that is, in my flesh,) dwelleth no good thing: for to will is present with me; but how to perform that which is good I find not.

James 4:6b ...God resisteth the proud, but giveth grace unto the humble.

I Cor. 4:7 For who makes you differ from another? And what do you have that you did not receive? Now if you did indeed receive it, why do you boast as if you had not received it? (NKJV)

Pr. 15:33 The fear of the LORD is the instruction of wisdom; and before honour is humility.

Dan. 4:37b And those who walk in pride He is able to put down. (NKJV)

I Pet. 5:5 Likewise you younger people, submit yourselves to your elders. Yes, all of you be submissive to one another, and be clothed with humility, for "God resists the proud, but gives grace to the humble." (NKJV)

I Jn. 2:16,17 For all that is in the world, the lust of the flesh, and the lust of the eyes, and the pride of life, is not of the Father, but is of the world. And the world passeth away, and the lust thereof: but he that doeth the will of God abideth for ever.

---

[1]Charles Bridges, <u>A Commentary on Proverbs</u> (Carlisle, Penn.: The Banner of Truth Trust, 1987), p. 521.

[2]Bridges, p. 491.

[3]Bridges, p. 222.

Self-Righteousness

(See also Pride, Hypocrisy)

General information and commandments about this sin:

Gal. 6:3 Deceives self.

Pr. 20:9 No one can say he is free from sin.
Help child to review sin in his life. Can he claim perfection?

Pr. 21:2 His way is right in his own eyes, but God weighs the heart.
Use a small balance scales to "weigh" righteousness and sin in the child's life. Review actions of the day, placing a coin for each action recalled, either on the sin or the righteous side. Any coins on the sin side means that we fail to meet God's standard.

Lk. 18:11-14 Compares himself to other men, depends on works.
Teach the child to compare himself to God's standards, not to compare himself to other people.

Matt. 6:6-8 Should pray in secret, not vain repetitions.

Deut. 9:4-6 Israelites took land because of the wickedness of their enemies, not because of their own righteousness.

Pr. 12:15 Way of fool is right in his own eyes.

Pr. 16:2 Man's ways are clean in his own sight.
Make a maze of boxes connected together and have child try to find his way out.
Observe an animal in a maze.

Pr. 26:12 There is more hope for a fool.
Study the fool. How much hope is there for him?

Pr. 28:26 Is a fool.

Lk. 16:14,15 One highly esteemed among men may be an abomination to God.
Read historical biographies.
Review the lives of popular figures of our day, and how they measure up to God's standards.
Recount the lives of acquaintances that were highly esteemed by men but proved to be disobedient to God.

Rom. 10:3 Doesn't submit to righteousness of God, ignorant of God's righteousness.

Pr. 30:12 Pure in his own eyes, but still filthy.

Is. 64:6 Our righteousness is filthy rags.
Compare a new, clean, bleached diaper with a dirty one.

Pr. 23:4 Should cease from our own wisdom.

Rom. 12:16 We should not be wise in our own conceits.

What happens, or should happen, to the self-righteous person:

Pray for God's hand in events that will lead to repentance, and pray for a teachable spirit in the child.

Pr. 28:13 He who covers his sins won't prosper.
Teach child to confess sin.
Deny money, privileges, rights, freedom.

Matt. 6:1-4 Don't do alms to be seen of men, or there will be no reward.
Pray for the ability to discern a child's motives when they seem questionable. Discuss with the child.

Pr. 14:12 Death.

Rom. 1:22 Profess wisdom, but become fools.
Allow the child to act on his own "wisdom," and then let him live with the consequences.

Ps. 19:12 Pray for cleansing from secret faults.
Psalm 119:9 says that a young man's way is cleansed by taking heed to God's Word. Study the Word diligently with him. Teach him basic Bible study methods. Study man's sinful nature.

The sin of self-righteousness is likened to:

Jn. 15:4-9 Like branch not abiding in vine. Can do nothing. No fruit.
Trim grapes, fruit trees, or roses. Leave trimmed branches next to tree or vine on the ground. How much do they produce?

Pr. 27:7 Full soul loathing honey. Feels no need.
After a big meal and special dessert, offer more sweets.
Or notice how there is less desire for a meal if sweets have been eaten before.

Pr. 25:27 Eating too much honey is like searching out one's own glory.

Eating too much honey is a detriment to one's health and well-being. It causes fatness, dulls the appetite for more essential nutrients, rots the teeth, causes nausea.

Seeking one's own glory causes something good (honor) to become a detriment in one's life -- it dulls one's appetite for God's Word, causes the "fatness" of pride, "rots" the heart, and takes glory away from God.

Is. 64:6 Our righteousness is filthy rags.
Send the child for a wash cloth out of the diaper pail, laundry hamper, etc.

Is. 65:3-5 Smoke in nose, fire burning all day.
Observe how irritating constant smoke is -- field burning, a smokey campfire, a burning pile of fall leaves.

Is. 5:20, 21, 24 Fire to stubble, chaff. Rottenness of roots. Blossom to dust.
Fire destroys. Observe remains after field-burning.
Observe plants that die from the roots up. We occasionally lose a few broccoli plants to a root rot, which very graphically demonstrates this principle.
Toss a beautiful flower into the compost pile. How good does it look a couple days later?

Jer. 2:13 Forsaking fountain of living water, hewing out broken cisterns that hold no water.
Have a day where no running water can be used (turn off water at its source). Stock up some water ahead of time in buckets, jugs, etc. that are cracked and leaky. How much water is available to use now?

Matt. 23:25 Cup that is clean on the outside but dirty inside.
Prepare a special hot or cold drink to enjoy together. Give the self-righteous child a special cup to use, but have it grossly dirty on the inside. Does he want you to serve him his drink in it? Why not?

Matt. 23:26-28 Whitewashed tomb.
May be beautiful on the outside, but is still full of dead man's bones and decaying body.

The blessings of acknowledging our sinful state before God:

(See also the blessings of humility listed in the "pride" section)

Matt. 6:6 God will reward openly.
Recognize and encourage a child when he is clearly honest in his relationship to the Lord, and in his estimation of himself.

I Jn. 1:9 Confess sin, will be forgiven and cleansed.
Show child mercy when he openly confesses his sin.

Pr. 28:13 Confess and forsake, will find mercy.

Pr. 3:6 Acknowledge God and He will direct your path.

Pr. 3:7-8 Will be health to your body.
Observe the affects on one's health when one disobeys and relies on his own wisdom and righteousness. Read about famous people who are suffering disease, mental unrest, etc. as a result of their sin.

Stories that illustrate the consequences of self-righteousness and the blessings of confession:

Pharisee and publican, Lk. 18:10-14 Pride in self and works, compared self with others. Publican recognized his sin, confessed, and asked mercy.

Korah, Dathan, and Abiram, Num. 16:3 Self-righteous attitude toward Moses and his leadership. Led to death.

Saul, I Sam. 13:8-14 Offered sacrifice without authority, and lost the kingdom.
I Sam. 15:13-31 Disobeyed for the sake of "sacrifice." Lost kingdom.

David, II Sam. 12:13 David sinned grievously, but confessed, and was forgiven.

Verses to memorize:

Ps. 19:12 Who can understand his errors? cleanse thou me from secret faults.

1 John 1:9 If we confess our sins, he is faithful and just to forgive

us our sins, and to cleanse us from all unrighteousness.

Pr. 12:15 The way of a fool is right in his own eyes, But he who heeds counsel is wise. (NKJV)

Ps. 130:3-4 If You, LORD, should mark iniquities, O Lord, who could stand? But there is forgiveness with You, that You may be feared. (NKJV)

1 Sam. 16:7b "...for man looks at the outward appearance, but the LORD looks at the heart." (NKJV)

Pr. 28:13 He who covers his sins will not prosper, but whoever confesses and forsakes them will have mercy. (NKJV)

Isa. 64:6 But we are all as an unclean thing, and all our righteousnesses are as filthy rags; and we all do fade as a leaf; and our iniquities, like the wind, have taken us away.

Ps. 139:23-24 Search me, O God, and know my heart: try me, and know my thoughts: And see if there be any wicked way in me, and lead me in the way everlasting.

Pr. 3:7-8 Do not be wise in your own eyes; Fear the LORD and depart from evil. It will be health to your flesh, and strength to your bones. (NKJV)

Jer 17:9 The heart is deceitful above all things, and desperately wicked: who can know it?

Pr. 21:2 Every way of a man is right in his own eyes, but the LORD weighs the hearts. (NKJV)

Ps. 32:5 I acknowledged my sin unto thee, and mine iniquity have I not hid. I said, I will confess my transgressions unto the LORD; and thou forgavest the iniquity of my sin.

Ps. 51:5 Behold, I was shapen in iniquity, and in sin did my mother conceive me.

Ps. 69:5 O God, thou knowest my foolishness; and my sins are not hid from thee.

2 Cor 10:18 For not he that commendeth himself is approved, but whom the Lord commendeth.

Shifting Blame/Making Excuses
(See also Self-Righteousness, Lying)

This is an essential problem to deal with. We want our children to be honest in examining themselves against God's standard, and to learn to readily confess and forsake sin. Excusing our sin and blaming our actions on others is dishonest and self-deceptive, and can lock us into immaturity and stagnation. It can also add a great burden of guilt to a life.

General information and commandments about this sin:

Pr. 21:2 Ways are right in our own eyes.

Pr. 12:15 Way of a fool is right in his own eyes.

Pr. 16:2 Man's ways are clean in his own sight.

Pr. 30:12 Pure in own eyes, but still filthy.
All these verses point to our need to establish God's Word as the authority in our lives. Man is not able to establish his own standard of morality; every man will do what is right in his own eyes, which leads to anarchy.

Ezek. 18:4b Soul that sins, it will die.

What happens, or should happen, to the person who makes excuses:

Pr. 28:13 He who covers his sins will not prosper.
Do not allow the "blame-shifter" to prosper. Deny privileges, discipline him firmly, and more severely when he tries to make excuses.

Matt. 7:1-5 Will be judged.
Add to his discipline. If he has earned a spanking, add one extra "swat," etc.

Pr. 19:3 Blames God.
A child will often blame the authority over him, instead of acknowledging his wrong. Sulking over discipline should not be allowed since it is evidence of an unrepentant and rebellious heart. Pray for the Holy Spirit's working in the child's heart, to bring him to a point of true humbling and recognition of his sin.

Job 9:20 Mouth will condemn.
*Conduct a "trial." Question the child about what he did.
Do not allow him to tell you what someone else did.*

Ezek. 18:4 The one who sins will be punished.
*Be consistent. Take the time and energy to thoroughly investigate
a situation, asking God for wisdom in properly disciplining those
who deserve it.*

Blessings of acknowledging and confessing our sin:

Js. 5:16 Confess sins, will be healed.

I Jn. 1:9 Will be forgiven and cleansed.
*Spend time with the child after confession and discipline to
restore fellowship and to express your pleasure in his action.*

Mic. 7:9 Will behold God's righteousness.

Pr. 28:13 Confess and forsake sin, will receive mercy.
*Lessen discipline when child readily, and sincerely, confesses.
(i.e. if spanking, give one less swat.)*

Stories that illustrate the consequences of blaming others:

Adam and Eve, Gen. 3:12-13 Banished from the garden, spiritual
death, cursings.

Aaron, Ex. 32:1-24 Aaron took what the people gave him, at his
request, and fashioned the golden calf. He built the altar.
Then he blamed the people.

Saul, I Sam. 15:1-23 Blamed people for his actions. Lost his
leadership and kingdom.

Pilate, Matt. 27:24 Tried to deny his responsibility.
*Saul, Aaron, and Pilate were all attempting to blame those under
their authority. They were not exercising their authority over
their inferiors, and were denying their own will and choice in
the matter. This is a good reminder to us as parents! We are
responsible for our actions.*

Sarah, Gen. 16:5 Blamed Abraham for situation with Hagar.

Esau, Gen. 27:36 Blamed Jacob for his foolish action in giving
up his birthright.

Verses to memorize:

Pr. 21:2 Every way of a man is right in his own eyes, but the LORD weighs the hearts. (NKJV)

Ezek. 18:4b ...the soul that sinneth, it shall die.

Pr. 28:13 He that covereth his sins shall not prosper: but whoso confesseth and forsaketh them shall have mercy.

Hypocrisy

(See also Lying, Pride, Self-Righteousness, Flattery)

General information and commandments about this sin:

Js. 3:17 The wisdom that is from above is without hypocrisy.

I Tim. 1:5 Love from a pure heart, good conscience, with unfeigned faith.

Matt. 6:2 Hypocrite sounds trumpet, seeks glory of men.

Matt. 6:5 Hypocrite prays with the intention of being seen by men.

Matt. 6:16 Hypocrite disfigures himself and makes it obvious when he is fasting.
Be sensitive to outward manifestations of a child doing something for the praise of men, with an insincere heart. Do not allow him to "show off." Teach him to serve God quietly, for the glory of God, rather than his own glory.

Matt. 7:3-5 Critical. Ignores beam in own eye.

Rom. 16:17-18 Serves own belly, deceives the simple.

Rom. 12:9 We are to love without hypocrisy.

Pr. 11:9 Destroys neighbor.

Matt. 23:5-7 Proud, wants to be seen by men.

Matt. 23:23 Concerned with details, but not with weightier matters, such as justice, mercy, and faith.

Mk. 7:7-8 Replaces God's laws with man's laws.
We, as parents, can set an example in this area, by being sure our family "laws" and the laws by which we live are firmly based on God's law as revealed in Scripture. Use the Bible to help explain why an action is wrong, and why you are disciplining in the way you do.

Eph. 6:6 We should not perform eyeservice, to please man, but be servants of Christ.
What does Jesus want us to do?

I Jn. 3:17-18 Should not love in word or tongue, but in deed and truth.
What can the child do to show his love, not just talking about it.

Josh. 24:14 Serve the Lord in sincerity and truth.

I Pet. 1:22 We should have unfeigned love for the brothers, love with a pure heart.

What happens, or should happen, to the hypocrite:

Lk. 12:1-3 What is covered will be revealed.
Reveal the child's dishonesty.
Point out examples of this in everyday life.

Matt. 23:14 Greater condemnation.
If child is caught in hypocrisy, discipline him for lying as well
 as the other wrong he has committed.

Matt. 22:12,13,18 Cast into outer darkness.

Job 36:14 Die in youth.
Shorten the child's day with an earlier bedtime or curfew.
Deny playtime or other privilege.

Job 20:5 His joy is temporary. Will fly away as a dream and not be
 found. Will be chased away as a night vision.

Matt. 7:5 Cast beam from own eye.
Help the child to examine his motives and his involvement in a
 problem.

Job 8:13 Hope will perish.
Do not allow child to participate in planned activity.

I Cor. 13:3 Profits nothing.
Take away from the child what he had hoped to gain through his
 hypocrisy.

Rom. 16:17-18 Avoid hypocrites.
Avoid association and friendship with hypocrites.
Isolate the hypocritical child from the family temporarily.

Matt. 6:1 No reward.
Do not pay for chores when heart is not serving.

The sin of hypocrisy is likened to:

Lk. 12:1 Leaven.
Infects others. Infects entire life. Grows.
Conduct some experiments with yeast. What is its effect on
 flour and water? Does plain flour and water do the same thing
 that flour, water and yeast does?

Matt. 23:25 Cup and platter, clean on outside, dirty on inside.
Serve special meal with special dishes. Have a bowl or cup very dirty inside. Does the child want to eat out of it?

Ps. 5:9 Throat is an open sepulchre.
What is an open grave waiting for? The hypocrite destroys his victim.

Ps. 55:21 Words are smoother than butter, softer than oil, but are drawn swords.
Appear inviting and pleasant, but mean to harm.

Jer. 9:8 Tongue is an arrow shot out.
Shoot an arrow and try to call it back.
The hypocrite's tongue is a weapon. It does damage that can not be re-called.

Hos. 6:4 Goodness like morning cloud, dew that goes away.
Observe the clouds some summer morning. How long do the morning clouds last on a hot summer day? How much do they produce?
Watch the morning dew. How long does it last?

Matt. 23:24 Blind guides.
Blindfold one child. Blindfold another child to serve as his guide throughout the house. How well can he guide?

Matt. 23:24 Strain out gnat, and swallow camel.
Imagine a camel in your soup!
Serve soup or ice cream or some other food that has two foreign objects in it, one very small, and one large and more disgusting. (Maybe a fake fly, spider, etc.?) Make a big point of removing the small object. Then start serving the food without removing the larger object.

Matt. 23:27 Whitewashed tomb, full of dead man's bones.

Matt. 23:33 Serpents, brood of vipers.

Lk. 11:44 Like graves, not seen, walked over.

Lk. 14:34 Like salt without savor.
Bake bread without salt, serve Chinese food without salt/soy sauce, etc. Does it taste the same?
Study up on salting fish, meat, etc. and try it. What happens to fish you do not salt?
I haven't figured out what to use yet, but I would like to think of some other white substance that I could grind up and put into the salt shaker at the table. Then I would serve a meal that is very obviously lacking salt, and watch the results when the

family used the salt shaker.

I Tim. 4:2 Conscience is seared with a hot iron.
*Observe a burn on the skin. First it stings a lot, then it hurts
very little, and then it sometimes has no feeling at all.*

Js. 1:22-24 Like looking in a mirror and forgetting.
*Take a shower, wash hair, and come to the breakfast table without
combing hair, etc.*
*Come out ready to go out for a special event with hair unkempt, face
visibly dirty, etc. "I looked in the mirror! Isn't that enough?"*

Jude 12, 13 Clouds without water, carried by wind.
Only promise, no profit.

Trees with withering fruit, plucked up.
*Find an example in your yard, or if you're too blessed to have
a diseased or unproductive tree, search one out in an orchard
during U-pick season. We know an unfortunate example at a
peach orchard we have always picked from for canning. The
owner lost almost his entire orchard to disease.*

Raging waves, foaming out own shame.
*Observe the waves along the beach, as they stir up sand and
dirt in the foam.*
*Go beachcombing, and notice all the debris that the waves throw
onto the shore.*

Wandering stars, blackness reserved forever.

Pr. 25:14 Like cloud without rain.
Holds promise, but doesn't produce. No blessing comes from it.

Blessings of sincerity and honesty:

(See also "blessings" section under "Lying")

Matt. 5:16 Brings glory to God.
I Cor. 10:31 Do all to the glory of God.

Stories that illustrate the consequences of hypocrisy:

Herod, Matt. 2:8 Attempt to deceive simple.

Judas, Matt. 26:25, 48; 27:3-5 Betraying Jesus led to injustice, his death, and to Judas's own suicide.

Pharisees, Matt. 15:1-9 Heart far from God, worship in vain.
Matt. 22:15-22 Manufactured questions with the purpose of ensnaring.
Mk. 12:13,14 Trickery.
Jn. 8:4-9, 9:24 Trickery.

Ananias and Sapphira, Acts 5:1-10 Their dishonesty was revealed. There was no profit from their plot, died.

Saul, I Sam. 18:21-25 Under the pretense of honoring, tried to use daughter as a snare.

Haman, Est. 3:8-13 Pretense of loyalty could have destroyed entire nation.

Daniel's accusers, Dan. 6:1-24 Led to injustice toward Daniel, and then to the accusers' deaths.

Absalom, II Sam. 15:1-9 Deceiving people, feigned humility with the intent to usurp the throne.

Parable of the two sons, Matt. 21:28-32 One son said no, then repented and did his father's wishes. Other son said yes, but did not actually obey.

Verses to memorize:

1 Sam. 16:7b ...for man looketh on the outward appearance, but the LORD looketh on the heart.

Lk. 12:2 For there is nothing covered that will not be revealed, nor hidden that will not be known.

Lk. 16:15 And he said unto them, Ye are they which justify yourselves before men; but God knoweth your hearts: for that which is highly esteemed among men is abomination in the sight of God.

Jer. 17:9 The heart is deceitful above all things, and desperately wicked: who can know it?

Ps. 139:23-24 Search me, O God, and know my heart: try me, and know my thoughts: and see if there be any wicked way in me, and lead me in the way everlasting.

1 Cor 10:31 Whether therefore ye eat, or drink, or whatsoever ye do, do all to the glory of God.

Js. 3:17 But the wisdom that is from above is first pure, then peaceable, gentle, and easy to be entreated, full of mercy and good fruits, without partiality, and without hypocrisy.

Matt. 15:8-9 These people draw near to Me with their mouth, and honor Me with their lips, but their heart is far from Me. And in vain they worship Me, teaching as doctrines the commandments of men.

Stubborness/Self-Will

(See also Pride, Scoffer, Disobedience, Defiance)

General information and commandments about this sin:

(See general information in sections for "Disobedience," "Pride," "Scoffer.")

What happens, or should happen, to the stubborn person:

Pr. 1:24-31 Call, will be refused; stretch out hand, will not be regarded, ignores counsel and reproof, God will laugh at his calamity, mock at his fear. Fear will come as desolation, destruction as a whirlwind, distress and anguish. Will eat the fruit of his own way, filled with own desires.
Do not spare child from the natural consequences that result from his stubbornness.
Pray for God's sovereign and obvious discipline in the child's life.
Study whirlwinds. What is their effect? How does this same type of thing occur in one's life?
Withhold counsel and aid to the child when he has been willful and stubborn.

II Chr. 30:6-10 Should not be stiffnecked. Yield to God, enter His sanctuary, serve God.
Design projects of service for the child.
Diligently train the child in Bible study. Help him develop a habit of consistent study of the Bible; be consistent in family worship time, being careful to make this time practical and understandable to your children.

Ps. 95:8-11 Will not enter into God's rest.
Deny participation in special outing or recreation.
Deny participation in communion.

Pr. 29:1 Suddenly destroyed without remedy.

Pr. 28:9 His prayer is an abomination.
Help your child understand this concept -- that his willfulness destroys his fellowship with God. Encourage his repentance before family and private prayer times.

Pr. 13:18 Poverty and shame.
Deny belongings and earnings.

Do not allow child access to any of his spending money.
Levy fines for certain acts of stubbornness.
Do not pay child for work that would normally be rewarded with pay.

Pr. 28:13,14 Harden heart, will fall into calamity, not proper, will fall into mischief.
Pray for God's clear and just discipline.
Construct some sort of "calamity" for the child: No playtime. Take away privileges. Take away belongings. Isolate from other children. Give extra work.

Rom. 1:28+ Given up to a debased mind.

Deut. 21:18-21 Stoning for a rebellious son, under the Mosaic judicial law.
This is one of the areas of discipline that we believe calls for spanking, when dealing with young children. If the self-will and stubbornness is directed towards parents and their instructions, the child is rebelling against God and his delegated authorities.

The sin of stubbornness is likened to:

Pr. 26:11 A dog returning to his vomit.
What a graphic illustration!

Is. 48:4 Neck of iron sinew, brow of brass.
A stiff neck hurts, limits, and affects the entire body.
When the neck is stiff, it is hard to turn, which affects our ability to see around us.

Zech. 7:11+ Heart is adamant stone.
Pray for God to change the child's heart. Ezekiel 11:19-20 are verses of encouragement in this area. Only God can change a heart.
Experiment with a stone. What can pierce through it? A needle? A nail?

Matt. 23:37,38 Chicks not going under hen's wings.
Watch this happen, or observe other wayward baby animals.
We have enjoyed Janette Oke's series of children's stories about animals. Many of them give good illustrations of stubborn, wayward offspring and the mischief they find themselves in as a result.

Pr. 12:4 A self-willed wife is rottenness to the bones.
"Rotten" bones are unreliable and painful.
Soak chicken bones in vinegar overnight. Are they still hard and strong and able to support the body as they once did?

The blessings of a submissive spirit:

(See "Blessings" section under "Disobedience" and "Defiance.")

Stories that illustrate the consequences of stubbornness:

People of Noah's Day, Gen. 6: 3,5,7 Led to their destruction.

Sodomites, Gen. 19: 8,14 Led to their destruction.

Pharaoh, Ex. 7:14,22,23; 8:15,19,32; 9:7,12,35; 10:20,28 Resulted in numerous plagues, death of his own son, destruction of his army in the Red Sea.

Israelites, Num. 14:22-23 Would not see the Promised Land.
*Verse 24 makes it very clear that Caleb served with "another spirit."
God blessed his obedience by bringing him into the Promised Land,
and allowing his children to possess it.*

Sons of Eli, I Sam. 2:22-25 Led to death.

Verses to memorize:

Ps. 51:17 The sacrifices of God are a broken spirit: a broken and a contrite heart, O God, thou wilt not despise.

1 John 1:9 If we confess our sins, he is faithful and just to forgive us our sins, and to cleanse us from all unrighteousness.

Disobedience
(See also Stubbornness)

General information and commandments about this sin:

Heb. 13:17 We should obey and submit to the authorities God puts over us. They are watching over our souls.

Rom. 1:30 Reprobates.

Eph. 6:6-7 Not men pleasers, but glory to God.

I Sam. 15:23 Rebellion is as sin of witchcraft, and stubbornness is as iniquity and idolatry.
Disobedience shows that we are placing ourselves over God's authority in our lives.

Eph. 6:1 We are to obey our parents.

I Sam. 15:22 Obedience is better than sacrifice.
We see this over and over in our children. They want to pick flowers for Mommy instead of coming in and getting ready for bed as they have been told to do. They want to help Bethany with her bottle instead of washing hands and coming to the table. Even though they are performing some other helpful task, if they are not obeying our directions, they are disciplined for disobedience, and reminded of this verse, and what happened to Saul when he chose to sacrifice rather than obey.

Col.3:20 Obey parents.

Col 3:22 Obey masters.

Titus 3:1 Obey magistrates.

What happens, or should happen, to the disobedient person:

Pr. 2:22 Cut off from the earth, uprooted.
Thin out non-productive branches from trees and bushes.
Pull weeds out of the garden.
Why can we not allow these plants to remain?

Pr. 10:7 Name of the wicked will rot.
Write the child's name, perhaps in extra fancy script, then bury it someplace in your yard. Dig it up in a few days. What happened?

Pr. 10:27 Years of the wicked will be shortened.
Limit the child's activities, put to bed earlier, longer nap, earlier curfew.
Imagine the literal meaning of this. The wicked may not have the pleasure of seeing their children and grandchildren.

Pr. 10:28 Expectation will perish.
Do not allow the child to participate in planned activity.
Deny requests.

Pr. 10:30 Will not inhabit the earth.
Deny inheritance, withhold deposit into long-term savings, levy a fine from long-term savings.
A child should understand that any potential inheritance of the family wealth is contingent on his faithfulness and obedience to God.

Pr. 17:2 Will be ruled by wise servant.
Place the disobedient child under the authority of an obedient child while performing a job. (Watch out for pride in the obedient child, and bitterness in the disobedient.)

Pr. 21:7 Violence of wicked will destroy them. Refuse to do justice.

Pr. 28:9 His prayer is an abomination.
Teach the child to confess and repent of the sin of disobedience, so that his fellowship and communication with God will not be interrupted.
Do not grant the requests of the child, when he has been disobedient and unrepentant.

Rom. 1:28 + Given over to debased mind.
Disobedience has a long-term effect on the child. If he is given up to his own desires, he is destined for a life of misery as he attempts to be his own master.

Lev. 26:14-39 Enemies reign, spend strength in vain, no increase or harvest from efforts.
Deny profit or earnings from labor.
Pray for God's obvious discipline in various situations -- in his employment in or outside the home, in gardening efforts, in family events.

Pr. 1:28 Will call on God, and He will not answer.
Deny requests, allow the child to suffer the natural consequences of his disobedience. Do not bail him out.

Is. 1:20. If willing to obey, will eat the good of the land.
If we refuse to obey, but rebel, will be devoured by the sword.

Make it clear to the child that he can make the choice between blessing and cursing, or rewards and discipline, in his life. He can choose to obey or disobey, but he will be disciplined when he chooses to disobey.

Deut. 28 Cursed: in the city and field, in the fruit of body and land, in the increase of their livestock, in pestilence, disease, no benefit from labor, no harvest, plagues, brought to nought, scattered, no rest, fear. Children will be taken into captivity, will serve enemies.

Study this passage together as a family. Write up two lists, one about the obedient, one about the disobedient, and then list the appropriate cursings and blessings under the proper section.
Which events would your children prefer to have in their lives?
Our children are working on little illustrated books on this chapter. One page shows cursings of the disobedient; the facing page shows the contrasting blessings of the obedient.
Deut. 4 is another good chapter to study.
Withhold pay from the child.
Put child in the position of servanthood for a specified period of time.
Pray for God's clear hand of discipline in the events of the child's life.

Lev. 26:36 Fear of enemies, flee when not pursued.

II Thess. 3:6 Withdraw from the disorderly.
Temporarily isolate the child from other children.
Limit child's association with other habitually disobedient children.

II Thess. 3:14-15 Do not keep company with the disobedient, that he may be ashamed. Do not treat as enemy, but admonish as a brother.
I think there is a place, if done carefully and with prayer, for explaining to other parents that you have chosen to not allow your children to play with their children because of the disobedient spirit you see in the children. This is difficult to do, and can offend people, but is part of our responsibility to our children, and to our brothers in Christ. We must do it with a humble and loving spirit.

Ps. 68:21 God will wound.
Pray for God's discipline.

Ezek. 5:12 Pestilence, famine and sword.

Ex. 20:5, Num. 14:33 Children suffer.
Deny inheritance or long-term savings deposit.

The sin of disobedience is likened to:

Clay tablet depicting besieged city, Ezek. 4:1-3
Read this passage, and follow God's instructions to Ezekiel for acting out this lesson for your children. The boys will especially enjoy this one!
This also could be done with matchsticks, constructing a city-like structure and then lighting it on fire, or construct a city out of paper and destroy with fire.

Shaved hair, Ezek. 5:1-4
After a haircut take the hair and throw outside into the wind, cut with a "sword," and burn, following instructions to Ezekiel in this passage.

Darkness, the disobedient doesn't know what makes him stumble, Pr. 4:19
Try to operate in a totally darkened house.
Go for a walk outside at night, away from other light sources. Start with a flashlight, and then turn it off and walk in complete darkness.
I recall a party in my junior high days that included a darkened room that we had to walk through, barefooted. The floor was covered with cooked spaghetti noodles. Yuck! We sure didn't know what made us stumble!

Foolish man building house on sand, Matt. 7:24-27
Build a sand castle, or a model fort with sand as its foundation. Then create your own storm and see how long the building stands.

Horse or mule with no understanding, Ps. 32:9
Attend a rodeo and watch how the bucking broncos, bulls, and steer must be handled when they have no self-control of their own.
Read about horses, or visit a riding stable. Why does the horse have a bridle in his mouth? Why must he have outward control?

Deaf adder, ignoring charmers, Ps. 58:3-5
Is useless to his masters.

Ruined sash, Jer. 13:1-11

Broken pottery, Jer. 19:1-11
The sash and the pottery are both rendered useless, irreparable, and only garbage to be disposed of.
Talk about these verses when a dish gets broken.

Stories that illustrate the consequences of disobedience:

Eli's sons, I Sam. 2:12-4:18 Led to their death. Were replaced by obedient. Eli was also punished for his negligence.

Adam and Eve, Gen. 3:6-24 Led to shame, blame, cursing, and were driven from the garden.

Lot's wife, Gen. 19:26 Led to her death.

Israelites and manna, Ex. 16:16-20, 23-27 Manna spoiled when they hoarded it. People suffered hunger on the Sabbath when they did not gather a double portion on the previous day.

Israelites and the Amorites, Deut. 1:26-43 Denied promised land, plagues, then went and fought after being told not to, and were defeated.

Saul, I Sam 13:8-15 Lost his kingdom after assuming role and authority that were not his. He lost the responsibility that *was* his.

Jonah, Jonah 1-2 Cast off the ship, swallowed by fish.
Jonah was isolated and allowed to suffer the consequences of his disobedience.

Moses and Aaron at Meribah, Num. 20:2-13 Failure to glorify God, didn't hallow God in eyes of people. vs. 12, Moses and Aaron not allowed to take people into the Promised Land. vs. 24, Aaron not allowed to enter Promised Land.

Study Exodus, Numbers and Deuteronomy and note the times of the Israelites' obedience and disobedience and the consequences of their decisions.

The blessings of obedience:

Pr. 16:7 Enemies at peace with him.

Jn. 13:17 Happy.

Pr. 1:9 Graceful ornament on head, chains about the neck.
Allow child to wear a special crown (real or homemade from fabric or paper) at dinner, on an outing, etc.
Wear special necklace or medal-of-honor.
Give young child shiny beads to string into special necklace.
Give special necklace or locket with Pr. 1:9 written on it.

Note: Doorposts carries a set of patterns which includes instructions for making cloth crowns and medals of honor. See ordering information at back of book.

Pr. 1:33 Listens, will dwell safely, secure, without fear of evil.

Ex. 20:12 Days are long.
Allow later bedtime or curfew, no nap, longer playtime, shorter schoolday.
Give a new clock or wristwatch.

Pr. 2:5-9 Understand fear of God, find knowledge, wisdom, God is his shield. Guards paths of justice, preserves way, will understand righteousness and justice, equity and every good path.
Make a special shield with the verse, Ps. 28:7a written on it.

Pr. 2:21 Will dwell in the land.
Make a deposit into a special savings account that will aid the child in purchasing a house or land in the future.

Pr. 3:1-2 Length of days, long life, peace.
See last two listings under Ex. 20:12 (above).

Matt. 5:19 Great in kingdom of God.
Grant the child more responsibility, honor, and privilege.

Ps. 1:3 Will be like a tree, will flourish.
Give the child his own fruit or flowering tree to plant and care for. Perhaps you could even put a sign beneath the tree with this verse on it.

I Jn. 5:14-15 Will receive what we ask of God.
Give the child the opportunity to ask a special request, and then grant it for him.

Lev. 26:3,5,9,12 Eat bread to the full, looked upon favorably, fruitful, God will walk with him.
Go out to eat at an "All-You-Can-Eat" restaurant.
Make homemade bread and eat together warm from the oven with butter or jam.
Have a special cinnamon toast bedtime snack.
Serve first at mealtime.
Give first choice in sharing situations.
Take the child on a special walk, hike, or backpacking trip.
Make a special fruit salad and enjoy while you talk about fruitfulness of trees and of obedient lives.

Matt. 25:20-23 Faithful in little, ruler over many things.
Give the child added responsibility and privilege.
Put him in charge in different situations.

Ex. 19:5 Will be a peculiar treasure.
*Give the child a special "treasure" at an appointed time in his
life. Base this reward on true, consistent obedience. The
treasure could be an ounce of gold, silver, heirlooms, etc.
We are planning to give this to our children at the age of 12 or
13, after they have attained a certain standard. We are listing
goals in memory work, character development, service, and other
areas that we want each child to reach by that age.*

I Ki. 3:14 Lengthen days.
See previous listing above for Ex. 20:12.

Is. 1:19 Eat good of land.
*Go out to eat.
Make special treat to enjoy together.
Give child extra portion of special fruit dessert.*

I Jn. 3:22 Will receive what we ask of Him.
Allow the child to ask for a special favor, and then grant it.

Stories that illustrate the blessings of obedience:

Shadrach, Meshach, and Abednego, Dan. 3, especially vs. 30 Were
promoted after their deliverance from the fiery furnace.

Sarah, I Pet. 3:6 Honored.

Abraham, Heb. 11:8, Acts 7:3-8 Blessed with son, descendants
inherit the land.

Noah, Gen. 6:9,22; 7:5; Heb. 11:7 Saved with family when rest of
the world was destroyed.

Caleb, Num. 14:24, Josh. 14:6-14 Granted inheritance of land.

Daniel and friends, Dan. 1:8-21 Granted good understanding,
dwelt safely, flourished.

Israel, Ex. 12:28; 39:42-43; Num. 9:20-21 Spared in the Passover,
protection and guidance.

Hezekiah, II Kgs. 18:1-7 Prospered.

Verses to memorize:

Eph. 6:1 Children, obey your parents in the Lord: for this is right.

Ps. 119:9 How can a young man cleanse his way? By taking heed according to Your word. (NKJV)

Ps. 143:10 Teach me to do thy will; for thou art my God: thy spirit is good; lead me into the land of uprightness.

1 John 2:3 Now by this we know that we know Him, if we keep His commandments. (NKJV)

Heb. 13:17 Obey those who rule over you, and be submissive, for they watch out for your souls, as those who must give account. Let them do so with joy and not with grief, for that would be unprofitable for you. (NKJV)

Ps. 119:11 Thy word have I hid in mine heart, that I might not sin against thee.

Defiance

(See also Pride, Stubbornness, Disobedience)

General information and commandments about this sin:

Ps. 50:17 Hates instruction, casts words aside.

Pr. 15:32 Despises own soul.
  Leads to his own destruction.

Pr. 21:29 The wicked hardens his face.
  A defiant spirit is often evident in a child's face.
  Pr. 29:1 Hardens neck.
  The neck is designed to bend and curve. A stiff neck leads to pain and injury.

Jer. 7:24 Go backward instead of forward.
  Set out a "prize" in front of a young child, a treat to eat or some favorite toy, etc., and have him step backward over and over in an attempt to reach it. Defiance will never help us reach our goal of being more like Jesus, and bringing glory to Him.

Pr. 19:26 Brings shame of reproach.

Rom. 1:30 Reprobates.

Rom. 13:1 Should subject ourselves to the authorities that God has placed over us.

Rom. 13:7 Render to all their due.

Ex. 22:28 Should not curse rulers.
  We need to set an example of this, as parents, in our response to the authorities that God has placed over us. We should submit with the right attitude to employers, civil authorities, husbands. We should not be bitter towards ungodly authorities, but pray for them and obey when they are not requiring us to disobey God's higher authority.

I Pet. 2:13-14 Submit to man's ordinances. Kings and governors are to punish evildoers and praise them that do well.
  A good reminder to us as parents. We need to punish when the child does evil, and praise when he does well.

What happens, or should happen, to the defiant person:

We need to be diligent to consistently and lovingly discipline a child before he reaches this point of defiance. Act firmly with the young *child. Do not allow him to exert his will over yours.*

Rom. 1:28+ Given over to a debased mind.

Ex. 21:15-17, Lev. 20:9, Deut. 21:18-21   Death.
Spanking is appropriate for acts of willful disobedience and defiance against authority.

Deut. 29:19-21 Anger of the Lord, curses, blot out name from under heaven.
Defiance against family authority is grounds for "blotting" a child's name from the family inheritance. This does not mean that the child is "excommunicated" from the family.   There is still communication and love shown. But good stewardship of God's blessing in a family requires that its wealth be passed on to children who are obedient to God and His Word. Defiance against parental authority reflects defiance against God and His sovereign authority.

Pr. 10:17 Goes astray.
Leads to other sins and loss of fellowship.

Jer. 6:19 Brings evil and the fruit of their thoughts.
Allow the child to suffer the natural fruit/consequences of his defiance.

Rom. 2:4-5 Wrath. Revelation of the righteous judgment of God. Will not escape.
Don't bail child out. Let him experience the fruits of his sin.

Pr. 28:13-14 Falls into mischief.

Pr. 29:1 Destroyed without remedy.

Pr. 20:20 Lamp put out in deep darkness.
Do this. Go for a walk on a dark night with flashlight, then turn the flashlight out. Go to the basement with a lantern, then put the lantern out. How well can you see? Is it comfortable to be in such darkness?

Lev. 26:21 Seven times more plagues.
Pray for God's clear discipline in the child's life.
Do not cease to discipline the child.

Deut. 28:15-68 Cursing in crops, disease, failure, drought, famine, defeat, madness, oppression, ruined plans, theft, offspring taken into captivity.
Study all the areas of cursing in this passage. Outline them. How could God discipline you in the same ways?

Tit.1:10-11 Should stop the mouths of subversive teachers.

Do not tolerate a defiant child spreading his sinful attitude among his siblings or friends.
Do not let the child voice his rebellion in front of other children.

Deut. 21:18-21 Defiant toward elders. Was stoned under Mosaic judicial law.

Ex. 21:15 Strike parent, put to death.

Ex. 21:17 Curse parent, put to death.

Lev. 20:9 Curse parents, put to death.
All the above verses list punishment as it existed under the Mosaic judicial law, which reflects the gravity of these sins.
These sins call for spanking, and for counsel from church authorities.

Rom. 13:2-4 Bring judgment on self, should do what is good, and not be afraid of authorities. The appointed authority is the avenger to execute God's judgment.

Eph. 5:20-21 Give thanks and submit in fear of God.
Pray with the child and then have him work on writing out a list of qualities he can be thankful for in the authorities he is rebelling against. (If rebellion is aimed at your, perhaps another respected adult could lead him in this activity.)

Ps. 81:11-12 Given up to own lusts, walk in own counsels.
Withhold counsel from defiant child.

Ps. 107:10-12 Heart brought down with labor. Falls with none to help.
Give the child extra work.
Arrange for the child to work under the authority of another person, a person who understands the child's problem with authority and is willing to work with him.

Pr. 1:24-31 God will laugh, not answer, mock at fear, eat fruit of own way.
Allow the child to live with the consequences of his defiance. Do not spare him from the pain and divine discipline that will come into his life.

Ps. 68:6 Will dwell in dry land.
Deny some of the natural blessings of being a member of your family. (i.e. have him buy his own clothes, pay partial room and board, deny younger child his toys, etc.) Do this with a loving, not vindictive, spirit.

Isa. 42:22-25 Robbed and spoiled, snared in holes, hidden in prison houses. Prey, none delivers.

The sin of defiance is likened to:

I Sam. 15:23 Sin of witchcraft, iniquity, idolatry.

II Sam 23:6 Thorns thrust away, burned with fire.
Watch brush pile burning.

Ps. 32:9 Horse or mule without understanding. Needs bit and bridle.
*Attend a rodeo and observe the bucking broncos and bulls. What do
the cowboys do to bring the animals under control?
How does the cowboy control the horse he is riding?*

Ps. 58:3-5 Deaf adder. Won't listen to charmers.
How useful to snake charmers is a snake with a mind of his own?

Is. 48:4 Neck is iron sinew, brow is brass.
*A stiff neck is painful and limits our movement and abilities.
A stiff neck does not flex and give when it needs to.*

Pr. 26:11 Dog returning to his vomit.

Matt. 23:37,38 Chick that won't go under hen's wings.
What will happen to that chick?

Zech. 7:11-13 Heart is adamant stone.
*Can't be pierced, bent, formed. Try piercing a stone with various
tools. Can only be crushed and broken.*

Matt. 11:16-21 Like children that call out and are never pleased.
*Observe a cranky, fussy child or baby. No matter what any one tries
to comfort him with, he is not happy.*

The blessings of quiet submission:

Eph. 6:2-3 Honor parents, will be well with you, and days will
be long.

Ex. 20:12 Honor parents and days will be long on the earth.
*Allow the child to go to bed earlier, stay out later, go out in
the evening for a special date with his parents, no naptime,
shorter school day, longer playtime, less chores.*

I Pet. 2:15 Will put to silence the ignorance of foolish men.
*True submission brings glory to God.
Teach child that he is serving God when he submits to the
authorities over him.*

Eph. 5:20-21 Give thanks, submit to one another.
Have older child complete a writing assignment in which he lists

*all that he can be thankful for as he lives under this authority
that he is resisting.*
Help a younger child perform this same task.
*Pray with the child for God's help in being thankful for the
authorities that He has placed in the child's life.*

*(See also "blessing" section under "Disobedience,"
"Stubbornness," and "Pride.")*

Stories that illustrate the consequences of defiance and rebellion:

Korah, Num. 16:3-35 His rebellion against God and Moses led to
his death and the deaths of all in his family and his associates.

Saul, I Sam. 15 Rejected Word of the Lord, and was then rejected
as king.

Eli's sons, I Sam. 2:25 Destroyed, along with their father.

Amaziah, II Chr. 25:16 Led to his captivity and subsequent murder.

Jehoiakim, Jer. 36:22-24 Destroyed scrolls without fear. Led to
loss of heirs to the throne, destruction, and captivity to Babylon.

Amon, II Chr. 33:23-24 Murdered by own servants.

Belshazzar, Dan. 5:22-23 Led to his death and division of the
kingdom.

Verses to memorize:

Pr. 15:32 He who disdains instruction despises his own soul, but
he who heeds rebuke gets understanding. (NKJV)

Pr. 21:29 A wicked man hardens his face, but as for the upright, he
establishes his way. (NKJV)

Lam 3:27 It is good for a man that he bear the yoke in his youth.

Pr. 29:1 He who is often rebuked, and hardens his neck, will
suddenly be destroyed, and that without remedy. (NKJV)

Scoffer/Scorner

(See also Defiance and Pride)

General information and commandments about this sin:

Job 21:14-15   Doesn't desire knowledge of God's ways.

Acts 13:45, Lk. 16:14   Motivated by envy.
Deal with envy in the child's life, as well.

Pr. 1:22   Delights in scorning.

Pr. 9:7-8   Hates reprover.

Pr. 12:1   He who hates reproof is stupid.

Pr. 13:1   Doesn't listen to rebuke.

Pr. 15:12   Won't go to the wise.

Pr. 15:32   Despises own soul.

Pr. 17:21   Brings sorrow to mother.

Pr. 21:24   Proud and haughty, arrogant pride.
Deal with pride problem in child's life.

Ps. 1:1   Starts by walking with ungodly, then standing with sinners,
then sits in the seat of the scornful.
Limit association or friendships with scornful children.
Protect your child from the tempting influence of ungodly friends.

What happens, or should happen, to the scorner:

Pr. 24:9   He is an abomination to other men.

Pr. 3:34   God scorns scorners.

Pr. 14:6   Seeks wisdom but cannot find.
Withhold your counsel from a scornful child.

Pr. 19:29   Judgment.
Discipline consistently. Make the wrong clear to the child.

Pr. 22:10   Cast out scorner, contention, strife, and reproach will end.
*Remove the scornful child. Isolate him. Do not allow him to go
unpunished, because other children will be noticing what happens
to him.*

Pr. 13:18   Poverty and shame.
Deny the child pay and privileges.
Take away belongings and rights.

Ps. 107:11-12 Bring down heart with labor, fall down, no help.
Give extra work without pay.
Do not spare or protect from the consequences of his scornful
attitude.

Pr. 21:11 Punish, and it will make the simple wise.
Make the child an example, not by publicly disciplining him, but
by making sure that onlooking children understand that the scoffer
is not going to go unpunished.

Isa. 29:20 Consumed.
Spank.

Pr. 15:10 He who hates reproof will die.
Talk about the consequences of scorning with the child.
Read books and Bible stories that illustrate this truth.

Pr. 13:13 Will be destroyed.
Spank.

II Chr. 36:16 Those who mocked and despised the prophets fell
under
the wrath of God without remedy.
Study in the Bible about what happened to the people who mocked
God's prophets.

Pr. 9:12 Will bear punishment alone.
Don't excuse behavior or protect the child from the consequences of
his sinful actions.

Isa. 5:24-25 Kindles God's wrath.
Display controlled, righteous anger.

Pr. 19:25 Smite the scorner and the simple will beware.
Make the child an example.

Pr. 10:17 Refuse reproof, go astray.
Tell stories from your own life of when you scorned reproof, and
then went astray.
Read books that illustrate this sin.

Pr. 29:8 Brings city into a snare.
Must be disciplined or will endanger the entire family.

The sin of scorning is likened to:

Isa. 5:24 Root as rottenness, blossom as dust.

Examine the roots of shriveled plants in the garden.
Observe what happens to flowers after they are picked.

Isa. 10:15 Ax, rod, staff speaking against their maker/user.
How much can an ax do by itself? Tell your child to send
the ax outside to chop the wood. What is his reaction?

Isa. 5:24 Stubble devoured by fire, chaff consumed by flame.
Watch field burning and what happens to the stubble on the ground.
Burn a dry brush pile, and see how long the brush lasts.
Watch how fast a dry Christmas tree burns to ashes.

Stories that illustrate the consequences of scornfulness:

Rabshekah and Sennacherib, II Kgs. 18 and 19 Assyria ends up
defeated.

Hagar, Gen. 21:9-10 Cast out of the household to restore peace.

Youths and Elisha, II Kgs. 2:23-24 Destroyed.

People of Judah, II Chr. 36:16-17 Mocked prophets, went into
captivity.

Pharaoh, Ex. 5:2, 10:24-29 Plagues, death of son, destruction of
part of his army.

Asa, I Kgs. 15:14, II Chr. 16:10-13 Anger with prophet led to wars
and disease.

Ahab, I Kgs. 18:17; 21:20; 22:8-37 Went to battle in disguise but
was still killed.

Ahaz, II Chr. 28:22-23 Defeated by Syria. Led to idol worship.

Sanballat, Neh. 4:1 Jews defended themselves.

Noah's generation, Gen.6:5-7 Destroyed in flood.

Sodomites, Gen. 19:7-9 City destroyed.

The blessings of humility and a teachable spirit:

Pr. 13:13 Fear commandment, will be rewarded.
Grant privileges and responsibilities.
Express thankfulness to the child after he has humbly accepted
correction. Pray with him and thank God for his repentance.

Pr. 13:18 Regard reproof, will be honored.
Honor and commend the child when you see his godly response to your reproof.

Pr. 14:6 Knowledge is easy to him.

Pr. 15:32 Gets understanding.

Pr. 19:25 Reproof leads to understanding.
Help the child see his own growth and progress as he correctly responds to discipline.

Pr. 15:31 Will abide among the wise.
Help child recognize when God blesses him with good counsel and righteous friendships.

Pr. 19:20 Will be wise in latter years.
Tell the child stories of the fruit in your own life from correctly responding to discipline and correction.

Pr. 3:34 God gives grace to lowly.

Stories that illustrate the blessings of a teachable spirit:

David and Nathan, II Sam. 12:1-13 David's humble response to Nathan's reproof led to his forgiveness. But he also suffered discipline.

Sergius Paulus when Elymas was stricken, Acts 13:6-12 Led to his salvation. Learned from the example of discipline to the scornful.
Others learn when they observe the discipline of a scoffer.

Verses to memorize:

Ps. 1:1-2 Blessed is the man that walketh not in the counsel of the ungodly, nor standeth in the way of sinners, nor sitteth in the seat of the scornful. But his delight is in the law of the LORD; and in his law doth he meditate day and night.

Pr. 13:1 A wise son heeds his father's instruction, but a scoffer does not listen to rebuke. (NKJV)

Pr. 3:34 Surely He scorns the scornful, but gives grace to the humble. (NKJV)

Pr. 15:10 Harsh discipline is for him who forsakes the way, and he who hates correction will die. (NKJV)

Scriptural principles to follow when dealing with a scoffer:

The scoffer has a rebellious heart, no reverence for God, no humility of mind, no submission of will. He hates reproof and the reprover.

The scoffer is good motivation for us to be continually faithful and diligent in the "little" areas of discipline. Bring the child under subjection early, deal quickly with rebellion, teach a reverence and fear of God, do not accommodate or encourage pride. Do not allow "walking" with the ungodly. (Ps. 1:1)

PRAY: For a responsive heart, for God to work in the child's life. Ezekiel 11:19 says, "Then I will give them one heart, and I will put a new spirit within them, and take the stony heart out of their flesh, and give them a heart of flesh."

God alone can change the stony heart of the scorner. The scorner is rebellious and proud and not open to reproof. Pray that the child will have a listening ear, tender conscience, and teachable spirit.

"The plough enters most effectually when the earth is softened."[1]

Do not be discouraged. Heb. 12:3, "For consider Him who endured such hostility from sinners against Himself, lest you become weary and discouraged in your soul."

Consider Christ's example in dealing with scoffers. In Matt. 16:1-4 and 21:23-27, He did not answer the Pharisees. In Matt. 22:41-46 and Lk. 13:14-17, He did answer them. Eccles. 3:7 reminds us that there is a "time to keep silence, and a time to speak."

Eccles. 8:5 also tells us that a "wise man's heart discerneth both time and judgment."

Pr. 9:7-9 says, "Reprove not a scorner, lest he hate thee."

Amos 5:13 says that there are times when "the prudent shall keep silence in that time."

Matt. 7:6 warns us not to "cast...your pearls before swine, lest they trample them under their feet, and turn again and rend you."

When Rabshekah was taunting Hezekiah's people, Hezekiah ordered the people not to answer.

There is precedent for *silence* when dealing with a scoffer.

However, this doesn't mean that we should never reprove the scorner. There is also "a time to speak." We just need to exercise wisdom in discerning the proper time for reproof, and we need to reprove with a humble, loving spirit.

Prov. 26:4 advises us, "Answer not a fool according to his folly, lest thou also be like unto him."

We must not argue and become emotional. We should wait until we are calm, and not attempt to reprove during the heat of a challenge. We must be very careful to not reprove with the wrong attitude.

Prov. 26:5 counsels us to not answer a fool in his own foolish manner when we are in a position where we must answer.

I Peter 3:9 says, "Not rendering evil for evil, or railing for railing, but contrariwise, blessing."

Study Moses and the prophets. They generally made rebellion against God the issue when people rebelled and scoffed.

In Num. 16:11 Moses accuses Korah and his associates of "gathering together against the Lord." Later, in Num. 20:12, God pronounced judgment against Moses and Aaron because they did not "sanctify [Him] in the eyes of the children of Israel." Their rebellion against God was not the focal point in this event. Moses was angry and impatient and asked, "Must *we* fetch you water out of this rock?"

Psalm 106:32 and 33 says, "...it went ill with Moses for their sakes: because they provoked his spirit, so that he spake unadvisedly with his lips."

This mistake cost the meekest man on earth his entrance into the Promised Land! His action with the people under his leadership had not brought glory to God.

David, when refused by Nabal, responded in anger and planned to take revenge. He responded to Abigail's humble reproof and repented of his planned wrongdoing.

"How forcible are right words!" Job 6:25

"A word spoken in due season, how good it is!" Pr. 15:23

Abigail's words were well chosen and timed, and they fell upon a soft and teachable heart.

"A needle pierces deeper into flesh, than a sword into stone."[2]

When disciplining a scorner, we must pray -- for a prepared heart in the scorner, and for a prepared and godly reprover.

We must also remember that the discipline of a scorner is an example to others, even if the scorner doesn't respond. In Acts 13, when Elymas, the sorcerer, was stricken blind for his scornful attitude, the Roman deputy, Sergius Paulus, became a believer.

Pr. 19:25 reminds us that when we "smite a scorner, the simple will beware."

---

[1]Charles Bridges, A Commentary on Proverbs (Carlisle, Penn.: The Banner of Truth Trust, 1987), p. 468.

[2]Bridges, p. 262.

Arguing/Contention

(See also Pride, Selfishness, Anger, Gossip,
Brawling Woman, Bitterness, Unkind Speech)

General information and commandments about this sin:

Pr. 29:22 An angry man leads to strife.
  Remove an angry child from a group to end strife.

Pr. 15:18 An angry man stirs up strife.

Pr. 3:30 Do not strive without a cause.
  Teach the child to ask himself, "Is there really an issue worth arguing over?"

Pr. 17:14 Stop arguing before contention starts.
  Help the child stop before quarrels begin.
  Remove the child who insists on arguing.
  Enforce a stop to argumentative conversations.

Pr. 18:6 Is a fool, calls for blows.

Pr. 20:3 Any fool can start a quarrel.
  This is a good verse to post on a wall in your home.
  Point out that it takes strength to abstain from a quarrel, more strength than it takes to participate.

Pr. 21:9 Is better to live in the corner of a housetop than with a contentious woman.

Rom. 13:13 Should not walk in strife.

Pr. 21:19 Better to live in the wilderness than with a contentious woman.

Pr. 28:25 Is proud.

Pr. 13:10 Comes only from pride.
  Deal with the pride in the child's heart.

Js. 3:16 Strife leads to confusion and evil.

Js. 4:1-2 Comes from lust.
  Deal with selfishness in the child's heart.

Pr. 10:12 Strife stirred up by hatred.
  Deal with the problem of hatred.

II Tim. 2:23 Avoid foolish, ignorant disputes which lead to strife.
  Teach to walk away from arguments, avoid disputes, recognize foolish disputes.

II Tim. 2:24 Must not quarrel, be gentle to all.

Rom. 12:18 Live peaceably.
Do not allow quarrelling. Separate those involved.

Pr. 25:24 Is not desirable.

Col. 3:12-13 Should be longsuffering and forgiving.
Help the child learn to forbear. Take him aside during an argument and talk to him. Pray with him. Send him back with instructions to be patient and forbearing in the situation.

Pr. 16:28 Froward man sows strife.
Give the child a package of flower seeds labeled "strife." Ask him to plant them and point to the picture on another package of vegetable seeds labeled "peace" and tell him that you want this kind of plant to grow from his seeds. Will it work?

What happens, or should happen, to the contentious person:

Rom. 1:28+ Given over to a debased mind.

Gal. 5:15 Will be consumed by one another.
Must put a stop to habitual quarreling, or household peace will be destroyed.

Mk. 3:25 A house divided cannot stand.
Build a house out of Legos, cardboard, wood, etc. Break it in half. Can it still stand? Can it offer the same protection?

Pr. 21:19 Should be avoided.

Titus 3:9 Avoid.
Isolate the arguing child.
Do not allow friendships with contentious children.

Rom. 14:19 Follow peace and that which edifies.
Help the child to think of words and actions that will build up instead of destroying.
Then help him to carry these actions out.

Rom. 15:5,6 Pray. God grants us to be likeminded.
Diligently pray for peace amongst family members, church family, and friends.

Js. 3:18 The fruit of righteousness is sown in peace.
Will righteousness grow and produce fruit if sown in the soil of contention?

Plant seeds (righteousness) in gravel (contention). Do they grow?

Pr. 22:10   Cast out the scorner, contention will cease.
Remove the contentious child from a group. Isolate, or have him work alongside of a parent.

Pr. 26:20-21   Where there is no talebearer, there is no strife. Contentious man kindles strife.
Remove contentious child. Do not allow to play or socialize with others.
Do not tolerate gossip. Discipline the talebearer.
Train the child to talk first to the person with whom he disagrees.

Matt. 5:25   Agree quickly.
Assure the children that if they do not settle a disagreement quickly between themselves, that you will step in and probably help settle the problem in a less pleasant way.

Matt. 5:39-41   Don't insist on rights.
What rights is the child demanding?
What rights do any of us really have?

Matt. 18:15-17   Talk alone to one who offended you. Then take 2-3 witnesses, then go to the church authorities.
Teach the child to carefully follow this sequence when resolving differences. He should talk to the person who offended him first before he involves any one else in the problem.

Eph. 4:26   Don't let the sun go down with you still angry.
Train children, by words and actions, and by your own example, to resolve arguments and come to peace, to forgive and to cease from anger before going to bed.
We have this verse calligraphed and hanging in the main hall of our house.

Gal. 5:19-21   Won't inherit kingdom of God.
Deny deposit into long-term savings.
Deny heirlooms that would have been passed on to the child.
Levy a fine from the child's long-term savings.

Pr. 18:18   Cast lots.
Teach children to do this to settle arguments over disputed items or privileges (i.e. toss coin, draw straws, etc.)

Note: We have published a chart-and-book-set that specifically deals with the Biblical resolution of differences with other people. It outlines step-by-step what the Bible says to do when we are offended by others or disagree with others. It is entitled "The

Brother-Offended Checklist: What to Tell a Tattletale." (See ordering information at the back of this book.)

The sin of contention is likened to:

Pr. 26:21 Contentious man is like coals to coals and wood to fire.
  Observe the briquets in a barbecue.
  What happens to a fire if no fuel is added to it?
  "Some persons make it their occupation to sit by the fire, to feed and fan the flame, lest it be extinguished..." A Christian should bring water, not fuel, to the fire. "[1]

Pr. 17:14 Releasing water.
  We have a "mud pit" in the back yard (an unplanted section of flower garden that the kids quickly appropriated) that very graphically helps illustrate this principle. The boys build a network of rivers and dams, and then flood the whole complex with the hose. Once one dam starts to give way, there is little hope of stopping the force of the water from destroying the whole system.
  Build a city in the sand or dirt, construct a dam, and then watch what happens if water is allowed to escape through even a small breach.
  Our local science museum has a fun sand table that kept us amused for a long time, studying the effects of erosion while we also saw the effects of the "releasing of water."
  It is easier to not allow any breach to form in a dam than it is to try to repair a breach once it is there. Protect the peace of your home by not allowing breaches of fellowship to exist. "Let not the sun go down upon your wrath." Eph. 4:26

Pr. 18:19 Contentions are like the bars of a city, and an offended brother is harder to win than a strong city.
  These are great pictures for Middle Ages-crazed young boys! Talk about these verses when reading Medieval history. Imagine participating in a siege against one of the fortified castles of that day -- the battering rams, catapults, boiling tar, etc. -- all the weapons and armor that the knights employed in an attempt to gain the advantage over those inside the castle walls. It is much better to not offend our brothers to start with than it is to try to repair the relationship after the offense has occurred.

Pr.19:13 Contentious wife is like continual dripping.
  This verse makes me think of the very annoying drip we have right over our garage side door. Everytime I go through that door on a

rainy day that drip drips right down the back of my neck! And when it can't find a neck to drip on, it drips onto the ground in front of the door, which makes an annoying mess there, too! (I guess we should fix that someday; in the meantime, it is a very good reminder to me as a potentially contentious wife!)

A drippy faucet is also a good illustration of this principle, especially if the drip falls into a basin of water or onto a metal surface so that it makes plenty of noise. That little drip can become very irritating to the ears, and it is also wasting an amazing amount of water over a period of time. A constant drip also leaves its permanent mark in the sink over a long span of time.

Pr. 25:24 It is better to live on a housetop than with a contentious wife.

Life on a rooftop sounds pretty uncomfortable and inconvenient to me!

Pr. 27:15-16 Like a continuous dripping on a rainy day.
Restraining a contentious woman is like trying to restrain the wind or grasping oil.

If the house leaks so that the rain leaks into the house, the husband cannot escape, whether he is inside or outside. The rain will find him either way. A contentious wife becomes a curse and annoyance rather than a haven and helpmeet as she should be.

Try to restrain the wind or to hold oil in your hands. Have a relay: Start with 1/2 cup of oil in your cupped hands, pass it on to the next family member, have him pass it on, and so forth. How much oil is left when you are done? (Do this outside since trying to grasp oil is usually unsuccessful!)

Pr. 26:17 Meddling with strife that doesn't involve us is like taking a dog by the ears.

The meddler will be bitten!

Talk about this verse when a young child is too rough with an animal and the animal snarls or nips in his defense.

Pr. 30:33 Like churning milk makes butter, like wringing the nose brings blood.

The inevitable result of anger and quarrelling is strife.

Make butter and watch the results.

The blessings of a peaceable spirit:

Rom. 15:6 Glorifies God (which is our purpose in life!)

Pr. 15:1 A soft answer turns away wrath.

Point out to the child when this happens.
Send the child back into an argument with a soft answer, and see what happens!

Ps. 133:1-3 Like ointment on Aaron's head, and the dew on Mt. Hermon.
Give special perfume, bath oil, skin lotion, etc.
Notice how refreshing and beautiful the dew is on an early, sunny morning.

II Cor. 13:11 God of peace will be with you.
Help child notice the sense of peace in his soul when he is willing to be peaceful with his brothers.
Take the child out for a special outing or date, or for a walk with you.

Pr. 12:20 Joy!
Create a joyful occasion for your child in recognition of his peaceableness. Let him have a special party, grant a special privilege, celebrate a family feast.
Work on the goal of peaceableness as an entire family, and then have a special family feast, party, or outing to celebrate your progress.

Pr. 17:1 Better to have a dry morsel and quietness, than a house full of sacrifice with strife.
Serve a meal of dry bread after an especially contentious day.
(But don't serve it with a contentious and vindictive spirit!)

Pr. 20:3 It is an honor to cease from strife.
Honor the peacemaker. Fly his special name flag from the front porch.
Make public mention of his peacemaking.
Have a special family feast in honor of peacemakers in your household. Invite friends or grandparents. Give a little "speech" about peacemaking and your delight in your peaceable children.

Ec. 4:6 Better to have one hand full, than to have strife with both hands full.
Take away the object of contention. (i.e. If children are fighting over toys and cannot come to an agreement, take away the toys they are fighting over. Do not allow them to play with them.)

Matt. 5:9 Called a child of God.

Heb. 12:14 Will see the Lord.
Enjoy a special outing or meal out with the child.
Give him a gift of your time. Let him choose what he would like to do with you.

I Pet. 3:10-11 Will love life and see good days.
Grant a special day out (the child chooses the location and activities.)
Have a special day of honor at home.
Have a special friend over for the day.
No homeschool for the day!

Pr. 15:18 Slow to anger appeases strife.

Stories that illustrate the consequences of contention and arguing:

Joseph and his brothers, Gen. 37:3-5, 18-27; 45:24 Contention rooted in jealousy. Led to conspiracy, lying, and kidnapping.
Joseph was still willing to forgive, recognizing God's hand in his life. Joseph's life was blessed with prosperity and rulership; his brothers' lives were haunted with guilt.

Disciples, Mk. 9:34 and Lk. 22:24 Pride, striving without a cause. Led to reproof.

Ephraimites, Jg. 12:1-6 Contention rooted in pride. Led to defeat.
Compare Jephthah's response to the Ephraimites, and its results, with Gideon's soft answer in Jg. 8:1-3.

Paul and Barnabas, Acts 15:39 Disagreement over whether to take Mark with them or not. Separated.

Jephthah's brothers, Jg. 11:1-11 Strife originating from hatred and pride. Jephthah ended up head and captain over his brothers.

David's brother, Eliab I Sam. 17:28-29 Accusing David of pride and scheming. David did not continue the argument.

Rehoboam, II Chr. 10:14-16 Provoked people to rebellion. Strife without a cause.

Amaziah, II Chr. 25:17-24 Strife out of pride, led to defeat and captivity.

Absalom, II Sam. 13:22 Contention from hatred and desire for revenge. Led to murder of Amnon.

Jacob and Esau, Gen. 27:41-45; 33:5-11 Hatred and desire for revenge. Originated from lust and pride. Esau forgave.

Stories illustrating the blessings of peacemaking:

Abraham with Lot, Gen. 13:6-9 Lived peaceably, treated Lot better than himself, was content with "one hand full" with peace. Was blessed with prosperity.

Abimelech, Gen. 21:22-32 Made a covenant with Abraham.

Isaac's herdsmen, Gen. 26:20-22 Dug new wells when others were stolen.

Abigail, I Sam. 25:23-33 Gave a soft answer which turned away David's anger. Wanted to make peace. Led to her honor in marriage to David.

Verses to memorize:

Ps. 34:14 Depart from evil, and do good; seek peace, and pursue it.

Ps. 133:1 Behold, how good and how pleasant it is for brethren to dwell together in unity!

Pr. 12:20 Deceit is in the heart of those who devise evil, but counselors of peace have joy. (NKJV)

Pr. 20:3 It is an honour for a man to cease from strife: but every fool will be meddling.

Mark 9:50 ...and have peace one with another.

Rom. 12:18 If it be possible, as much as lieth in you, live peaceably with all men.

Rom. 14:19 Therefore let us pursue the things which make for peace and the things by which one may edify another. (NKJV)

2 Tim 2:24a And a servant of the Lord must not quarrel but be gentle to all... (NKJV)

1 Th. 5:13b And be at peace among yourselves.

James 3:17 But the wisdom that is from above is first pure, then peaceable, gentle, and easy to be entreated, full of mercy and good fruits, without partiality, and without hypocrisy.

Heb. 12:14 Follow peace with all men, and holiness, without which no man shall see the Lord.

Heb. 13:1 Let brotherly love continue.

Rom. 12:21 Be not overcome of evil, but overcome evil with good.

Gal. 5:15 But if you bite and devour one another, beware lest you be consumed by one another! (NKJV)

Phil 2:2-3 Fulfill my joy by being like-minded, having the same love, being of one accord, of one mind. Let nothing be done through selfish ambition or conceit, but in lowliness of mind let each esteem others better than himself. (NKJV)

1 Pet. 3:8 Finally, be ye all of one mind, having compassion one of another, love as brethren, be pitiful, be courteous.

Phil. 2:14-15 Do all things without murmurings and disputings: that ye may be blameless and harmless, the sons of God, without rebuke, in the midst of a crooked and perverse nation, among whom ye shine as lights in the world.

James 4:1-2 Where do wars and fights come from among you? Do they not come from your desires for pleasure that war in your members? You lust and do not have. You murder and covet and cannot obtain. You fight and war. Yet you do not have because you do not ask. (NKJV)

2 Cor. 13:11b Be perfect, be of good comfort, be of one mind, live in peace; and the God of love and peace shall be with you.

Pr. 13:10 Only by pride cometh contention: but with the well advised is wisdom.

Pr. 15:18 A wrathful man stirs up strife, but he who is slow to anger allays contention. (NKJV)

---

[1]Charles Bridges, <u>A Commentary on Proverbs</u> (Carlisle, Penn.: The Banner of Truth Trust, 1987), p. 208-209.

Complaining/Ingratitude

(See also Selfishness, Envy, Covetousness, Hatred, Bitterness)

General information and commandments about this sin:

Ex. 16:8, 12 Murmur against God.

Pr. 19:3 Foolishness perverts their way.

Mal. 3:14 Say it is vain to serve God, that there is no profit.

Phil. 2:14 Should do all without murmuring or disputing.
   Do not tolerate complaining. Discipline it.

Js. 5:9 Do not grudge.

Jude 16 Walk after own lusts.

Ps. 106:7 Doesn't remember multitude of God's mercies.

Jer. 2:5-6 Forgets God's blessings and great works.
   *Read through the Psalms, especially those in which God's blessings
      to Israel are recounted.*
   Review God's blessings in the child's life. Make a list and keep it.
   *List qualities the child can be thankful for in the person he is
      complaining against.*
   *List elements the child can be thankful for in the circumstances he
      is complaining against.*
   *Give thanks to God and to the appropriate people for these qualities
      and circumstances.*

Hos. 13:6 Have forgotten God.
   Study the Bible together.
   Study God's attributes, His omniscience, omnipotence, holiness, etc.
   *Study the Israelites and what happened to them when they forgot or
      murmured against God.*

Isa. 1:2-3 Forgets maker. (Ox knows owner, ass knows master's
   crib.)
   *Lead the child to a place of thankfulness for the way God has made
      him and the circumstances He has placed in his life. Pray together
      with thanksgiving.*

Rom. 1:21 Vain in imaginations.

II Tim. 3:2 Lovers of themselves, unthankful.

I Tim. 6:6 Godliness and contentment are great gain.
   *Contentment allows us to enjoy the great blessings God puts in our
      lives.*

What happens, or should happen, to the complainer:

A complaining attitude tends to be contagious. Look at the Israelites! Maybe that is one reason for a contagious plague being their discipline.

We as parents must avoid the temptation to complain. We can even start complaining about everyone complaining. Deal with murmuring quickly before it infects the entire family.

Complaining and ingratitude are related to the sin of envy, comparing our lives to the blessings of God in others' lives. We question God's wisdom and sovereignty. That leads to bitterness and rebellion against God. "Why aren't I blessed the same way that person is? Why do I have all these testings in my life?"

To allow a child to develop the habit of complaining is to prepare them for a life of bitterness and grief.

Num. 14:26-37 Die in wilderness, not see Promised Land, children wander.
Deny blessings, privileges and gifts. If child complains about a gift given to him, take it away and give to someone more thankful. If he complains about work, take away his pay but give him more work.

Ps. 78:21 Kindles God's wrath.
Explain to child that his ingratitude angers God and you.

I Cor. 10:10 Destroyed.
Spank.

Num. 21:5-6 Plague.
Place limitations on the child. Take away freedom, privileges. Isolate.
Do not allow him to spread his complaining attitude among his siblings and friends.

Phil. 4:6 Prayer and thanksgiving.

Col. 4:2 Continue in prayer with thanksgiving.

I Thess. 5:17-18 Pray without ceasing. Give thanks.
Pray with the child. Give thanks to God.

Eph. 5:19-20 Sing!
Read and sing Psalms with the child.
Sing hymns together in family worship.
Play tapes of music that voices gratefulness. I remember the great ministry that music played in my heart when our 2-1/2-year-old was hospitalized with a ruptured appendix. A family in our church had

graciously lent us their wonderful, <u>dependable</u> car while my husband and I traded shifts at the hospital for a week. One of the greatest encouragements to me during that time, besides all the faithful support from our church family, was the stack of cassette tapes that I was invited to enjoy in that borrowed car. The Psalms lifted up my heart, and helped me to thank God even in that time of testing and stress.

Js. 5:9 Condemned.

Deut. 28:47-48 Will serve enemies. Hunger, thirst, nakedness, want of all things.
If the child complains about the food, take it away.
If he complains about his clothes, take them away.
Let him supply and take care of his own things.
Give him work!

Ec. 5:12 Labor leads us to sweet sleep, whether we have little or much.

The sin of complaining is likened to:

Rom. 9:19-20 Creation complaining to creator.
Imagine the child drawing a picture that starts to complain about how it was drawn, what colors it is, etc.

The blessings of gratefulness:

Pr. 15:13 Merry heart makes a cheerful countenance.
Award the child with the "Cheerful Face Award."
Have a special portrait photographed or painted of the child.
Buy the child a special mirror.

Pr. 15:15 Merry heart creates a continual feast.
Go out to eat, have a special family feast.

Phil. 2:14-15 Are as shining lights.
Give the child a new flashlight, bedroom lamp.
Paint or affix stick-on glow-in-the-dark stars onto the ceiling of the child's room.

Ps. 50:14-15 God will deliver.

Sacrifices and feasts of the Old Testament helped the Israelites review and give thanks to God for His many blessings. Study the feasts and memorials that God established for His people.

Passover, Ex. 12 and 13

First Fruits, Deut. 16:9-12

Feast of Booths, Deut. 16:13-15, Lev. 23:39-44

Omer of manna in the tabernacle, Ex. 16:32

Shoulder stones on the priests' ephod, Ex. 28:12

Communion, Lk. 22:19, I Cor. 11:24-26

Pillar at Jordan River, Josh. 4:1-9

Ebenezer, I Sam. 7:12

(We have enjoyed Martha Zimmerman's Celebrate the Feasts, a book that has given new meaning to the Old Testament feasts in our family.)

We have instituted some of our own family memorials:

We remember what we call Benjamin's Purim, the day that God spared him from death when his appendix ruptured and went undiagnosed for over a week.

We pasted a paper $1000 bill in our prayer notebook. That same $1000 was originally pasted to the top of a paper mountain while we prayed for God to provide that amount to pay for a van that looked like the perfect van for our family. When God clearly provided that money through the gracious offer of a family member, we moved the $1000 to the prayer notebook as a reminder of His great provision. (We have a "Family Prayer Notebook" in which we record specific prayer requests and God's very specific answers to our prayers.)

Although I have horribly failed in maintaining family picture albums, I have made a determined effort to keep detailed, up-to-date baby books for each of the children. I paste in our favorite pictures, write in memorable occasions, etc. and our kids love to review their lives over and over again. We make it a special tradition to read through a child's baby book on his birthday. It is a wonderful time of thanksgiving for all that the Lord has blessed the child and our entire family with.

Stories that illustrate the blessings of thankfulness:

Ruth, to Naomi, Ruth 1:10-17 Ruth's grateful loyalty to Naomi led to great blessing and honor in Ruth's life.

Naomi, to Boaz, Ruth 2:19-20 Saw God's faithfulness and provision through Boaz's kindness. Led to her provision, and the birth of a grandson.

Spies, to Rahab, Josh. 6:22-25 Spared Rahab and family when city was destroyed.

Moses' and Miriam's Song of Deliverance, Ex. 15:1-21

Stories that illustrate complaining and ingratitude:

Ex. 5:21 Israelites against Moses after Pharaoh increased their labor.

Ex. 14:11-12 "I told you so!" Israelites insisted that they would be better off as slaves.

Num. 11:1-10 and 14, Israelites angered God. God sent fire. Complained about the manna, wanted meat. Moses was discouraged.

Num. 16:41 Israelites complained against Moses and Aaron after God killed Korah and other rebels.

Num. 20:2-5 Complained because of lack of water, wished they had died. Led to Moses' anger and sin.

Num. 21:5-6 Complained about no food, no water. Serpents came and bit the people.

Deut. 1:27-28 Moses recounts their complaints when facing the Amorites.

Ps. 106:24-27 Overthrown in the wilderness, and children scattered.

Ps. 78 Recounts God's discipline.

Notice God's gracious provision even in the midst of the Israelites' complaints in the following passages:

Ex. 15:23-24 Bitter water, led to 12 wells at Elim.

Ex. 16:2-4 No food, complained that Moses brought them out to kill them. God provided manna.

Num. 11:4-6 and 16-20 Complained about the manna. God gave them meat, LOTS of meat!
Perhaps giving the child an overabundance of what he thinks he wants would be an appropriate punishment at times. I remember reading, as a young girl, a story about a boy that was allowed to eat ice cream, and nothing but ice cream, until it was "loathsome" to him.

Ex. 17:2-3 No water. Moses went to God for instructions, and God provided water from the rock.

Rachel, Gen. 30:1 Complained to and blamed Jacob. Envied Leah.

Martha, Lk. 10:40 Complained about sister not doing her share of the work.
(Does that sound familiar?)

Korah, Num. 16:1-41 Complained against leadership and led others into rebellion. Were separated and destroyed.

Jonah, Jon. 4 Complained about Nineveh's repentance. Wanted to die.

Verses to memorize:

Eph. 5:20 Giving thanks always for all things unto God and the Father in the name of our Lord Jesus Christ.

Col. 3:17 And whatsoever ye do in word or deed, do all in the name of the Lord Jesus, giving thanks to God and the Father by him.

1 Th. 5:18 In every thing give thanks: for this is the will of God in Christ Jesus concerning you.

Phil. 4:8 Finally, brethren, whatsoever things are true, whatsoever things are honest, whatsoever things are just, whatsoever things are pure, whatsoever things are lovely, whatsoever things are of good report; if there be any virtue, and if there be any praise, think on these things.

Ex. 14:14 The LORD shall fight for you, and ye shall hold your peace.

Brawling Woman

(See also Arguing, Complaining)

This chapter can provide material for training young women, and for counseling young men as they wait on the Lord for a wife.

General information and commandments about this sin:

Pr. 12:4 An excellent wife is a crown to her husband.
Let your daughter wear a special crown or tiara when she displays a submissive, gentle spirit.
Have a special dinner of appreciation where you honor your daughter before guests. Have her wear a crown or give her a special gift of jewelry.

I Cor. 11:3-7 Man is the head, woman is his glory.
Model this in your marriage.

Gen. 2:18 Woman is the helpmeet.

I Tim. 2:9-11 Should practice moderation, good works, and learn in silence.
Keep your daughter busy with projects of good works and service.
Teach her to learn quietly, and to direct her spiritual questions to her father primarily, and to her mother.

Pr. 31:10-31
Study this example of a virtuous woman with your daughter or with your son, just as King Lemuel's mother did.

Titus 2:5, I Pet. 3:2 Woman should be chaste.
Train daughter in modesty and purity.
Do not put your daughter into tempting, compromising situations.
Practice courting instead of dating.

Eph. 5:22-23, I Pet. 3:1, 4-6 Should be obedient.
Train daughter diligently in the area of obedience. Her habit of obedience to you will aid her in obeying God and her future husband. (See "Disobedience.")

Titus 2:4 Should be affectionate.

Pr. 14:1 Should be prudent.
Train daughter to apply Scripture's wisdom, to anticipate

evil, to discern, and to plan and prepare.

Pr. 31:27-28   Should be conscientious in household duties.
*Train daughter to be faithful and industrious in domestic
duties.*
Train daughter in how to perform specific household duties.

We need to diligently train our daughters, from their births, in *obedience, submission, and humility. We need to train them to control their tongues; we should not tolerate whining, complaining, pouting, backbiting. By our examples, and by our direction, we should raise our daughters to be cheerful, faithful servants. They, and their husbands, will someday "rise up and call [us] blessed." And we will be able to rejoice as we see our labors bear fruit in the lives of our daughters, and then in the lives of our grandchildren.*

These Scriptures should be used in training and preparing a daughter for future marriage. We can train our sons to observe these qualities in young ladies. And we can go back to the time-honored tradition of courtship, rather than dating, which not only protects our children from overwhelming temptation, but also gives them and their parents time to observe potential mates in their own families, relationships, and responsibilities.

One idea that we plan on implementing with our own daughters centers around a hope chest. We would like to give each of them a nice hope chest, and then, yearly, probably on their birthdays, we will evaluate the year and the daughter's progress toward the goals we have outlined for her. If we can look back on that year as a year of growth and greater preparation for mature womanhood, we will make a special occasion to go out for lunch, and to shop for a new and special item to add to her hope chest.

What happens, or should happen, to a brawling woman or girl:

Pr. 14:1   Foolish woman tears down her own house.
Fine her from her dowry savings. (We have our daughters save a portion of their earnings in a fund that we have labeled "dowry." This is for her use, as a young wife, in establishing a home business someday, and also serves as a form of "insurance" should she somehow be left without a husband for some reason.)
Deny her portion in the family inheritance, or withhold the passing on of family heirlooms, or contributions to her hope chest.
As a very young girl, a daughter can see this principle in action when she experiences the loss and destruction that results from

negligence in caring for her belongings. A foolish girl tears down her possessions with her own hands. She has been blessed, but she destroys those blessings with her own hands.
Read about Herodias, Job's wife, Sarah, Delilah, Eve, and Rebekah. As women who stepped out from under their God-appointed authorities, they ceased to be helpmeets and became a source of temptation, leading their husbands into evil. We should be alert to any sign of this tendency, leading others astray, in our daughters, and discipline them.

To what is the brawling woman likened:

Pr. 12:4 A wife is a crown to her husband or rottenness to his bones.
Are rotten bones a sign of good health?

Pr. 11:22 Pig with gold ring in snout.
What about buying your daughter a stuffed pig, and then sewing a gold ring (real or pretend, depending on the age of your daughter) onto its snout? Place it up on a shelf somewhere in her room, as a decoration and reminder, rather than a toy. At the age of 16 (or whatever age you choose) review your daughter's character with her. If she shows true discretion, give her the ring to wear. If she later proves to be indiscreet in her relationships, sew the ring back onto the pig's snout.

Pr. 21:9, 25:24 Better to live on a housetop than with a contentious woman.
Imagine together the discomfort and inconvenience of living on a housetop!

Pr. 21:19 Better to live in the wilderness.
Living in a wilderness (or desert) would be uncomfortable, inconvenient and lonely.

Pr. 19:13 Constant dripping.

Pr. 27:15-16 Continual dripping on rainy day.
Destroys household comfort.
Leave water dripping, or watch a drip outside. What are its effects? (See listing under this verse in "Arguing/Contention.")

The blessings of a virtuous woman:

Pr. 11:16 Retains honor.

Study the verses in the following section and make note of the women of the Bible that retained honor.
Honor your daughter with praise, recognition, a special privilege or gift, while commending her for her gentle, God-fearing spirit.

Matt. 23:11 One who is willing to serve will be greatest.
Honor a daughter's servant heart with privileges, responsibility, praise, "rank," and leadership over others.

I Pet. 3:4 A gentle, quiet spirit is precious in God's sight.
It is her glory.
Demonstrate the value you place on your daughter and her right spirit. Give her precious jewelry, a precious heirloom, and locket with this verse in it, silver or gold for her dowry/savings.

Pr. 12:4 Crown to her husband. Advances her husband.
A good wife cannot be envious of her husband.

Pr. 31:23 Husband is known "in the gates."
The virtuous wife brings glory to her husband, and advances him, which in turn brings blessing to her.

Pr. 31:28-31 Husband and children praise her. Her works also praise her.
Praise your daughter for her God-fearing spirit and obedience to you and·God.
Help her see when her works "praise" her, and the blessing of diligence and faithfulness.

Pr. 31:11 Husband trusts her.
Show trust in a faithful daughter by giving her extra privileges and freedom.
Offer financial assistance for a cottage industry venture.

These blessings are all directed to our daughters. We can also encourage our sons in their respect for honorable young girls by drawing attention to God-fearing character in the young ladies that they know. Do not praise girls for their beauty, clothing, and outward characteristics. Praise them for their servant's heart, for their gentleness, modesty, industry, prudence, and wisdom. These are the qualities that will make good helpers and wives to our sons.

Stories that illustrate the blessings and cursings that come to women:

Study these passages (and others) that tell about the lives of women in the Bible. Were they obedient, Godly women, or were they contentious and scheming stumblingblocks? Did God bless them with honor, or discipline them?

Jezebel, I Kgs. 16:31-33; 21:24-25; II Kgs. 9:30-37
Tempted her husband to evil.

Herodias, Matt. 14:8
Tempted her husband to evil, beauty without discretion, trickery, murder.

Esther, Est. 4:16
Strength and honor as clothing, courage, prudence.

Job's wife, Job 2:9
Temptress, not supportive, did Job evil.

Eunice, II Tim. 1:5
Taught Timothy. (Lois also did.) Feared the Lord, and was praised.

Hannah, I Sam. 1
Faithfulness, taught Samuel, opened mouth with wisdom, rejoiced in the future, led to fruitfulness in own life and blessing to nation.

Jochebed, Ex. 2, Heb. 11:23
Faithfulness, prudence, creativity, looked well to ways of household, didn't fear king's command, led to blessing to family, son, nation.

Sarah, Gen. 12:11-20, 16:1-6, Gen. 20, I Pet. 3:5-6
Example of submission and trust, later became temptress, contentious, tearing down own house.

Rebekah, Gen. 24:16-28, 58; 25:28+
Diligent, kind, hospitable, stretched out hand to the needy, led to honor and marriage, was not afraid to go with servant, later became unjust mother that encouraged her son in deceit against his father and brother, which led to separation of the family.

Rachel, Gen. 30:1-2
Contention, discontent, blaming husband.

Delilah, Jg. 16
Scheming temptress, dishonest, immoral, led man astray.

Dorcas, Acts 9:36
Full of good works, which praised her. Stretched out hand to needy.

Eve, Gen. 3
Disobedient, deceived, tempted Adam.

Ruth, Ruth 1-4

Chaste, loyal, diligent, worked willingly with her hands, reached out to her mother-in-law's needs, led to honor and blessing.

Sapphira, Acts 5
Conspiring, dishonest, did not encourage her husband to be honest, led to death for husband and herself.

Miriam, Ex. 2:4-7, Ex. 15:20-21, Num. 12:1-16
Faithful, prudent daughter, prophetess, later rebelled and was punished with leprosy and shame.

Abigail, I Sam. 25:18+
Prudent, wise tongue, industrious, led to honor and blessing.

Haman's wife, Est. 5:14, 6:13
Encouraged her husband in his pride, scheming, and sin.

Rahab, Heb. 11:31, Josh. 2:1-22, Josh. 6:25
Fear of God led to brave action, kindness. Saved family.

Verses to memorize:

Pr. 11:16 A gracious woman retaineth honor: and strong men retain riches.

1 Pet. 3:3-4 Do not let your adornment be merely outward; arranging the hair, wearing gold, or putting on fine apparel; rather let it be the hidden person of the heart, with the incorruptible beauty of a gentle and quiet spirit, which is very precious in the sight of God. (NKJV)

Pr. 12:4 An excellent wife is the crown of her husband, but she who causes shame is like rottenness in his bones. (NKJV)

Pr. 19:13 A foolish son is the calamity of his father: and the contentions of a wife are a continual dropping.

Pr. 31:30 Favour is deceitful, and beauty is vain: but a woman that feareth the LORD, she shall be praised.

Vanity/Overconcern for Beauty

(See also Pride, Immodesty, Hypocrisy)

General information and commandments about this sin:

Much of this information is aimed primarily at women, but many principles can be adapted for boys. It can also provide good counselling material for boys who are preoccupied with the appearance of girls rather than the character of girls.

Pr. 31:30 Charm is deceitful, beauty is vain.

Ezek. 28:17 Heart lifted up, corrupted wisdom

I Pet. 3:3+ Outward apparel, arranging of hair, wearing of gold is
not beauty. Beauty is hidden person of the heart.
Adorn with incorruptible gentle and quiet spirit, submission
to husband/authority.
Holy women who trusted God were adorned in their subjection to
their husbands.
*Do not allow daughter to indulge in, and do not help finance, a
preoccupation with outer appearance.*
Teach humble submission to authority.

I Tim. 2:9-10 Should adorn self in modest apparel with sobriety,
and with good works.
Help daughter develop the habit of good works, Keep her busy.
Keep son busy with service and works.

I Sam. 16:7 God looks on the heart.
*Draw a picture of a heart. Then list what is inside the child's
heart; do this together, and then talk about how it compares with
what God wants to be in our hearts.*

I Pet. 1:24 Flesh is grass, withers. Flower fades.
*Buy or pick a beautiful bouquet. Perhaps you could even have them
delivered. Enjoy its beauty, but watch what happens to the flowers
as time passes. Talk about the brevity of physical beauty.*

What happens, or should happen, to this person:

Ps. 39:11 Beauty melts away like a moth.

Physical appearance can become an obsession. Trying to maintain a certain standard of beauty can consume much time, thought, and energy. It can lead to anorexia, bulemia; it can affect a woman's menstrual cycle and fertility. It can limit a person's social contacts. We need to help our children realize that physical beauty is very temporary. We should not make it an idol in our lives.

We should not allow it to consume the time and energy that God wants us to use for His glory, not ours.

Take away ornaments, jewelry and clothing when it becomes an idol. Give away some of these items to other needy families.

Isa. 3:16-24 God's judgment for haughtiness -- stink, baldness, sackcloth and burning. Destruction of all the beauty they were proud of.

Limit a child's time and money that he can spend on physical appearance. Fill his time with other profitable activities.

Ezek. 28:17 Shame.

Ps. 49:14 Beauty of the foolish is consumed in the grave.

I Tim. 4:7-8 Exercise godliness. Bodily exercise profits little.
Work out a list of spiritual "exercises" for the child: Bible study projects, good works of charity and service, prayer, singing.

I Tim. 2:10 Clothe in good works.
Involve in projects that serve others -- the needy, children, elderly, church, etc.

Prov. 31
Study this description of a virtuous woman. What is truly valuable and attractive? Write up a list of these qualities. Think up projects and goals that will help develop this character in your daughter. Apply her energies to these projects.

To what is outer beauty likened:

Vapor, Ps. 39:11
Watch a vapor -- steam from breath, steam over a boiling pot, fog on a hill. Can you touch it? Does it last? Can you "catch" it and save it?

Moth, Ps. 39:11
Notice what happens to moths flying around the lightbulbs. Find them dead in the windowsill, trapped in spiderwebs, etc.

Gold ring in pig's snout, Pr. 11:22
Misused beauty is an object of disgust.
(See suggestions listed under this verse in the "Brawling Woman"
section.)

The blessings of inner beauty:

Pr. 11:16 Gracious woman retains honor.
Give honor and attention for godly character, rather than praise
for outer beauty.

Ec. 8:1 Wisdom makes the face shine.
Train diligently in wisdom.
Compare the faces of different women -- "beautiful" but ungodly
women, older godly women, etc. Study a godly woman's face.
What do you see even in old age?

Pr. 31:25 Strength and honor are a virtuous wife's clothing.
What do you notice most about a godly woman? There were several
older women that I admired in my girlhood -- devout and godly
women. What I remember most about them was their gentle
demeanor, their eyes that reflected such great inner beauty,
their kindness, their example and counsel, their unselfish interest
in others. They are the women I want to be like. They are the
women we name our babies after.

Ps. 31:30 Woman who fears God will be praised.
Praise a daughter who exhibits godly character through her godly
actions.

I Peter 3:4 A quiet spirit is precious in God's sight.
Communicate the value you place on your daughter's quiet and godly
spirit.
Give her a precious gift -- jewelry, heirlooms, etc. that will
remind her of the preciousness of her spirit to God and to you.

Stories that illustrate the value of outer and inner beauty:

Moses, Acts 7:20

Joseph, Gen. 39:6

David, I Sam. 16:12
In the lives of all three of the above men, their outer attractiveness
is mentioned, but their strength of character is what was important,

and what God used.

Esther, Est. 2:7 Outer beauty was given to accomplish God's purpose.

Job's daughters, Job 42:15 Beauty was a gift and blessing from God.

Bathsheba, II Sam. 11:2 + Indiscreet use of beauty. Led to sin and great punishment.

Sarah, I Pet. 3:6 Sarah remembered for her submission, even though her beauty is also mentioned in the Old Testament.

Saul, I Sam. 9:2 Most handsome man in Israel, but ended life in shame and madness.

Verses to memorize:

1 Pet. 3:3-4 Do not let your adornment be merely outward; arranging the hair, wearing gold, or putting on fine apparel; rather let it be the hidden person of the heart, with the incorruptible beauty of a gentle and quiet spirit, which is very precious in the sight of God. (NKJV)

Ec. 8:1b A man's wisdom maketh his face to shine, and the boldness of his face shall be changed.

Pr. 31:30 Favour is deceitful, and beauty is vain: but a woman that feareth the LORD, she shall be praised.

Ps. 90:12 So teach us to number our days, that we may apply our hearts unto wisdom.

Judging Others

(See also Meddling, Disobedience, Complaining,
Revenge, Pride, Gossip, Bitterness)

General information and commandments about this sin:

Pr. 18:13 To answer before hearing is folly and shame.

Js. 4:11+ Don't speak evil or judge the law. God is only lawgiver.
We need to constantly remind ourselves of this truth: God is Judge.

Rom. 14:13 Should not judge. Resolve to not be a stumblingblock.

Rom. 14:3-4 Man stands before his own master. He is not
responsible to us.

Gal. 6:1 Should help restore with meekness.
Teach a child to humbly reprove his friends or siblings.

I Thess. 5:11 Should comfort and edify.
*Help the child think of ways that he can build up and encourage
the person instead of judging and criticizing him.*

Matt. 7:5 Take the beam out of own eye first.
*Teach the child to examine himself and to discern his part in the
problem.*

Rom. 2:1 When we judge, we are often doing the same things
ourselves. We condemn ourselves.

Matt. 7:1,2 Judge not.

Jn. 7:24 Judge not by appearance.
*Help a child remember that he cannot see all sides of a
situation, so he is not qualified to judge in the situation.
He also does not have the authority to judge.*

Pr. 18:17 First party sounds right, should search matter out.

I Cor. 4:3+ Is a small thing to be judged by another man. God
is our judge.

Eph. 4:2 Forbear one another in love with lowliness, meekness,
longsuffering.

Rom. 14:10-12 Will all stand before the judgment seat of Christ
and give account.
Will I be able to defend this action to Jesus Christ?

I Pet. 4:8 Love covers a multitude of sins.
*A child needs to learn to overlook and not make an issue of every
minor offense against him, and every imperfection he sees in*

*another. We are all at different stages of growth and maturity.
We need to show each other grace, just as God is gracious.*

Pr. 14:21 Despising neighbor is sin.

What happens, or should happen, to the person who criticizes others:

Rom. 1:28+ Is given over too a debased mind.
*Maliciousness, backbiters, whisperers, malignity are all listed
here along with fornicators and murderers. We tend to justify our
critical words, but God says we're just as sinful as a murderer
when we are angry.*

Js. 2:13 Will be judged without mercy.
*Judge the child more sternly for his wrongdoing.
Remind the child of the great mercy that God has shown us. How
much has He forgiven us?*

Matt. 7:3-5 Remove beam from own eye.
*Examine self first, and confess your part in the problem first
before going to the other person.*

Matt. 18:15 Show brother his fault.
*Teach the child to humbly go to the person that he perceives as
wrong and talk to him, not to anyone else.*

Matt. 18:16 If the offender does not repent, go back to him with
witnesses.
*Train your child to do this. Confront the wrongdoer again with
other children that witnessed the wrong. This needs to be done
humbly, in love, not as an attack.*

Matt. 18:17 If the offender still does not repent, tell the church.
*After following the above two steps, if the offender still has
not repented, then your child should come to you, the authority
in the home.
As parents, if we are dealing with habitual, unrepented sin in the
lives of our children, we need to follow these steps, turning to
the church authorities for their counsel when the child's heart
is hard.
Note: We have developed a chart-and-book-set, "The Brother-
Offended Checklist," which takes the problem of disagreements
and offenses, and outlines the Scriptural steps the offender,
offended, and authority need to take to resolve the problem in a
godly fashion. (See ordering information at the back of this book.)*

Matt. 7:1-2 Will be judged by own standard.
*Often a child that is judging a sibling for wrongdoing is also
disobeying.*
*When a child comes to you, criticizing or judging another without
first*
*going to that person, ask him, "What do you think I should do to
him?" Then discipline this child by that same standard.*

Lk. 6:37-38 Don't judge, won't be judged. Don't condemn, won't be
condemned. Forgive, will be forgiven.

To what is a critical person likened:

Lk. 6:39 Like blind leading the blind.
*Blindfold two children. Appoint one of them as the leader of the
other, and send them through an obstacle course in the living room
or backyard. How well does a blind leader do?*
*Peter Bruegel painted a very graphic illustration in his painting
entitled "Blind Leading the Blind." Locate this and study it
together.*

Lk. 6:41-42 Pointing out a speck in brother's eye, when there is
a beam in your own eye.
*How well can you see, and how clearly will you think, if you have
a piece of lumber poking you in the eye?*
*This would be a fun, and useful, principle to draw a picture of.
Draw a rough cartoon yourself, and show it to your children. See
if they can figure out what is happening, and explain the principle.
Or have them draw their own illustrations.*

The blessings of peacemaking and forgiveness:

Pr. 17:9 One who covers a transgression seeks love.

Lk. 6:36-37 Don't judge, won't be judged. Don't condemn, won't be
condemned. Forgive, will be forgiven.
*Use this principle in your discipline. Show more mercy to one who
has been merciful. Judge more sternly the child who is judging
everyone else.*
*This should not be carried to the point that a child thinks that if
he constantly overlooks blatant sin committed by others, that his
sin will not be recognized or punished.*

Pr. 11:17 Does good to own soul.

Pr. 21:21 Follow righteousness and mercy. Will find life, righteousness, and honor.
Honor a child with the honor of your praise when he has been merciful.

Matt. 5:7 Will obtain mercy.
Show mercy to the merciful child.
Do a word study of "mercy" together with the child. How can he show mercy?

Stories that illustrate the consequences of a critical spirit:

Parable of workers, Matt. 20:1-16 Criticized employer for supposed injustice. Were reproved. Were assuming authority that wasn't theirs.

Pharisees, Lk. 5:29-30 Criticizing Jesus for eating with publicans. Were reproved.

Michal, II Sam. 6:16-23 Criticism of David led to her barrenness.

Judas Iscariot, Jn. 12:3-6 Criticizing Mary for wasting expensive ointment that could have been sold to gain money for the poor. Motivated by his own greed. Was reproved.

Miriam, Num. 12:1-15 Criticizing Moses' marriage and his right to authority. Motivated by jealousy and pride. Led to her shame and leprosy.

Israelites, Num. 14:1-4 (and others) Continually criticizing Moses when they didn't like God's leading. Attack his leadership, and are continually disciplined by God.

Eliab, I Sam. 17:28 Judged David's motives in challenging Goliath.

Princes of Amnon, II Sam. 10:2-3 Judged David's motives when he conveyed sympathy to Hanun. Led to military defeat.

Martha, Lk. 10:38-42 Criticizing Mary for not helping her. Easily provoked. Was reproved.

Stories that illustrate the blessings of forgiveness and peacemaking:

Joseph, Matt. 1:19 Was not going to make a public example of Mary.

David, I Sam. 24:10-17 Recognized that God was judge. Led to his great blessing as king.

Stephen, Acts. 7:59-60 Didn't condemn his murderers.

Jesus, Lk. 23:34 Forgave those who crucified him.

Joseph, Gen. 45:4-15 Did not judge and condemn his brothers for the great wrong they had committed against him.

Verses to memorize:

Matt. 7:1-5 Judge not, that you be not judged. For with what judgment you judge, you will be judged; and with the measure you use, it will be measured back to you. And why do you look at the speck in your brother's eye, but do not consider the plank in your own eye? Or how can you say to your brother, 'Let me remove the speck from your eye'; and look, a plank is in your own eye? Hypocrite ! First remove the plank from your own eye, and then you will see clearly to remove the speck from your brother's eye. (NKJV)

1 Cor. 16:14 Let all that you do be done with love. (NKJV)

Col 3:13 Forbearing one another, and forgiving one another, if any man have a quarrel against any: even as Christ forgave you, so also do ye.

1 Pet. 4:8 And above all things have fervent love for one another, for "love will cover a multitude of sins." (NKJV)

Eph. 4:2 With all lowliness and meekness, with longsuffering, forbearing one another in love.

Pr. 18:13 He that answereth a matter before he heareth it, it is folly and shame unto him.

Rom. 14:4 Who are you to judge another's servant? To his own master he stands or falls. Indeed, he will be made to stand, for God is able to make him stand. (NKJV)

Pr. 18:17 The first one to plead his cause seems right, until his neighbor comes and examines him. (NKJV)

Selfishness/Greed/"Me First"

(See also Pride, Arguing, Covetousness, Gluttony)

General information and commandments about this sin:

Pr. 23:4-5 Don't overwork to be rich. Riches make wings.

Pr. 27:20 Eyes are never satisfied.

Rom. 15:1,2,5 Bear infirmities of weak. Should not please ourselves.
Train your children to please and serve others.

Eph. 4:28 Work so you can give.
Teach your children the habit of giving.
Establish portions of their budget and savings that are specifically set aside for giving.
Have children purchase gifts for others from their own earnings.

I Jn. 3:17 Love of God doesn't dwell in him.
What would God do to us if He gave us what we deserve? Because of His love, we have eternal life and forgiveness.

Matt. 5:42 Give to him who asks.
Help a child learn to say "yes" unless he has a very good reason to say "no." (I have to remind myself of this, too, when I am tempted to say "no" as soon as I hear "Mommy" called out in a I'm-going-to-ask-for-something tone of voice!)

I Cor. 10:24 We should seek the other man's wealth.
Teach your child to ask, "What can I do for this person to bless him and make his life more happy and pleasant?"
Teach him to promote others rather than himself.

II Cor. 5:15 Live unto Christ.
How would Jesus want you to treat another person?

Gal. 6:2 Bear one another's burdens.

Phil. 2:4, 20, 21 Look on the things of others.
Help the child learn to ask himself, "What can I do to help this person?"

Js. 2:15,16 Don't just talk. Do something. Give to people's needs.
When you know that a person is in need, make a list of everything you can think of that you could do to help them. Then pick at least one of those things to do right away.

Gal. 6:10 Take opportunity to do good.

Pr. 14:21 To despise our neighbor is sin.

I Tim. 6:10 Love of money is root of all evil.
Draw a picture of a plant. Down by the roots draw a heart with a dollar sign inside it. Draw leaves growing out of the main stem and label each of them with other sins that grow out of love for money: theft, envy, covetousness, lying, etc. Hang this picture up in your house.

Acts 20:35 More blessed to give than to receive.
Have your child save money which he can use to purchase his own gifts to give, so that he will appreciate the full blessing of giving of themselves when they give.
Make a practice of having the child give something to another person whenever they have received something (a gift, etc.)

Ec. 5:10,11 He who loves silver will not be satisfied. The more we have, the more we consume.
Observe the truth of this statement. After a child has gained a longed-for item, and has enjoyed its newness, he will quickly wish for more.
Tell your children stories from your life that illustrate the truth of "when goods increase, they are increased that eat them."

Matt. 6:21 Where our treasure is, there is our heart also.
Talk with the child. Where is his treasure? Is that where he wants his heart to be?
Work together to decorate a little box like a treasure chest.
Throughout the day write down the child's activities on slips of paper and put them into the treasure chest box. At the end of the day read through all the slips and divide them into two piles -- heavenly treasures and earthly treasures. Where is the child's treasure?

Rom.12:13 Should distribute to the needs of saints, practice hospitality.
Teach your child basic rules of hospitality and manners. Help him to be a good host to company. Take him aside when company is at your house and teach him and watch how he applies what you have taught.
Take children along with you, and have them help, when you go to help a brother in need.
Have one child act as host, and pretend the rest of the family is "company." Teach the host to graciously think of his "company," serving them, making them comfortable, putting them first. And no grumbling!

I Pet. 4:9 Use hospitality without grumbling.

II Cor. 9:7 Should give from the heart, not grudging or forced. God loves a cheerful giver.
Help child to see the blessings that come into his life when he shares and gives.

Matt. 6:1-4 Give in secret. God will reward.
Giving should not be a performance done for our own glory.
Perhaps the child could give an anonymous gift to someone in need, or leave a simple homemade gift on the widow-neighbor's porch.

I Cor. 13:3 If we give without love, it is worth nothing.

What happens, or should happen, to the selfish person:

Matt. 25:41-46 Cast into hell. When we ignore man's needs, and do not minister to him, we are doing the same to Jesus.
Teach the child to ask, "How would I treat Jesus if He had this need?"

Ec. 5:11 Goods increase, users increase.

Pr. 13:7 He that makes himself rich has nothing.
If child is not sharing with others, it is sometimes appropriate to temporarily take away the items he is being selfish with. We do this especially when a child is attempting to dominate several items at once.

Pr. 1:19 Selfishness takes away the life of owners.

Pr. 15:27 Troubles own house.
Fine from spending portion of savings.
Deny privileges and belongings.

Pr. 28:27 Many curses when we hide our eyes from the poor.
Discipline child when he does not help or share with his younger siblings.
Deny privilege of playing, or deny toys, etc.

Pr. 11:26 People will curse.

Pr. 24:11-12 God will render to them according to their works.
Deny the child when he requests a special privilege, use of your tools, possessions, etc. Gently explain that you have observed his unwillingness to share and to put others first, and that you do not think you should share with him this time, but "render to him according to his works." (This needs to be done with a loving attitude.)

Pr. 13:25 Shall want.
Take away belongings or privileges of the greedy child.

Matt. 19:21,22; Lk. 12:33,34 Our treasure is in heaven.
*Try this project: Label two jars or boxes, "Heavenly Treasure"
and "Earthly Treasure." Write down each activity throughout the
day on slips of paper, and put each slip in the appropriate jar.
Which jar is fullest?*

Pr. 25:16 Will vomit.

Pr. 11:24; 23:21 Come to poverty.
*Make the child poor: Fine from spending money, take away
belongings and toys he was unwilling to share.*

II Cor. 9:6 Sow sparingly, reap sparingly.
Give less to this child, and explain why.
*Plant two rows of seeds, one sparingly and one generously. What
do you reap?*

Phil. 2:3 No selfish ambition or conceit. Should have lowly mind,
esteem others better than ourselves.
*Ask the child, "What would you do for this person if he was the
King?"*
Think of self as servant.

I Tim. 6:9-10 Fall into temptation and snare. Err from faith.
Sorrow.
Don't spare child from natural consequences of his selfishness.

Phil. 2:5 Have the mind of Christ.
Study Jesus' actions. What would He do?

Rom. 12:10 In honor, prefer one another.
*Think of an action, and do it, that demonstrates that you prefer
that person more than yourself.*

I Cor. 10:24 Seek other person's wealth.

Ec. 5:13 Possessions kept to own hurt, riches perish by evil
travail.
*Pray for God's direction of events to clearly demonstrate this to your
child.*

Hag. 1:6 No satisfaction. Eat, but not full. Drink, but not full.
Clothed, but not warm. Sow, but small harvest.
*Point out to the child the sinful tendency to never be satisfied.
When he is greedy about food, give him very little, etc. Deny
satisfaction when he is greedy.*

To what is the greedy man likened:

Greedy dogs and shepherds without understanding, Isa. 56:11
Watch a greedy dog. Is that how we want to look?

Clouds and wind without rain, Pr. 25:14 One who falsely boasts
of giving.

Putting earnings into bags with holes, Hag. 1:6
*How much does a pocket with holes hold? Does it work to put
groceries into a grocery bag that has holes in it? Try it!*

The blessings of generosity:

Ps. 112:5-9 Rewarded, not moved, not afraid, honored.

Ps. 37:25-26 Never lacks, children blessed.
*Make a deposit into the child's long-term savings account.
Set up a special savings account into which you deposit sums
for the child's future children (your grandchildren!)*

Isa. 58:10,11 Deliverance in time of need.

Pr. 3:9-10 Honor Lord with firstfruits and your barns will be
filled with plenty, presses will burst with new wine.
Teach your child to tithe as soon as he has any money.

Deut. 24:19 Bless work of hands.
Pay for chores.
Pray for God's clear blessing of the child's generosity.

Pr. 28:27 Shall not lack.

Ps. 41:1-3 God will deliver in time of trouble, preserved, blessed,
not delivered to enemies, strengthened.
Show grace, give financial assistance.

Ps. 112:5,9 Shows favor and lends, horn exalted with honor.
Show special generosity to the generous child.

Matt. 23:11 Servant will be greatest.
*Exalt the generous, unselfish child: give him a special "Honor-the-
Servant" party, a special day in his honor when he chooses
activities and meals. Have rest of family serve him for a day.*

Pr. 11:24-25 Scatters, yet increases, soul made fat.

Pr. 13:7 Has great riches.
*Bless the generous child with occasional gifts, but also remind
him of the riches he is storing up in heaven when he gives and*

shares.

We enjoy a game called "The Richest Christian" by Ornament Publications which helps communicate this principle while also teaching various proverbs. (See Resources.)

Pr. 14:21 Show mercy, will be happy.

Pr. 19:16-17 God will repay.

Pr. 22:9 Will be blessed.

Matt. 6:4 God will reward.

Lk. 6:38 Give, will be given, running over.
Demonstrate with a glass of water. Pour part of the water from the glass into another glass. Then fill the first glass again to overflowing with a pitcher.

II Cor. 9:8 God enables us to abound in every good work.

II Cor. 9:10 Supply and multiply seed sown, increase fruits of righteousness.
Project: Give child package of flower or vegetable seeds. Let him plant them. Notice how the seed multiplies, especially if you let one or two plants "go to seed" so that you can harvest more seeds from them. One flower seed can produce one flower or many flowers which can all produce many, many seeds.

II Cor. 9:11 Causes thanksgiving and glory to God.
Point out how unselfish actions can bring glory to God.

Stories that illustrate the consequences of selfishness:

Ananias and Sapphira, Acts 5 Did alms before men. Led to death.

Nabal, I Sam. 25 Caused contention, led to death.

Achan, Joshua 7:11-26 Led to theft, dishonesty and then death. Nation defeated in battle.

Ahab, I Kg. 21:1-4 Covetousness and selfishness led to false accusations, murder and theft.

Judas Iscariot, Lk. 22:1-6 Greediness led to betrayal and eventual suicide.

Haman, book of Esther, God rendered to him according to his works, troubled own house. Led to his death and the deaths of all in his family.

Rich fool, Lk. 12:16-21 Preoccupation with riches took away life.

Rich man, Lk. 16:19-25 Hid eyes from poor, no treasure in heaven, rendered to him according to his works, cast into hell.

James and John, Mk. 10:35-37 Desire to be first.

Stories that illustrate the blessings of generosity:

Virtuous woman, Pr. 31 Not afraid, honored, work blessed.

Dorcas, Acts 9:36-41 Praised, honored, delivered from death.

Ruth, Book of Ruth Not afraid, deliverance, honor, children blessed, God repaid.

Good Samaritan, Lk. 10:30-37 Not delivered to enemies, will be repaid.

Poor widow, Lk. 21:1-4 Honored.

Verses to memorize:

Acts 20:35b It is more blessed to give than to receive.

Matt. 6:1 Take heed that ye do not your alms before men, to be seen of them: otherwise ye have no reward of your Father which is in heaven.

Mat 25:40 And the King shall answer and say unto them, Verily I say unto you, inasmuch as ye have done it unto one of the least of these my brethren, ye have done it unto me.

Mat 5:16 Let your light so shine before men, that they may see your good works, and glorify your Father which is in heaven.

1 Cor 13:3 And though I bestow all my goods to feed the poor, and though I give my body to be burned, and have not charity, it profiteth me nothing.

2 Cor 9:6-7 But this I say, He which soweth sparingly shall reap also sparingly; and he which soweth bountifully shall reap also bountifully. Every man according as he purposeth in his heart, so let him give; not grudgingly, or of necessity: for God loveth a cheerful giver.

Ps. 112:5 A good man deals graciously and lends; he will guide his affairs with discretion. (NKJV)

Phil. 2:4 Let each of you look out not only for his own interests, but also for the interests of others. (NKJV)

Rom 12:10 Be kindly affectioned one to another with brotherly love; in honour preferring one another.

Luke 12:34 For where your treasure is, there will your heart be also.

Gal 6:10 As we have therefore opportunity, let us do good unto all men, especially unto them who are of the household of faith.

1 Cor. 10:24 Let no one seek his own, but each one the other's well-being. (NKJV)

Gal 5:13b By love serve one another.

1 Pet. 4:9 Be hospitable to one another without grumbling. (NKJV)

Greedy for Gain/ Confidence in Riches

(See also Covetousness, Selfishness,

General information about this sin:

Matt. 19:23 Hard to enter kingdom of God.

Matt. 6:24 Can't serve God and mammon.
Help child to see that he cannot serve two masters at the same time. Mom and Dad can both give him directions at the same time that conflict throughout an evening, to help him understand this principle.

Pr. 23:4 Don't labor to be rich.

Ec. 2:4-11 Is vanity.

Matt. 6:25-34 Take no thought about tomorrow. Follow example of birds and flowers.
They are obedient to the way God created them, and He is faithful to care for them.

Pr. 28:11 Is wise in own conceit.
Help child remember that __anything__ he has is a gift from God.

Ec. 5:13-14 Wealth is a gift of God.

Jer. 9:23 Don't glory in riches.
Give the child a gift of money or other possessions. Ask him if it makes sense for him to boast of his accomplishment, if what he has was __given__ to him.

Ezek. 7:19, Zeph. 1:18 Silver and gold won't deliver them in day of wrath.
Can the child's possessions and money deliver him from discipline?

I Tim. 6:17 Not high-minded or trust in uncertain riches. Trust in living God.
Trusting in possessions can become a form of idol worship. Can an idol protect or deliver us?

Matt. 16:26 If we gain the world, but lose our soul, it is no profit.
Draw a picture to illustrate this: a house full of possessions, but the person in hell.

Pr. 11:4 Won't profit in day of wrath.

Lk. 12:15 Man's life doesn't consist of possessions.

Make a list: What <u>should</u> our lives consist of?

Ps. 62:10 Set not heart upon riches.

Ps. 49:6-7 Trust in riches, can't redeem soul.

What happens, or should happen, to the person who puts his trust in riches:

Matt. 13:22 Is unfruitful.

Ec. 5:10 Loves silver, but is not satisfied.

Pr. 11:28 Will fall.
Help child see when his confidence in possessions leads him to fall.

I Tim. 6:17-19 Trust in God, do good works, distribute, willing to communicate, lay up good foundation.
Involve child in service and good works, in the giving up of some of his wealth for others.

I Tim. 6:9 Leads to temptation and snare, foolish lusts which drown men in destruction.
Have a treasure hunt, complete with treasure map! Hide some coins for the treasure inside the garage, a closet, or other room where you can close the door and "trap" your treasure hunters while they are engrossed in examining their treasure.

I Tim. 6:10 Love of money is root of all evil. Err from faith, pierced with sorrows.
Observe when this happens in the lives of others, and in the child's life.
Draw a picture of a plant to help illustrate this concept. Draw the roots underground with a heart and a dollar sign around them. Then draw a main stem coming up with leaves growing out of it. Label the leaves with different sins that grow out of man's love of money (theft, envy, lying, etc.).

Pr. 13:7 Has nothing.
Remove income, possessions.
Keep earnings in savings, but deny spending privileges. Put all earnings into savings.

Ec. 5:12 Can't sleep.
Consider this with a child (or Mom or Dad!) who has trouble sleeping. Is he worrying about possessions, greedy for more?

Ec. 5:11 Goods increase, consumption increases.
Put more financial pressure on him. Give him more responsibility financially. Have him buy his own clothes, etc.

Ec. 5:15 We can take nothing with us at death.
Spend a day trying to function only with what you can take with you when you die. What was important?

Pr. 30:8-9 Prayer for no riches lest we become full and deny God.
Deny wealth if it tempts the child to pride and despising God.
Pray for the lessening of wealth for an older child tempted in this area.

Pr. 23:4-5 Riches fly away, make themselves wings.
Make a paper airplane out of a dollar bill and fly it away!
We enjoy Richard "Little Bear" Wheeler's devotional history tapes. In his volume that deals with the Gold Rush, he tells a fun story about a man that struck it rich with a gold find. The man came home with cash, which the wife nervously moved all over the house before finally hiding it in the unused woodstove overnight. She then went to bed, and the husband, who had been out, came back home, thought he'd light up the fire to take off the chill, and proceeded to unwittingly burn up his "riches." The amazing part of the story is that he and his wife had a good laugh over it! And they went on later to strike an even richer claim!
Tell stories from your own experience, when you thought you had "extra" money (a bonus, tax return, gift, etc.), and how quickly it was consumed with extra unanticipated expenses or foolish spending.

Deut. 8:10-18 Can lead to pride and forgetting God.

Ezek. 28:5 Can lead to pride.
Deal with the problem of pride in the child's life.
Take riches away, or limit their use, when pride becomes a problem.

Mk 10:17-23 Trust in riches makes it hard to enter kingdom.

Col. 3:2 Set affections on things above.
Design projects of eternal value for the child: projects of service for others, Bible study, etc.
Make a list: What things are important to you in life? Where are your affections?

Lk. 12:34 Where your treasures are is where your heart is.
Keep a daily time journal for a few days. Write down everything you do. Study it. Where is your heart?

Matt. 6:19-21 Earthly treasures are vulnerable to moth, rust, thieves.

Should lay up treasure in heaven.
Examine a favorite sweater that has been plundered by moths.
Observe a once-treasured object that has been left outside and ruined by rust.

To what are riches (and confidence in riches) likened:

Thorns choking out seeds, Matt. 13:22
Plant seeds for some beautiful flowers in an unprepared patch full of weeds. Plant more seeds in a flower bed that has been carefully prepared and weeded. Which seeds grow best?

Flowers, Js. 1:9-10 Sun will wither them, will pass away.
Watch the morning glories out in the garden.
Pick or buy a beautiful bouquet, and watch how long its beauty lasts.

Strong city, Pr. 18:11 A rich man's confidence is in his riches.
The story of the "Trojan Horse" would be a good illustration of some people that mistakenly placed their confidence in their strong city.

Camel going through eye of needle, Matt. 19:24
Look at a needle together. It's hard to get a thread through the eye. How about a camel?

Eagle, Pr. 23:5 Fly away.
Watch a bird flying. We saw a "Birds of Prey" show at our city's zoo, and I was amazed at how fast and effortless an eagle could fly!
Study eagles. How can you compare them with riches?

We should consider the raven and lilies, Lk. 12:24-28 God provides for them.
Observe flowers and birds. Do they worry and overwork? They spend much of their existence glorifying God with their beauty and songs, and God takes care of them.

Stories that illustrate man's response to riches:

Parable of rich man, Lk. 12:16-21 Ended life with nothing.

Rich man, Lk. 18:22-26 Unwilling to give up possessions, hard to enter kingdom of God.

Rich man and Lazarus, Lk. 16:19 + Ignored prophets, led to eternal torment.

Achan, Josh. 7:11-26 Greed led to theft and lying, defeat for Israel, death for him and his family.

Parable of the sower, Matt. 13:22 Sowed seeds among thorns, which were choked out.

Solomon, I Kgs. 3:11-14 Blessed with riches becaused his desire and request was for wisdom. With wisdom, he knew how to use riches.

Job, Job 42:10 Doubly blessed after he did not deny God when he lost all his possessions.

Verses to memorize:

Ps. 62:10b ..If riches increase, set not your heart upon them.

Phil. 4:19 But my God shall supply all your need according to his riches in glory by Christ Jesus.

Matt. 6:24 No man can serve two masters: for either he will hate the one, and love the other; or else he will hold to the one, and despise the other. Ye cannot serve God and mammon.

Deut. 8:18 But thou shalt remember the LORD thy God: for it is he that giveth thee power to get wealth..

1 Tim. 6:17 Command those who are rich in this present age not to be haughty, nor to trust in uncertain riches but in the living God, who gives us richly all things to enjoy. (NKJV)

1 Sam. 2:7 The LORD maketh poor, and maketh rich: he bringeth low, and lifteth up.

Pr. 10:22 The blessing of the LORD, it maketh rich, and he addeth no sorrow with it.

Matt. 6:21 For where your treasure is, there will your heart be also.

Luke 12:15 And He said to them, "Take heed and beware of covetousness, for one's life does not consist in the abundance of the things he possesses." (NKJV)

Col. 3:2 Set your affection on things above, not on things on the earth.

Luke 12:31 But rather seek ye the kingdom of God; and all these things shall be added unto you.

Luke 12:34 For where your treasure is, there will your heart be also.

Envy/Jealousy

(See also Pride, Hatred, Complaining, Covetousness, Sinful Thought
Life, Bitterness, Hypocrisy, False Witness, Gossip)

The sin of envy can lead to a very unhappy and spiteful life. We, out of love for our children, and out of obedience to God, must help our children conquer this sin. An envious person can't endure the excellency of others, and is unhappy over the advantage or prosperity of others. He ends up spending his life competing with, and trying to defame others. Reading through Bible stories that tell of envy and its consequences is pretty sobering. The envious person can grow to be bitter, self-centered, and hypocrital. He can become blind to God's many blessings in his life.

Little children so often have a hard time rejoicing in others' successes. We need to be sensitive to this problem in our families.

General information and commandments about this sin:

Pr. 23:17, Ps. 37:1, Pr. 24:19 Don't envy sinners.

Pr. 3:31 Don't envy oppressor.

Pr. 24:1 Don't envy evil men or desire to be with them.

I Cor. 3:3 Envy is carnal.

II Cor. 12:20 Envy is associated with backbiting, strife, etc.

Gal. 5:26 Don't desire vainglory, provoking and envying one
  another.
Envy has its roots in pride. Deal with pride in the child's heart.

Pr. 27:4 Worse than anger. Can't stand before envy.

Ec. 4:4 Man is envied for his toil and skillful work.

I Cor. 13:4 Love doesn't envy.
  Do a word study of love in the Bible.
  *Ask the child what he could do to show the person love. Have him
    do it!*

Ps. 49:16 Don't be afraid when someone else gains glory or riches.

What happens, or should happen, to the envious person:

Job 5:2 Envy slays the simple one.

Pr. 14:30 Leads to rottenness of the bones.
Envy affects our health and happiness.

Rom. 1:28-29 Given over to debased mind.
Thinking becomes distorted.

I Tim. 6:4-5 Withdraw yourself from an envious person.
Do not let your child develop a strong friendship with an envious person.
Isolate your child when he is voicing his envy.
Train your child to not listen to an envious person who is complaining and slandering.

Titus 3:3-5 Need to be renewed, regenerated through the Holy Spirit.
Pray for the child's open heart, and the Holy Spirit's work.
Work on renewing the child's mind with Scripture reading, study, and memorization.

Js. 3:16 Leads to confusion and every evil work.
Envy produces misery in the heart of the envious, but also causes great evil and confusion among those who associate with him.

I Pet. 2:1-2 Should desire God's Word for growth.
Teach Bible study methods to the child, and guide him in a consistent daily study time.
Be consistent in family worship time.
Do a Bible study on contentment.

Gal. 5:19-21 Won't inherit kingdom of God.
Deny deposit into long term savings.
Help child understand that he will be excluded from family inheritance if he is envious.

Rom. 13:13-14 Put on the Lord Jesus Christ. Make no provision for the flesh.
Do a Bible study together on temptation.
Study and memorize the "Armor of God" in Eph. 6. Make a drawing of a soldier and his armor; label each part of the armor. Post the picture in an obvious place, and when envy becomes a problem, look at the soldier and decide which part of the armor the child has "taken off."
Note: We sell two products that deal with the "Armor of God." One is patterns for making actual cloth and wood armor for your child to wear. The other is a set of paper dolls, a Bible-times man and woman and the Christian soldier with his armor. (See ordering information at back of book.)

Ezek. 35:11 God will do to us according to our anger, envy, and hatred against others.

To what is envy and jealousy likened:

Cruel as grave, Song of Sol. 8:6
Can't escape.

Coals of fire, Song of Sol. 8:6
Can you touch coals without injury? What do coals do if they come in contact with other wood or fuel?

Vehement flame, Song of Sol. 8:6
Watch a fire. What happens to anything that is put in the fire?

Stories that illustrate the consequences of envy:

Miriam and Aaron, Num. 12 Their envy of Moses' leadership responsibilities led to rebellion. Miriam was stricken with leprosy temporarily and sent out of the camp.

Cain and Abel, Gen. 4:4-8, I Jn. 3:12 Cain envied the favor that God showed to Abel. His envy led to murder.

Joseph's brothers, Gen. 37:4-11, 19-20; Acts. 7:9 Envied the favor that Jacob showed to Joseph. Led them to conspire against him, kidnap him, and lie to their father.

Korah, Num. 16:3, Ps. 106:16-18 Envied Moses' position of leadership. Led to his gathering of others to his side, to rebellion, and to the death of Korah, his family, and his associates.

Haman, Est. 6:6-12 Envied the favor and honor Mordecai received. Led to conspiracy, and to the death of Haman and his family.

Princes and Daniel, Dan. 6:4 Princes envied Daniel's character, wisdom and favor. Led to conspiracy and slander to snare him. Daniel was spared from unjust execution, and his accusers were then justly fed to the lions.

Rachel, Gen. 30:1 Envied God's blessing of fruitfulness in Leah's life. Led to contention between Rachel and Jacob, and between Rachel and Leah.

Philistines and Isaac, Gen. 26:13-21 Envied Isaac's prosperity, which led to strife and theft.

Saul, I Sam. 18:7-9 Envied the favor God and people showed to David. Led to hatred, injustice, conspiracy, attempted murders, Saul's insanity and his eventual loss of the kingdom and his death.

Brother of prodigal son, Lk. 15:25-32 Envied the favor his father showed to the son who had been unfaithful and wasteful. Was bitter and questioned his father's wisdom and fairness.

Parable of workers, Matt. 20:1-16 Workers who started at beginning of the day ojbected to the employer's payment for those who only worked a short time. They envied the favor shown to the later workers. The employer points out that he has the right to do what he wants to do with his own possessions.

Both of the last two stories illustrate a principle that we each need to learn early in life. Favor is not equally distributed among all men. God does not owe any of us any blessing. His blessing is all grace. Rain falls on the just and the unjust. To envy others insinuates that God is unfair and is not giving us what we deserve. We need to remember that we don't want God to give us what we <u>deserve</u>!

Stories that illustrate men that rejoiced in the success of others:

Jonathan, I Sam. 18:1-4; 19:1-7; 20; 23:16-18 Jonathan did not question God's sovereignty. He recognized David's annointing, admired him, and was his loyal friend until death.

John the Baptist, Matt. 3:11-13; Mk. 1:7-8; Jn. 3:26-31 Did not envy Jesus' position, but pointed people to Jesus. "I must decrease," he said.

Verses to memorize:

Js. 5:9 Grudge not one against another, brethren, lest ye be condemned: behold, the judge standeth before the door.

1 Cor. 13:4 Love suffers long and is kind; love does not envy; love does not parade itself, is not puffed up. (NKJV)

1 Cor. 3:3 ...for you are still carnal. For where there are envy, strife, and divisions among you, are you not carnal and behaving like mere men? (NKJV)

Matt. 20:15 'Is it not lawful for me to do what I wish with my own things? Or is your eye evil because I am good?' (NKJV)

Jer. 29:11 For I know the thoughts that I think toward you, saith the LORD, thoughts of peace, and not of evil, to give you an expected end.

1 Pet. 2:1-2 Wherefore laying aside all malice, and all guile, and hypocrisies, and envies, and all evil speakings, as newborn babes, desire the sincere milk of the word, that ye may grow thereby:

Ps. 9:2 I will be glad and rejoice in thee: I will sing praise to thy name, O thou most High.

Ps. 16:11 Thou wilt show me the path of life: in thy presence is fulness of joy; at thy right hand there are pleasures for evermore.

Ps. 119:165 Great peace have those who love Your law, and nothing causes them to stumble. (NKJV)

Matt. 19:19b Thou shalt love thy neighbour as thyself.

Ps. 34:10 The young lions do lack, and suffer hunger: but they that seek the LORD shall not want any good thing.

Pr. 19:23 The fear of the LORD leads to life, and he who has it will abide in satisfaction; He will not be visited with evil. (NKJV)

Rom. 12:15 Rejoice with them that do rejoice, and weep with them that weep.

1 Jn. 2:10 He who loves his brother abides in the light, and there is no cause for stumbling in him. (NKJV)

1 Jn. 4:12 No man hath seen God at any time. If we love one another, God dwelleth in us, and his love is perfected in us.

1 Cor. 10:24 Let no one seek his own, but each one the other's well-being. (NKJV)

1 Cor. 2:9 But as it is written, Eye hath not seen, nor ear heard, neither have entered into the heart of man, the things which God hath prepared for them that love him.

Covetousness

(See also Confidence in Riches)

General information and commandments about this sin:

Pr. 21:25 Lazy man covets greedily all day. Desire kills him.

Heb. 13:5 Be content with what you have.
Ask the child, "What do you need that you do not have?" Help him see that what he wants is not always what he needs. Help him recognize how faithfully God supplies all that he really needs.

Lk. 12:15 Man's life doesn't consist of possessions.
Make a list: What does man's life consist of?

Ex. 20:17 Shall not covet.

Ps. 10:3 God hates covetousness.

Ec. 1:8 Eyes and ears are never satisfied.

Hag. 1:6 The covetous find no satisfaction. They earn money to put in bags with holes.
Give your child money in the form of coins. Then give him a bag with holes cut in it to put the money in. How well does it stay in?

Col. 3:5 Coveting is idolatry.
As a graphic illustration for your child, make a collage of magazine pictures pasted onto a sheet of paper. Cut out pictures of things your child especially longs for. Put the picture up on the wall, and then call your child to come in for his devotion time. Suggest that he kneel down and pray to the picture. His reaction will probably be one of confusion and surprise. Use this moment to help him see how his desire for things has become an idol, a god, to him.

Ps. 39:6 Busy in vain, doesn't know who will gather riches.

I Tim. 6:10 Love of money is the root of all evil.
Stop to analyze arguments and strife in the home. How many conflicts can you trace back to the love of possessions?

Matt. 6:24 Can't serve two masters.
Hire your child for a day of work (on a day when both Mom and Dad are home.) Tell the child that he will not be paid unless he follows your instructions exactly. Then, Mom and Dad, give him conflicting instructions. How does he do trying to follow two sets of opposing orders?

Mk. 7:21-23 Comes from the heart, defiles.

Eph. 5:3 Coveting should not be named among you.
This means we should discipline this sin out of our child's (and our) lives.

I Tim. 3:3, Titus 1:7 Disqualifies for office of bishop.

I Tim. 6:6-8 Godliness and contentment is great gain. Will take nothing with us.
Contentment allows us to truly enjoy what God has given us.

I Jn. 2:15 Don't love things of the world, or the love of the Father is not in us.

What happens, or should happen, to the covetous person:

Pr. 15:27 Greedy of gain, troubles house.
Bring "trouble" into the child's life: take away privileges, belongings, levy fines, etc.

Matt. 13:22 Becomes unfruitful, distracted.
Deny the child profit from his labor, or do not allow him spending access to his money.

I Cor. 5:11 Don't keep company with Christian who is covetous.
Isolate the child temporarily.
Limit associations with covetous children or families.

Eph. 5:5 No inheritance in kingdom.
Withhold long-term savings deposit.
Withhold inheritance or passing on of heirlooms.

Col. 3:6 Brings wrath of God.

Col. 3:2 Set affections on things above.
Keep a journal of activities. Study it. What does it reveal about what is most important to you?

I Tim. 6:11 Follow righteousness, faith, love, patience, meekness.
Read stories together -- from the Bible, history, biographies -- about people that exemplify these qualities.

Jer. 8:10 Will give wives to others, fields to heirs.

Jer. 6:11-13 Houses, fields and wives given to others.
Give possessions away.
If child is coveting what another child has (ie. thinks he has not recieved his share of ice cream, etc.) take away the portion he does have. Give to others.

Ps. 119:36 Should incline heart to God's testimonies.
Study and memorize the Bible together.
Help child strive for eternal riches: set a goal for reading a
certain number of chapters in the Bible each day, memorizing a
specified number of verses during a week, studying a certain
topic or question in the Bible over a period of time, etc.
If child is young, keep a chart to check off. If older, set
up some system of accountability. And design some sort of
reward when the goal is reached -- a special outing, gift,
etc.

Ps. 106:14-15 God grants desires, but sends leanness to soul.
Pray for this in the child's life, and then help him understand it.

The blessings of contentment:

Pr. 28:16 If we hate coveting, our days will be prolonged.
Later bedtime, no nap, longer playtime, shorter school day.

I Tim. 6:6 Godliness with contentment is great gain.

Stories that illustrate the consequences of covetousness:

Eve, Gen. 3:6 Ate forbidden fruit, led to sin and separation.

Lot, Gen. 13:10-13 Chose the plain of Jordan, lived among sinners,
Sodom destroyed. Exposed to temptation, danger to household,
death of wife.

Balaam, Num. 22, II Pet. 2:15 Coveted riches, went against God's
directions.

Achan, Josh. 7 Led to theft, dishonesty, nation's defeat in battle,
and Achan's death.

Eli's sons, I Sam. 2:13-17 Coveted and took sacrificial meat. Led to
their death.

Samuel's sons, I Sam. 8:3-5 Dishonest gain, accepted bribes and
judged unfairly. Led to the people asking for a king.

Saul, I Sam. 15:8-9 Kept best of booty from battle, led to rejection
as king.

David and Bathsheba, II Sam. 11:2-5 Coveting another man's wife led to adultery, deceit, murder, and rebellion and conflict in David's family.

Ahab, I Kgs. 21:2-16 Led to pouting, allowing wife to execute injustice, false witnesses, and unjust killing of Naboth.

Gehazi, II Kgs. 5:20-27 Coveting Naaman's gift led to dishonesty and leprosy.

Moneychangers in temple, Matt. 21:12-13 Defiled the temple, and were clearly rebuked by Jesus.

Rich fool, Lk. 12:15-21 His soul was required of him, and he had to leave his possessions behind.

Judas, Matt. 26:15-16; Mk. 14:10-11; Lk. 22:3-6; Jn. 12:6 Betrayed Jesus for silver, then committed suicide.

Israelites, Ps. 106:13-15 Lusted in the wilderness. God gave them what they wanted but brought leanness to their souls.

Verses to memorize:

Pr. 30:8 Remove falsehood and lies far from me; give me neither poverty nor riches; feed me with the food allotted to me. (NKJV)

Ec. 4:6 Better a handful with quietness than both hands full, together with toil and grasping for the wind. (NKJV)

Ec. 6:9 Better is the sight of the eyes than the wandering of desire. This also is vanity and grasping for the wind. (NKJV)

Heb 13:5 Let your conversation be without covetousness; and be content with such things as ye have: for he hath said, I will never leave thee, nor forsake thee.

Luke 12:15 And he said unto them, take heed, and beware of covetousness: for a man's life consisteth not in the abundance of the things which he possesseth.

Ps. 119:36 Incline my heart unto thy testimonies, and not to covetousness.

1 Tim. 6:6-8 But godliness with contentment is great gain. For we brought nothing into this world, and it is certain we can carry nothing out. And having food and raiment let us be therewith content.

Theft
(See also Covetousness)

General information and commandments about this sin:

Matt. 15:19; Mk. 7:20-23; I Pet. 4:15 Comes from the heart.

Ex. 20:15; Lev. 19:11-13 You shall not steal.

Pr. 28:24 One who robs mother or father is companion to one who destroys.

Lev. 19:13 Not paying hired labor quickly is theft.

What happens, or should happen, to the thief:

Pr. 13:11 Wealth will diminish.
Require restitution. If child cannot replace item, or has no money, he should work for you to earn money or work for the victim of his theft until satisfactory restitution has been made.

Pr. 21:7 Will be destroyed.

Pr. 6:30-31 Will not be excused. Must make full restitution.
Do not accept excuses. Any form of theft must require restitution to the victim.
In our family we consider the taking of a toy, without permission from the child who was using it, as theft. We also consider it theft when a child "borrows" someone else's personal possessions without permission.

Pr. 28:8 One who gains by usury or extortion gathers for him who pities the poor.
Levy a fine from spending money into charity savings, or pay fine to parents who can then put it into a fund for giving.

Eph. 4:28 Let him labor so that he can give to him who needs.
Give child extra work.
Make restitution.

Ex. 21:16 Kidnapping is a capital crime.
We consider the following examples as forms of kidnapping in our household: locking a child in a room, holding a child against his will, taking the ladder away from the treehouse when a child is up there, etc.
This offense calls for spanking.

Lev. 6:2-5 Restore full value plus 1/5 for the following offenses:
  Lying about something you are caring for.
  Lying about a pledge.
  Lying about a robbery.
  Extortion of neighbor.
  Lying about object that one finds after it was lost.
  Swearing falsely about item.
  Have the child restore the item, plus pay approximately 20% of
    its value to the owner.

Pr. 20:17 Bread gained by deceit will turn to gravel.
  I haven't tried this yet, but I may. I've thought about making
    a cupcake and throwing in some pieces of aquarium gravel before
    I bake it. It would create a great opportunity to talk about this
    principle, but I don't want to break any teeth, and some of my
    kids would probably swallow rocks and all without ever noticing!

Ex. 22:3 Thief should serve as slave if he is unable to make
  restitution.
  Give the child "slave labor" if he cannot make restitution. Have
    him work for you to earn money for replacing the object, or have
    him work for the victim of his theft.

Lev. 5:14-16, Num. 5:5-8 If thief voluntarily seeks to make
  restitution before being caught, he should return the object, plus 1/5
  of its value.
  If child confesses his theft before he is discovered, he should return
    the object, plus 1/5 of its value.

Ex. 22:4 If stolen object is found unharmed, the thief should
  make double restitution.
  If the child is making restitution for taking away a toy or some
    other item, he can give that item back and also give the victim
    another toy that he (the thief) was playing with. If a daughter
    "borrows" her sister's blouse without permission, she should return
    it, washed and ironed, as well as giving her sister opportunity to
    choose an item of hers to use or wear.

Ps. 50:18 One who consents with a thief is a thief.
  A child who was a knowing party to a theft should be punished in
    the same way as the actual thief.

I Cor. 6:8-10 Will not inherit kingdom.
  Deny deposit into child's long-term savings.
  Deny passing on of heirlooms when theft is habitual.
  Clarify to child that he will be excluded from inheritance of
    family wealth if he does not conquer the sin of stealing.

Ex. 22:5 If person causes another's field or vineyard to be
eaten by his animals, he should make restitution from the best
of his own field or vineyard.
*If the child causes damage to another's property (ie. leaves
felt pens open so they dry out, leaves crayons out so that baby
comes along and breaks them or decorates the walls with them)
the person responsible should replace the item with his own,
or purchase a new item as replacement.*

To what is the thief likened:

Partridge on eggs that don't hatch, Jer. 17:11 Person who gains
riches that are not his by right.
*We know from experience what happens to unhatched eggs that a
hen has set on -- they <u>rot</u>! Not only do they not produce a
cute little chick, but they do produce a very unpleasant odor.
(Fern and her brother, in <u>Charlotte's Web,</u> found this out
from Templeton's egg, too.)
These unproductive eggs consumed the time and energy of the hen,
without gain.*

The blessings of the honest man:

Mal. 3:8-10 Man who does not rob God by withholding the tithe,
will have no room to receive all of God's blessings.

Lk. 19:8-10 Zacchaeus received salvation when he repented and
made four-fold restitution to those he had robbed.

Stories that illustrate the consequences of stealing:

Achan, Josh. 7 Cost the lives of others in battle, and led to
the execution of Achan and his familly.

Rachel, Gen. 31:19, 34, 35 Stealing of father's idols, led to
lying.

Verses to memorize:

1 Pet 4:15 But let none of you suffer as a murderer, or as a thief, or

as an evildoer, or as a busybody in other men's matters.

Ex. 20:15 Thou shalt not steal.

Eph. 4:28 Let him that stole steal no more: but rather let him labour, working with his hands the thing which is good, that he may have to give to him that needeth.

Pr. 20:17 Bread gained by deceit is sweet to a man, but afterward his mouth will be filled with gravel. (NKJV)

Rules for Borrowers

General information and commandments about borrowing:

Pr. 27:1   Boast not of tomorrow, we don't know the future.

Pr. 22:7   Borrower is servant to the lender.

Matt. 6:24   Cannot serve two masters.
Let your child try this. Hire him for an afternoon of work at home. He must follow your instructions completely to receive his pay. Mom and Dad should both be his bosses. Give him opposing instructions (ie. "The next thing you should do is to wash the living room windows," while the other parent is telling him to not do anything else until he vacuums the rug). See how he does.

Ps. 37:21   Wicked borrows and doesn't repay.

Pr. 3:28   Don't put person off. Repay him on time.
Insist on prompt repayment of loans (if you allow borrowing at all). This can apply to returning library books on time, quickly returning tools, and other things people have lent, etc.
An example can be set in this area by parents who pay their bills on time. (Utility, insurance, etc. To really teach children properly about debt, I believe parents should not be going into debt with credit.)

Rom. 13:8   Owe no man anything but to love.

Lev. 19:13   Don't hold wages of hired man overnight.
We should pay our children for their chores at agreed-upon intervals.

Isa. 41:21-23   Only God knows the future.

Js. 4:13-15   We don't know tomorrow.
We're assuming we do know the future when we go into debt.

Ps. 84:11   God will withhold no good thing from the upright man.
If God "cannot" supply this for us without us going into debt, is it really a "good" thing that we really need?

Phil. 4:19   God will supply all our needs according to His riches in glory.
Is God not rich enough to supply this item without us going into debt?

What happens, or should happen, to the borrower:

Pr. 22:7 Becomes servant to lender.

Neh. 5:5 Servitude.
The borrower has sold a portion of his future increase.
When my children press me to lend to them I ask them, "Do you
really want to be my servant until you can repay me?" That is
usually enough to discourage them.

Ex. 22:10-11 If keeping care of animal and it dies, is injured,
or disappears, without witnesses, owner should accept
the caretaker's word, and no restitution should be required.

Ex. 22:14 If man borrows animal and it is hurt or dies, and the
owner is not present, the borrower should replace the animal.
If child borrows an item and breaks it while its owner is not
present, the child needs to replace the item. This is part of
the risk and responsibility of borrowing.

Ex. 22:14-15 If man borrows animal and it is hurt or dies, and
the owner is present, the borrower does not need to make
restitution.
If child borrows an item and it breaks while the owner is present,
the child should not be required to make restitution. The owner
still had responsibility over the object.

Lev. 24:18 If a man kills an animal, he must replace it.
If child willfully breaks or destroys someone else's property, he
should replace it.

We should be helping our children save for their futures. We have
taught our children a system of budgeting their earnings that divides
their money into 7 different categories: charity, living expenses, tithe,
short-term savings, spending, long-term savings, and "dowry" (for wife's
use in marriage).
(Note: Doorposts sells a booklet entitled "Stewardship Street" which
explains the budget system we use with our children, and provides
patterns for making a "street" of milk carton savings houses. See
ordering information at back of book.)
The purpose of our long-term savings is to provide the children with
capital to use for starting up small businesss ventures, to pay for
additional training for careers, to purchase future cars, property, building
materials, etc. With this money saved ahead, they can start a small
business that requires little investment -- yardwork, baking, sewing,
typing/word processing, etc. With the profit and experience gained in
that initial business, the child can expand into a related business that will

bring even greater profit and learning experience. From the humble beginnings of a little business started as a child, a potential lifetime career could blossom, without incurring any debt.

Neither my husband nor I had the foresight to save money before our marriage. When friends started encouraging us to print up some of the charts we used with our own children, and start a little home business, we could not even scrape up the money it would take to print up a small run of one chart. A family in our church gave us $100 venture capital, not a loan, with the agreement that we could pay them $.50 for each chart we sold until we sold out the first run of 250. If we didn't sell any charts, we didn't owe them any money.

The first fair we went to earned us enough profit to print up our next chart, and with two charts at the next fair we earned enough to print up more of our ideas. Three years later God is providing a portion of our family's income through our little business. God has accomplished all this without us ever going into debt.

We want our children to be able to develop businesses that will support their families, allow Daddy to stay home, and free them from the servitude of debt.

Stories that illustrate the consequences of borrowing:

Jews under bondage of usury, Neh. 5:1-13

Parable of forgiven debtor, Matt. 18:23-35 Vs. 25 says that the debtor, his family, and all his belongings were about to be sold to pay off his debt.

Widow and Elisha, II Kgs. 4:1-7 In verse 1 the widow is explaining that her late husband's creditor is coming to take her sons as slaves.

Verses to memorize:

Rom. 13:8 Owe no man any thing, but to love one another: for he that loveth another hath fulfilled the law. (NKJV)

Pr. 27:1 Do not boast about tomorrow, for you do not know what a day may bring forth.

Pr. 22:7 The rich ruleth over the poor, and the borrower is servant to the lender. (NKJV)

Easily Swayed / Backsliding / Double-Minded
(See also Faint-Hearted)

General information and commandments about this sin:

Js. 1:8 Is unstable in all his ways.

Rom. 12:1-3 Be not conformed to world, present bodies as living sacrifices.
Begin each day with your children, praying and presenting your bodies as sacrifices to God.

Js. 4:17 To know what is good, and not do it, is sin.

Pr. 24:21 Don't meddle with one given to sudden change.
Do not allow your child to develop deep friendships with others that are always wanting change.

Matt. 6:24 Can't serve two masters.
Try this! See listing for this verse in chapters on "Borrowing," "Greedy for Gain," and "Covetousness."

Eph. 4:14 Be no more children, tossed about.

Pr. 1:10 If sinners entice you, do not consent.

Heb. 4:14 Hold fast our profession.
It is easier to hold fast to something if we know and understand it. Does your child know what he professes as a believer?
Work through basic church doctrines, memorize a catechism, study the Bible seriously together, so that your children understand what they profess to believe.

Heb. 13:9 Should not be carried about with divers doctrines.

Gal. 5:1 Stand fast, not entangled.
Protect the child from entanglements -- harmful friendships, reading, media, overinvolvement in activities, etc.

What happens, or should happen, to the person who is easily swayed:

Job 34:26-27 Strike as wicked in sight of others.

Pr. 14:14 Filled with own ways.

Ezek. 3:20 His righteousness is not remembered.

Matt. 5:13 Cast out, trodden.

Mk. 4:15-19 Not fruitful.

Mk. 8:38 Jesus ashamed of him.

Js. 4:8 Double-minded, purify heart.
Purify your child's heart with Scripture. Study it, memorize it together. Encourage and train him in daily Bible reading. Be faithful in family worship.

Rom. 12:12 Rejoice in hope, patient in tribulation, continue in prayer.
Pray for your child and with your child.

Heb. 6:4-8 Bear thorns and briars, reject, burn.
Talk about what happens to weeds and briars that are pulled out of your yard.

Js. 1:7 Receive nothing from the Lord.
Deny benefits of family -- inheritance, finances, recreation, etc.

Gen. 49:3-4 Reuben was unstable as water, wouldn't excell.
Review child's life and accomplishments thus far. Is there evidence of stability or instability?

Pr. 24:21,22 Calamity rises suddenly.
Pray for God's clear discipline in your child's life.

Js. 1:6 Pray with faith.

Hosea 10:2 Heart is divided, God will break down their idols.
Look for "idols" and distractions in the child's life. Help remove them.
Pray for God to remove idols and the opportunity to "worship" them.

Rev. 3:16 Spew out of mouth.
What kind of things do you spit out of your mouth? Good things or "yucky" things?

Rom. 12:2 Should not be conformed to the world, but transformed by renewing of mind.

Acts 17:11 Search the Scriptures daily, like the Bereans.

Col. 2:7 Need to be rooted and built up in him.
Help the child be consistent in devotional life, fellowship with other believers, prayer, memorization, and Bible study.

Pr. 28:14 Leads to calamity.

Heb. 12:1.+ Lay aside every weight, and look to Jesus.
Working with your child, write up a list of "weights" that are hindering his growth and progress. Perhaps you could even write each "weight" onto rocks or other heavy objects. Then "lay aside"

these weights. (Put them in the garbage, bury them, or put them in a box where they can be retrieved for review when needed.)

I Thess. 5:21 Need to prove all things.
Take an area of question that the child is wavering over and study it thoroughly with him. Teach him Bible study methods, read commentaries together, ask your pastor for counsel, discuss it with friends over a meal.

Js. 1:5-6 Ask God, in faith, for wisdom.

II Pet. 1:5-10 Work towards maturity: Diligence + faith + virtue + knowledge + temperance + patience + godliness + brotherly kindness + charity.
Study Hebrews 11 and 12:1-4 for examples of faith and perseverence.
Read Foxe's Book of Martyrs and stories of Christians persecuted for their faith in hostile countries. These people were sure of what they believed and were willing to suffer and die for their beliefs. We want our children to be this sure of what they believe, so that they are willing to stand up for what is right, and turn against sin. Daniel and his friends, in Babylon, are testimonies that prove to us that young people are capable of resisting evil and standing up for their convictions, even in the midst of the enemy. Their parents must have faithfully trained them!

Eph. 6:10-18 Put on the armor of God.
Study and memorize this passage. Make actual armor that your boys can wear in their play, make a set of armor for a doll, draw a picture of a soldier and cut out individual pieces of armor to put on him. When he has doubts, or is being swayed in his beliefs, go to the passage and your armor and think about which piece of armor your "soldier" has forgotten to put on.
Note: See ordering information at back of book for materials related to the "Armor of God" that we offer for your help.

Matt. 7:24-25 Build on rock.
Build some model houses together outside -- one on mud or sand, and one on a rock base. Create a storm! Which house survives? How do we build on the Rock?

Pr. 14:14 Double-minded man is filled with his own ways.
This child needs to submit himself and his thinking to the authority of Scripture. Study God's Word together, and help it replace the foolishness of the child's own ways.

Lk. 9:62 Not fit for the kingdom.

II Tim. 2:12 If we deny God, He will deny us.

II Pet. 2:20-21 Better to have not known the way of righteousness than to know and turn from it.

Isa. 59:9-11 Justice is gone.
Look at our government! Many Christians have been easily swayed by man's reasoning and Satan's deception. The salt has lost its savor, and justice is quickly disappearing in our country.

Jn. 15:4 + We bring forth fruit if we abide in Him. If we do not abide in Him, we cannot bear fruit alone. We will be cast forth and burned.

To what is the double-minded, backsliding person likened?

Murky spring, polluted well, Pr. 25:26 This is a picture of the righteous man faltering before the wicked.
Wells, especially in Bible times, were precious. The cost for corrupting them was high. Polluted water cannot provide refreshment and cleansing.

Dog returning to vomit, Pr. 26:11 Returns to what body already rejected the first time.

Salt without savor, Matt. 5:13
Bake bread without salt or fix dish that definitely needs salt, but leave salt out. How does everybody like it?
Study the method of salting fish for preservation. Salt one piece of fish, and leave another without salt. Which one lasts the longest? What happens to the unsalted fish?

Seeds among thorns and on stony ground, Mk. 4:4-20 No root, choked out.
Experiment! Divide a package of seeds into 3 portions. Plant one portion in thorny, weedy ground. Plant another portion in stony soil, and the last portion in good, well-prepared soil. Watch to see what happens! What happens to the double-minded man who has no roots?

Looking back with hand to the plow, Lk. 9:62
If the plowman is looking backward instead of keeping his eyes fixed ahead, his furrow will be crooked.

Tossed to and fro in the wind, Eph. 4:14
Watch an object in the wind, or a toy in the water of a bathtub or fishtank. Observe how it has no control of itself, but is tossed about by the force of its surroundings.

Branch, Jn. 15:6 Withered, pruned and burned.
 *Prune trees or bushes together. Prune grape and berry vines.
 Talk about the need to prune for the plant's growth and health,
 and why you prune out unproductive and diseased branches.
 Our raspberry rows illustrated this for us, as they slowly
 browned and withered, bore shriveled and tasteless fruit, and
 eventually completely died.*

Shipwreck, I Tim. 1:19
 *How useful is a ruined ship? How much freedom does it have?
 Can it accomplish its purpose?*

Baby that needs milk instead of strong meat, Heb. 5:12 Cannot
 digest solid food.
 *Compare a newborn babe and a 3-year-old child. Do they eat
 the same things? Does a 3-year-old drink milk as its only food?
 What about a 10-year-old? What would happen if they did have
 milk as their only food?*

Blind, nearsighted, II Pet. 1:9
 *Look through an unfocused camera. How well can you see?
 If you or your child wears glasses or contacts, remove them. Try
 to read roadsigns or maps. Would it be safe to drive without
 glasses if you normally need them? Why not?*

Bird wandering from nest, Pr. 27:8
 *What happens to a little bird who falls out of, or leaves, his
 nest before he is old enough?*

Lukewarm, Rev. 3:15,16 Will be spit out.
 *Whet your child's appetite for a glass of cold, cold iced tea or
 a dish of ice cream. Then serve it to him warm. Is it as appetizing
 as it would have been when cold?*

Water, Gen. 49:4 Reuben
 *Study water. Is it stable? Can you walk on water? Does it hold
 it shape? Does water hold a constant temperature regardless of its
 surroundings? Does water stay clean regardless of it surroundings?
 Does water hold its shape? Try some experiments!*

Good soldier, II Tim. 2:3-4 If engaged in warfare, he cannot be
 entangled with affairs of life.
 *Read a story of a soldier in battle, or imagine a soldier in the thick
 of battle. Would he be sitting back in an easy chair reading a
 magazine or watching TV?*

Athlete, II Tim. 2:5 Must compete by the rules.
 *If athlete violates rules he will be sent out of game or disqualified.
 Discuss this parallel after a disappointing experience on the ball*

field, or while observing the results a fight on the hockey ice, etc.

Man looking in a mirror, Js. 1:23-25 Walks away and forgets what
he looked like.
*Come to the breakfast table in obvious disarray. Arrange with your
spouse to comment on your disheveled appearance, and go to a
mirror for repairs, but come back to the table in the same state.
After your family's reactions, talk about this verse and its truth.*

Wife departing from husband, Jer. 3:20
*Unfortunately, there are many examples of this to observe in our
culture. How well does a woman do on her own when she leaves
her husband? Does she have to make sacrifices? Does her life
change? Does she give up her protection?*

Wave of sea, tossed by wind, Js. 1:6 A man who doubts.
*Observe the waves on the ocean. They are always changing, always
driven by the wind.*

House on sand, Matt.7:24-27 No foundation, destroyed in storm.
*Build a sand castle or a house of sticks on the sand. What
happens to it when "storms" come?*

The blessings of returning from backsliding:

II Tim. 2:12 Will reign.
*Give child extra responsibility and privilege.
Honor the child with responsiblity over others.*

Lev. 26:40-42 God will remember His covenant with the one who
humbles himself and confesses his backsliding.
*Work within the structure of convenants with your children.
Your children should understand the blessings that will result
from their obedience, and they should understand the unavoidable
discipline that their disobedience will bring into their lives.
Study Biblical covenants together -- God's covenants with man,
man's covenants with man, man's covenants with God.
Note: Doorposts carries two charts, "The If-Then Chart" and "The
Blessing Chart," which can help you in the formation of informal
covenants regarding obedience and disobedience. See ordering
information at back of book.*

Deut. 30:1-10 Keep covenant, God will keep His covenant. Will
bring blessing and plenty.
*Give recognition and praise to the child who returns from the
error of his ways.*

II Chr. 30:9 Turn back, will have compassion from captors.

Job 22:23-30 Great blessing, gold, silver, prayer heard, light will shine on way.
What an example the prodigal sons' father sets for us! He bestowed great blessing on his returning son, and freely forgave him.

Jer. 6:16 Rest to souls.
Enjoy a brief retreat together after a period of indecision has been resolved. Rent a cabin in the woods, go to the beach, go fishing, some quiet, secluded activity that gives you time to talk and time to review the decisions that have been made.

Hos. 14:4 Heal backsliding, anger turned away.
Forgive your child if there has been wandering from the faith, and he has returned with a repentant heart. Do not bring up past failures and mistakes.

Isa. 26:3 Perfect peace.

Pr. 28:14 Happy.

Rev. 2:7 Eat tree of life.
Celebrate a family feast in honor of the repentant child. Perhaps you could serve foods that grow on trees, and explain this verse during the meal.

Rev. 2:10 Wear crown of life.
Give the child a special crown to wear during family meal.

Rev. 2:17 Eat hidden manna, white stone with new name written on it.
Perhaps you could keep a family book in which you record the spiritual milestones of family members. Write down an account of the restoration of a wayward child that can be reread as a testimony and encouragement in the future.
Note: Doorposts, in 1994, will have a product available entitled, "Our Pilgrim's Journey," which is a sort of spiritual "baby book" in which you can record spiritual milestones and remembrances for your child. See ordering information at back of book.

Rev. 2:26 Power over nations.

Rev. 2:28 Morning star.

Stories that illustrate the consequences of backsliding and being easily swayed:

Aaron, Ex. 32 Israel's worship of the golden calf. Aaron attempted to blame the people over whom he ruled.

After Joshua's death, Jg. 2 Anger of God, sold into hands of enemies.

Israelites that believed the 10 spies, Num. 14:1-45 Were not allowed to enter Promised Land.

Solomon, I Kgs. 11:4-40, Neh. 13:26 Swayed by idolatrous beliefs of wives. Kingdom taken away.

Lot's wife, Gen. 19:26 Turned back towards Sodom, and lost life.

Israel and Baal-Peor, Num. 25:9 24,000 killed.

Asa, II Chr. 16:1-9 Relying on King of Syria instead of on God. Cursed with a future filled with wars.

Pharaoh, Ex. 8+ His double-mindedness cost him and his country the loss of produce and livestock, much discomfort, firstborn children, and a portion of their army in the Red Sea.

Stories that illustrate the blessing of strong conviction and courage:

Gideon, Jg. 6:25+ Tore down the altars of Baal. Spared from death, and then led army in victory over Midian.

Shadrach, Meshach, Abednego, Dan. 3:16+ Spared from death and later promoted in responsibility.

Daniel, Dan. 1 Found favor, was given greater wisdom, blessing.

Daniel, Dan. 6 Spared from death.

Joshua and Caleb, Num. 14:24, 38 Spared from plague, given portion in land.

Verses to memorize:

Heb. 10:23 Let us hold fast the profession of our faith without wavering; (for he is faithful that promised.)

2 Tim. 2:12 If we suffer, we shall also reign with him: if we deny him, he also will deny us.

1 Thess 5:21 Prove all things; hold fast that which is good. (NKJV)

James 1:7-8 For let not that man think that he shall receive any thing of the Lord. A double minded man is unstable in all his ways. (NKJV)

Eph. 6:10-11 Finally, my brethren, be strong in the Lord, and in the power of his might. Put on the whole armour of God, that ye may be able to stand against the wiles of the devil.

Eph. 6:11 Put on the whole armour of God, that ye may be able to stand against the wiles of the devil.

Phil. 4:1b So stand fast in the Lord, my dearly beloved.

Luke 17:3 Remember Lot's wife.

Isa. 26:3 Thou wilt keep him in perfect peace, whose mind is stayed on thee: because he trusteth in thee.

Phil. 3:14 I press toward the mark for the prize of the high calling of God in Christ Jesus.

Matt. 6:24 No man can serve two masters: for either he will hate the one, and love the other; or else he will hold to the one, and despise the other. Ye cannot serve God and mammon.

Faint-Hearted/Easily Discouraged/Giving Up

(See also Fear, Worry, Depression)

We, as parents, need to carefully and prayerfully examine how we relate to our children. How do we correct them? What attitude do we have toward them? Are we discouraging them, or are we encouraging them to draw on the Holy Spirit's power to give them victory over their temptations and struggles? Are we upholding them in prayer, or scolding and nagging them in our own strength and sinful pride?

"Fathers, provoke not your children to anger, lest they be discouraged." (Col. 3:21)

General information and commandments about this sin:

Pr. 24:10 If you faint in day of adversity, your strength is small.
This means that we are relying on our own strength instead of on God's omnipotence.

II Tim. 2:3 Endure hardship.
It is tempting to protect our children from hardship. But hardship is part of God's training ground for mighty soldiers in His army.
We should not always shield our children from discomfort. In fact, we should be looking for ways to help them grow stronger in body, mind and spirit. Give your children work. Do not spare them when they think a task is too hard if you believe that they are capable of accomplishing it.
Spend time as a family in situations that will teach your children to endure physical hardship -- camping, backpacking, gardening, doing physical labor for others.
Read books together about Christians who have endured great hardship.
Read Foxe's Book of Martyrs for graphic stories of endurance.
I've always wondered about Daniel's parents -- what did they do that prepared their son to go into captivity with such integrity and strength of conviction? Were they still alive and praying for him? We need the commitment and wisdom to raise up such sons and daughters, "plants grown up in their youth" and "corner stones polished after the similitude of a palace." (Ps. 144:12)

I Pet. 4:12-14 Persecution leads to joy.

II Thess. 3:13 Should not become weary in well-doing.
Train your children to persevere, to finish a task, to not give up when it becomes difficult.

Set an example!

Eph. 3:13 It is our glory to not give up.

Acts 14:22 We enter the kingdom through much tribulation.
  Tribulation and hardship are designed to bring maturity. To allow a child to run from tribulation is to retard his spiritual growth.

Heb. 12:12-13 Strengthen hands that hang down.
  This part of a parent's responsiblity.

Heb. 12:3 Consider Jesus' endurance.
  Study Jesus' life. What did He do during all the times when we would be tempted to quit -- during temptation, denial, betrayal, false accusation, disciples arguing, crucifixion?

II Thess. 2:15-17 Stand fast, hold tradition taught.

What happens, or should happen, to the faint-hearted?

Eph 6:13 Put on armor of God.
  Study and memorize this passage together. (See suggestions for this Scripture passage in chapter on "Easily Swayed.")

Eph. 6:18, Js. 5:13 Pray.
  Pray for willingness and strength to persevere.

Deut. 20:8 Remove fearful so he doesn't affect others.
  Be careful to not let this attitude infect others in your household. Silence the child who is expressing discouragement, especially in the form of complaints, or you'll have an epidemic on your hands!

Mk. 6:31 Come apart from others and rest.
  Sometimes discouragement is the result of fatigue.
  If the entire family seems to be struggling with discouragement, maybe its time for a vacation, or at least a day away together.
  Taking a true day of rest on Sunday has been a real source of refreshment for our family. We might be exhausted and discouraged on Saturday evening, but resting and meditating and fellowshipping together, while taking a conscious break from our regular daily activities, always leaves us refreshed and ready to tackle the next week.
  Note: Our little book, "Day of Delight," tells the story of our family's discovery of real Sabbath rest, and gives dozens of ideas for family activities that will make Sunday the best day of the week for you. (See ordering information at back of book.)

Heb. 12:12-13   Strengthen feeble hands and knees, make paths straight.
Encourage your child with Scripture.
Make the child's paths straight by protecting him from overactivity and temptation.

Rom. 12:12   Continue in prayer.
Support this child with fervent prayer.
Pray with the child about his areas of discouragement.

Hab. 3:17-18   Rejoice in the Lord.
Make a list of encouraging Psalms for the child to read.
Study these Psalms together.
Point the child to God -- His character and His many blessings.

Heb. 4:15-16   Come boldly to the throne of grace.
Pray with and for the child.

Heb. 12:5-11   Accept God's chastening as a sign of His love.
Sometimes the circumstances that discourage us are the result of, and discipline for sin in our lives. Help the child recognize this, if it is the case, and encourage him to confess and repent of his sin.

Rom. 15:1   We should bear the infirmities of the weak.
We need to exercise a great deal of patience with the easily discouraged child.

To what is the faint-hearted person directed for examples:

Soldier, II Tim. 2:3-4   The soldier is held up as an example to the faint-hearted.
Read biographies of soldiers, and stories of Medal-of-Honor winners.

Athlete, II Tim. 2:5

Runner, I Cor. 9:24-25
Work with the child to select an athletic discipline to pursue.
The training and discipline of athletics can teach a child to persevere.
Watch sports events together and discuss the training and discipline that has been required for the athlete to develop his skill.

The blessings of perseverence:

Js. 1:12 Endure temptation, will gain crown of life.

I Cor. 9:24-25 Imperishable crown.
Let the child wear a special crown at the dinner table in recognition for perseverence or victory over temptation.

Matt. 24:13 Will be saved.

Ps. 37:24 Upheld by the Lord.

Gal. 6:9 Will reap if we don't faint.
Plant a special flower garden (or pot of flowers) during a period of discouragement. Watch it grow, anticipate the harvest, enjoy the beauty of seeds and labor brought to fruition.

II Tim. 2:12 If we suffer, we will reign.
Give leadership responsibility to a child who has faithfully weathered a period of testing.

Isa. 40:31 Will renew strength, will run and not faint.
Go running together. Talk about this verse when you grow weary and stop to walk.

Stories that illustrate discouragement and faint-heartedness:

People of Jericho, Josh. 2:24 Feared the Israelites.

Saul, I Sam. 28:16-25 Responding to the discipline that was to come because of his disobedience.

Cain, Gen. 4:13 Response to the discipline for his murder.

Hagar, Gen. 21:15,16 After being cast out from Sarah's household for her impudence.

Israelites under bondage in Egypt, Ex. 6:9

Elijah, I Kgs. 19:4 Fled from Jezebel, after great victory over the prophets of Baal.

Jonah, Jon. 4:3,8 Resenting God's mercy toward Nineveh.

Stories that illustrate perseverence:

David with Saul in pursuit, I Sam. 18-31

Read through the stories of Saul's jealous pursuit of David. David had plenty of reasons to become discouraged, but he did not give up. He remained faithful and obedient to the Lord. I Sam. 30:6 says, "..but David encouraged himself in the Lord his God."

The Psalms are testimony to David's constant calling upon the Lord for strength. In remembering God's character and His faithfulness in the past, he was encouraged, and has left us a rich collection of prayers to meditate on when we grow discouraged. Direct your child to the Psalms when he is faint-hearted.

Joshua and Caleb, Num. 14:6-9,24,38 Were not afraid of the people of Caanan. Remembered, and reminded the people, that God was with them. Were allowed to enter the land, when all the rest of their generation were not.

Joseph, Gen. 27-50

Study the life of Joseph together. In spite of continual testing and injustices, he remained faithful and obedient, and found favor from those over him, until God put him into a position of great leadership and influence.

Jacob, Gen. 29:18-30 Worked for fourteen years to be able to take Rachel as his wife.

Verses to memorize:

Phil. 1:6 Being confident of this very thing, that he which hath begun a good work in you will perform it until the day of Jesus Christ.

Phil. 2:13 For it is God which worketh in you both to will and to do of his good pleasure.

2 Cor. 12:9 And he said unto me, My grace is sufficient for thee: for my strength is made perfect in weakness. Most gladly therefore will I rather glory in my infirmities, that the power of Christ may rest upon me.

Ps. 147:3 He healeth the broken in heart, and bindeth up their wounds.

Ps. 138:8 The LORD will perfect that which concerneth me: thy mercy, O LORD, endureth for ever: forsake not the works of thine own hands.

1 Cor. 16:13 Watch ye, stand fast in the faith, quit you like men, be

strong.

Gal. 6:9 And let us not be weary in well doing: for in due season we shall reap, if we faint not.

Phil. 4:13 I can do all things through Christ which strengtheneth me.

Ps. 37:23-24 The steps of a good man are ordered by the LORD: and he delighteth in his way. Though he fall, he shall not be utterly cast down: for the LORD upholdeth him with his hand.

Ps. 46:1 God is our refuge and strength, a very present help in trouble.

1 Thess. 5:24 Faithful is he that calleth you, who also will do it.

2 Tim. 1:12 For I know whom I have believed, and am persuaded that he is able to keep that which I have committed unto him against that day.

2 Tim. 2:3 Thou therefore endure hardness, as a good soldier of Jesus Christ.

Isa. 40:31 But they that wait upon the LORD shall renew their strength; they shall mount up with wings as eagles; they shall run, and not be weary; and they shall walk, and not faint.

Isa. 50:7-9 For the Lord GOD will help me; therefore shall I not be confounded: therefore have I set my face like a flint, and I know that I shall not be ashamed. He is near that justifieth me; who will contend with me? let us stand together: who is mine adversary? let him come near to me. Behold, the Lord GOD will help me; who is he that shall condemn me? lo, they all shall wax old as a garment; the moth shall eat them up.

Ps. 68:19 Blessed be the Lord, who daily loadeth us with benefits, even the God of our salvation.

Phil. 3:13-14 Brethren, I count not myself to have apprehended: but this one thing I do, forgetting those things which are behind, and reaching forth unto those things which are before, I press toward the mark for the prize of the high calling of God in Christ Jesus.

Rom. 8:37 Nay, in all these things we are more than conquerors through him that loved us.

Ps. 66:12 Thou hast caused men to ride over our heads; we went through fire and through water: but thou broughtest us out into a wealthy place.

2 Tim. 4:7-8 I have fought a good fight, I have finished my course, I have kept the faith: henceforth there is laid up for me a crown of righteousness, which the Lord, the righteous judge, shall give me at

that day: and not to me only, but unto all them also that love his appearing.

James 1:2-4 My brethren, count it all joy when ye fall into divers temptations; knowing this, that the trying of your faith worketh patience. But let patience have her perfect work, that ye may be perfect and entire, wanting nothing.

Ps. 121:1 I will lift up mine eyes unto the hills, from whence cometh my help.

Depression

(See also Discouragement, Envy, Complaining, Covetousness, Fear, Worry, Bitterness)

Depression is not considered, by many, to be a problem of sin. It is very true that depression can originate from physical causes -- chemical imbalances in the body, illness, fatigue, allergy, etc. These possibilities should be carefully considered when dealing with depression.

God can use those periods of physically-caused depression to bring greater maturity into our lives. As I have been putting this book together, I went through a rather frightening period of depression which was caused by a hormone imbalance during pregnancy. In spite of all prayer, Bible reading, and meditation, my confused body was still determined to reign over my mind and spirit. It was a very sobering experience as I had to deal with fears and thoughts that I normally never have in my life. But, in the midst of it, God revealed to me areas that I have not fully trusted Him with, and has brought me to a place of greater faith in Him.

Depression can also be a response to sin in our lives, to guilt, to isolation, the result of our spiritual coldness or of bitterness and contention in our personal relationships. We can become depressed when we are not willing to accept God's wisdom and sovereignty in our lives. If we resist the events and circumstances that God brings across our paths we will become discouraged and depressed. Depression is the sinful handling of adverse circumstances that God allows into our lives, giving in to the temptation to despair.

We all have periods of discouragement and disappointment; depression results when we give in to these feelings and quit looking to God for our strength and comfort, when we quit trusting Him to give us what is truly best for our good.

When dealing with a depressed child, pray for wisdom in discerning sins in his life, and gently confront him about those sins. Teach him the Gospel and of God's forgiveness for those who will trust in Christ's finished work on the cross. Help him to resolve conflicts he might have with other people. He may need help in learning to forgive instead of nursing grudges.

We parents also need to prayerfully examine our relationship to our children. Are we loving them, encouraging and supporting them, and forgiving them for wrongs, or are we discouraging them with unfair expectations of perfection, in anger and constant criticism? These attitudes can be a great source of discouragement to the little ones God has given us.

General information and commandments about depression:

Ps. 73:2-14 Envious of foolish and wicked.
Discouragement over the wickedness of our world can cause depression. We must remember that we are "more than conquerors" in Him, and that God will "give [us] the heathen for [our] inheritance." (Ps. 2:8)

Ps. 32:1-4 Unconfessed sin and guilt.
The burden of sin and the guilt that comes from not confessing it can depress and immobilize us in our Christian walk. We need to help our children keep a pure conscience before the Lord by teaching them to quickly confess and repent of sin.

What happens, or should happen, to the depressed person:

Ps. 1:1-3 Delight in God's Word.
One of the keys to overcoming depression is God's Word.
Study God's Word with your child. Read the Psalms with him. Sing the Psalms with him. Memorize Scripture with him so that he is armed against the "fiery darts of the wicked."

Lk. 11:28 Hear and obey God's Word.

Jn. 13:17 Obedience leads to happiness.
If the child is not being obedient to the truth he knows, he may become depressed and burdened with guilt.
Help him remember the saving grace of Christ's death and resurrection. Help him come to a point of acknowledging his sin and repenting.
Give him projects that will help him move toward obedience, and work out a system of accountability to you or some other trusted person who loves your child enough to regularly ask him how he is doing.
Pray for an open and obedient heart in your child.

Ps. 32:1-2,5 Should acknowledge sin. Man whose sin is forgiven is blessed.
Pray for your child to be sensitive to unconfessed sin.
Talk with your child, attempting to uncover secret sins that may be causing his despair.
Pray with your child when you discipline. Teach him to quickly acknowledge his sin to God, ask His forgiveness, and pray for His

strength. He should confess his wrong to those he has hurt.

Js. 5:13 Pray.
  *Pray for the child's right response to the discouraging circumstances
    in his life.*
  *Pray that God's will might be accomplished in the circumstances that
    your child is in.*
  *Pray for wisdom in discerning ways to encourage and motivate your
    child.*

I Sam. 2:1-10 Prayer and praise.

Ps. 42:5,11 Hope in God. Praise Him.

Ps. 40:3 Praise.

I Thess. 5:16-18 Rejoice, pray, give thanks.
  Give thanks to God for all His many blessings.
  *Review the child's life and the way God has blessed and intervened
    and protected throughout it. Make a list of these blessings that an
    easily depressed child can review when he is discouraged.*
  *Praise God for His unchanging character, His faithfulness and His
    love. Discuss how these attributes call for our complete trust in
    God.*

Ps. 128:2 Eat labor of your hands, will give happiness.
  *Do not allow the child to wallow in despair to the point of
    neglecting his responsibilities and abandoning his normal routine.*
  *Require that the child participate in normal activities, and be
    responsible for normal duties.*
  Give him projects to do, interests to pursue. Work alongside him.

Jn. 13:14-17 Serve. Jesus was still serving others, even as Judas
went out to betray him.
  *Help the child take his eyes off himself. Involve him in projects
    of service to others -- helping a widow lady, babysitting without
    pay for a needy couple that needs a break, sorting through his
    belongings to set aside good usable articles for someone in need,
    writing letters to missionaries overseas, helping a family with
    illness or a new baby, etc.*

Neh. 8:10 Fellowship with other believers. "The joy of the Lord
is your strength."
  *Do not allow the child to isolate himself. Draw him into family
    times of fellowship. Do not allow him to abandon the fellowship
    of your church family.*
  *Allow and encourage times of special fellowship with good, edifying
    friends.*

Js. 1:12 Endure temptation.

Help arm your child against temptation through regular Bible study, prayer and fellowship.

Keep your relationship open enough with your child so that he will feel free to express his areas of temptation to you. This will enable you to give him counsel and support him with prayer. It will also enable you eliminate circumstances that might make this area of temptation more difficult for your child -- TV, certain types of books, etc.

Matt. 5:1-12 Blessed when we respond correctly to life -- pure heart, merciful, meekness, peacemaking.
Pray that your child will draw on the strength that enables him to respond correctly to all circumstances in life.

Phil. 4:8-9 Think on these things: whatever is true, honest, just, pure, lovely, of good report. Things of virtue and praise.
Help the child gain control of his thought life. Pray for him in this area.
Examine your household and your child's life. What is he exposed to? Is he viewing or participating in things that are not honest, pure, lovely? Purge your house of any questionable TV programming, reading materials; guard your conversations. Ask the Lord to reveal these areas to you.

Ps. 55:22 Cast burden on the Lord.
With your child, write out a description or list of his "burden." Pray over it and "give" it to the Lord.

Jer. 15:16 God's Word is the joy and rejoicing of our hearts.

Study David's life and the Psalms together. As a teenager, I used to wonder what was wrong with David, always moaning and groaning. Now, with a few more of life's experiences behind me, I understand a little more fully the beauty and comfort of the Psalms.

David's life brought many circumstances that would cause discouragement -- his friends turned against him, he was slandered, Saul conspired against him and doggedly pursued him, many returned his good with evil. He was the victim of repeated attempted murders. He succumbed to great sin, and then attempted to cover it with more sin. There was rebellion and sin in the lives of his children. He had to face and deal with sin in his nation.

David could have resigned himself to fear, despair, and bitterness. Instead he turned to God -- his salvation, his strong tower. He praised God, even in the midst of tribulation. He remembered God's character. He prayed for God's discipline of the wrongdoer. He appealed to God to defend His glory.

Compare David's life with that of Saul. Saul indulged in hatred, envy, pride, and fear, and lived a life of depression and madness.

The following is a list of verses from the Psalms to help you get started in a study of David and his trust in God:

Ps. 13:1, 5-6 "How long wilt thou forget me, O Lord? for ever? ...I will sing unto the Lord, because he hath dealt bountifully with me."

Ps. 27:1,10 "Whom shall I fear?" The Lord will take us up when even our parents forsake us.

Ps. 32 Confession of sin.

Ps. 35 "Plead my cause, O Lord, with them that strive with me... and my tongue shall speak of thy righteousness and of thy praise all the day long."

Ps. 38 Deep despair, abandoned by friends, "For in thee, O Lord, do I hope: thou wilt hear, O Lord my God."

Ps. 51 Confession, remembers God's forgiveness.

Ps. 55 "I mourn in my complaint... but I will trust in You."

Ps. 56:3 When afraid, trust in God.

Ps. 61:2 When heart is overwhelmed, go to Rock that is higher than us.

Ps. 62:11 "Power belongeth to God."

Ps. 69:29+ After despair of being forsaken by all, without cause.

Ps. 77:1-3 Crying unto God in day of trouble.

Ps. 77:7-9 Recalls God's favor, mercy, promise, grace.

Ps. 77:10 "...but I will remember the years of the right hand of the most High."

Ps. 78 Recounts history.

Ps. 88:1-9 Cried day and night before the Lord, stretched out hands to God.

Ps. 88:9b-12 Considers God's glory. How will he glorify God in the grave?

Ps. 94 Prayer to avenge wicked.

Ps. 102 Remembers his finiteness, God's infinity.

Ps. 106 Response to sin: confess, saved for God's glory. Recounts Israel's sins and God's faithfulness to His covenant.

Ps. 109:21-31 Despair, appeal to God to save for His glory.

Ps. 116:3-4 Trouble and sorrow, call on the name of the Lord.

Ps. 116:13 Take up cup of salvation.

Ps. 119:145-148 Meditate on Word.

Ps. 130:3-4 Man's sinfulness/ God's forgiveness.

Ps. 136 Recalls God's mercy. Give thanks.

Ps. 142 Prayer in cave hiding. Vs. 3 Spirit overwhelmed. God knows our path.

Ps. 143: 4-6 Spirit overwhelmed, remembers history, meditate on His works, muse on works of His hands, spread out hands to Him.

Ps. 143:11-12 Revive for His name's sake, righteousness' sake. "I am your servant." We are servants doing our master's bidding. He is not our servant.

David pours his emotions out to the Lord. Notice how many times the Psalm begins with a prayer of pain and despair, and ends with praise to God.

In connection with your study of the Psalms, try some of these activities with your child:

Write out some of your own Psalms. Pour out your emotions and close with a phrase of praise.

Compose your own song that expresses your heart and your trust in God.

Write out accounts of God's faithfulness in the child's life. Have him write them.

Read stories from the Bible and from other history that give testimony to God's faithfulness.

Write out a prayer of praise to God, reviewing His character and His many acts of mercy and blessing in the child's life.

Stories that illustrate the effects of depression:

Hannah, I Sam. 1:10-15; 2:1-10 Despair over barrenness, and then prayer of praise when taking Samuel to Eli.

Elijah, I Kgs. 19 Discouragement when pursued by Jezebel after victory over prophets of Baal.

Hagar, Gen. 21:15-16 Despair over what appeared to be Ishmael's imminent death.

Saul, I Sam. 28:20-25 Depression after Samuel's reproof and prophecy.

Verses to memorize:

Ps. 139:23-24 Search me, O God, and know my heart: try me, and know my thoughts: and see if there be any wicked way in me, and lead me in the way everlasting.

Ps. 147:3 He healeth the broken in heart, and bindeth up their wounds.

Ps. 32:1 Blessed is he whose transgression is forgiven, whose sin is covered.

Ps. 119:28 My soul melts from heaviness; strengthen me according to Your word. (NKJV)

Ps. 38:17-18 For I am ready to fall, and my sorrow is continually before me. For I will declare my iniquity; I will be in anguish over my sin. (NKJV)

Ps. 51:7-9 Purge me with hyssop, and I shall be clean: wash me, and I shall be whiter than snow. Make me to hear joy and gladness; that the bones which thou hast broken may rejoice. Hide thy face from my sins, and blot out all mine iniquities.

Ps. 51:12 Restore unto me the joy of thy salvation; and uphold me with thy free spirit.

Ps. 55:22 Cast thy burden upon the LORD, and he shall sustain thee: he shall never suffer the righteous to be moved.

Ps. 61:2 From the end of the earth will I cry unto thee, when my heart is overwhelmed: lead me to the rock that is higher than I.

Ps. 69:29 But I am poor and sorrowful: let thy salvation, O God, set me up on high.

Ps. 77:10-12 And I said, this is my infirmity: but I will remember the years of the right hand of the most High. I will remember the works of the LORD: surely I will remember thy wonders of old. I will meditate also of all thy work, and talk of thy doings.

Fear

(See also Worry, Faint-Heartedness)

Fear in itself is not a sinful emotion; it can protect us from foolish actions that endanger our lives. A child needs to learn a healthy fear of water, electricity, traffic, etc.

Fear becomes sinful when we fail to obey God because of our fears. A child often has many fears. We should not mock him in his fear, but gently lead him to an understanding of God's unfailing love and protection over him.

We want to help our children overcome unhealthy fear because fear can prevent them from truly serving our Savior. Fear also tends to be contagious and can infect an entire family if not controlled. And fear often leads to other sins -- lying, compromise, complaining, rebellion, depression, and injustice.

General information and commandments about fear:

I Jn. 4:18 Love casts out fear.

Deut. 20:8 Causes others to fear.

Gen. 42:21-28 Is sometimes the result of a guilty conscience.
  Joseph's brothers were fearful because of the guilt of their sinful dealings with Joseph.

Jn. 12:43 Loved praise of men more than praise of God.
  This man fears what man thinks of him more than he fears God.

Pr. 28:1 Wicked flee when no one pursues, but righteous man is bold as a lion.

Pr. 29:25 Fear of man brings a snare.
  Fear of man leads us into disobedience. We become more afraid of man and his opinions of us than we are of God's laws and discipline.

Isa. 51:12,13 If we fear man, we forget God.

II Tim. 1:7 God has not given us a spirit of fear, but of power, love, and sound mind.
  Teach the child to ask, "If we have a spirit of power, love and sound mind, what will we do in this fearful situation?"

Ex. 14:13 Fear not, stand still and see salvation of the Lord.

Deut. 31:6 Fear not, God is with us, won't fail or forsake.
  Teach your child the great truth of God's continual presence with him.

When he is afraid, always remind him that God is with him and that God will not leave him.

Matt. 8:26 Fear indicates little faith.

What happens, or should happen, to the fearful person:

Ps. 56:11 Trust in God.

Josh. 23:8 Cleave to God.

Ps. 34:4 Seek God, will deliver from all our fears.
Study God's character together -- His faithfulness, justice, love, omnipotence, omniscience, omnipresence, love, etc. <u>Knowing</u> our God and His unchanging character makes it more natural to trust Him when we are afraid. It is easier to trust someone when we <u>know</u> he is trustworthy.
Review God's faithful protection and deliverance in your child's life and in your life.
Keep a journal in which you record the many events of your child's life that are testimony to God's protection over him. Reading through this can be comforting and encouraging in a time of fear and testing.

Pr. 29:25 Will be snared.
Help the child to see when his fear has led him into a snare or place of helplessness.

Pr. 10:24 The fear of the wicked shall come upon him.

Matt. 25:14-25 Fear causes man to hide his "talent," to not use the abilities and blessings entrusted to him.
If "love casts out fear," our love for the Lord should overcome any fear we have that could keep us from doing what God wants us to do. When a child is afraid to talk to a new child at church, when he is afraid to play the piano for the Sunday School class singing time, when he is afraid to say "no" when enticed by other children, we can appeal to his love for the Lord. That love should be greater than any fear he has. He should focus on his desire to obey God, and turn away from the fear that would prevent him from obeying.

Heb. 2:15 Subject to bondage.
Help the child see how his fear can make him a prisoner, how it prevents him from freely exercising his abilities and performing his duties.

Take a rope or chain and talk about the child's specific fears. The rope/chain represents all those fears. Bind the child with it. Can he function in a normal way? Does the rope limit his freedom and ability?

Matt. 10:28-32 We should fear Him who is able to destroy both soul and body in hell.
Teach the child to ask, "If I fear <u>God</u>, what will I do in this situation?"

To what is the sin of fear likened:

Hearts became as water, Josh. 7:5
Experiment with water: How firm is it? Does it hold its shape regardless of what is done to it? Does its temperature remain constant in spite of its environment?

Stories that illustrate the consequences of fear:

Abraham, Gen. 12:11-19 His fear for his life because of Sarah's beauty led him to lie and to abandon his role as protector of his wife.

Isaac, Gen. 26:7-9 His fear led to the same action and sin as his father committed.

Aaron, Ex. 32:22-24 Fear of man led to blaming others for his sin, and to lying and idolatry. Fear of man caused him to set aside his responsibilities as an authority.

10 Spies, Num. 13:28-33, 14:1-10 Their fear led to the demoralization and panic of an entire nation. The spies were killed, and the Israelites rebelled and then went on to defeat in battle.

Israelites confronted by Goliath, I Sam. 17:24 Forgot God's power.

20,000 of Gideon's army, Jg. 7:3

Disciples in storm, Matt. 8:26; Mk. 4:38, Lk. 8:25 Forgot Jesus' power.

Peter, Matt. 26:69-74; Mk. 14:66-72; Lk. 22:54-60; Jn.

18:16,17,25,27 Fear of man led to lying and denial of Jesus.

Pilate, Jn. 19:12-16 Fear of man led to great injustice.

Stories that illustrate the blessings of courage and trust in God:

Joshua and Caleb, Num. 13:30, 14:6-12 Remembered "the Lord is with us." Led to entering the Promised Land when all the rest of their generation did not.

Gideon and 300 men, Jg. 7:7-23 Trusted God and saw great victory.

Deborah, Jg. 4 Remembered, "Is not the Lord gone out before thee?" Went on to military victory.

David, I Sam. 17:32-50 Recalled God's deliverance in the past. Recognized God's honor at stake, that the battle was the Lord's. Led to victory over Goliath and great favor of the people.

Esther, Est. 4:8,16, and chapters 5-7 Trusted God with her life. "If I perish, I perish." Led to deliverance of the Jews from death.

Shadrach, Meshach, and Abednego, Dan. 3:16-18 Knew that God was able to deliver them.

Daniel, Dan.6:10-22 Obeyed God rather than man. Was spared in the lion's den.

Jonathan and armorbearer, I Sam. 14 Protected and victorious. "For there is no restraint to the Lord to save by many or by few."

Verses to memorize:

Ex. 14:14 The LORD shall fight for you, and ye shall hold your peace.

Jer. 32:27 Behold, I am the LORD, the God of all flesh: is there any thing too hard for me?

Ps. 56:11 In God have I put my trust: I will not be afraid what man can do unto me.

Ps. 28:7 The LORD is my strength and my shield; my heart trusted in him, and I am helped: therefore my heart greatly rejoiceth; and with my song will I praise him.

2 Tim. 1:7 For God hath not given us the spirit of fear; but of power,

and of love, and of a sound mind.

Heb. 13:5-6 Let your conduct be without covetousness; be content with such things as you have. For He Himself has said, "I will never leave you nor forsake you." So we may boldly say: "The LORD is my helper; I will not fear. What can man do to me?" (NKJV)

John 10:27-29 My sheep hear My voice, and I know them, and they follow Me. And I give them eternal life, and they shall never perish; neither shall anyone snatch them out of My hand. My Father, who has given them to Me, is greater than all; and no one is able to snatch them out of My Father's hand. (NKJV)

Rom. 8:37-39 Nay, in all these things we are more than conquerors through him that loved us. For I am persuaded, that neither death, nor life, nor angels, nor principalities, nor powers, nor things present, nor things to come, nor height, nor depth, nor any other creature, shall be able to separate us from the love of God, which is in Christ Jesus our Lord.

Isa. 41:10 Fear not, for I am with you; be not dismayed, for I am your God. I will strengthen you, yes, I will help you, I will uphold you with My righteous right hand. (NKJV)

Isa. 43:2 When thou passest through the waters, I will be with thee; and through the rivers, they shall not overflow thee: when thou walkest through the fire, thou shalt not be burned; neither shall the flame kindle upon thee.

Rom. 8:31 What shall we then say to these things? If God be for us, who can be against us?

Worry/Anxiety

(See also Fear, Envy, Covetousness,
Confidence in Riches, Double-minded)

General information and commandments about this sin:

Lk. 12:22-31 Worry is forbidden.

Phil. 4:6 Be careful for nothing. Give thanks with prayer and
supplication. Peace of God will keep hearts and minds.
Pray with the child about his worries.
Make a list together of all the blessings God has put in the
child's life. Thank God for them.

I Pet. 5:7 Cast cares on Him. He cares for you.
With the child, write down the things that he is worrying about.
Then pray together over the list, giving all his cares over to
God. When the child worries again, review the list. Which "cares"
is he taking back from God?

Heb. 13:5 Be content with what you have.
Envy and covetousness lead to worry and anxiety.

Isa. 51:12,13 Forgets Maker.
When the child is worrying, ask him. "Who are you forgetting?
Who made everything? Who is all-powerful? What can God do
about this situation?"

Matt. 6:34 Take no thought for tomorrow.

What happens, or should happen, to the worrier:

Pr. 15:15, Ps. 38:6 Causes depression.

Pr. 28:1 Wicked flee when no man pursues.

Pr. 29:25 Brings snare when we fear man.
Help the child see the consequences of his worry, how it affects
his actions and the snares it leads him into.

Phil. 4:8-9 Think on these things: whatever is true, honest, just,
pure, lovely, of good report, any virtue and praise.
Examine what goes into your child's mind and spirit. Books,
magazines, newspapers, newscasts over radio and TV,
conversations with ungodly friends, etc. can give a child much
more to worry about than he is equipped to handle.

Lk. 8:14 Don't mature or produce fruit.
What happens to a tree that never matures to produce fruit?

Rom. 8:26 Pray.

Phil. 4:19, Ps. 37:25-26 Remember God's faithfulness.
Keep list of demonstrations of God's faithfulness in the child's life.
Review the list together when the child is tempted to worry.
Have him write an essay about God's faithfulness in his life.
Read biographies and histories that give testimony to God's faithfulness.
Study Bible stories together that demonstrate God's faithfulness.

Matt. 6:33 Seek God's kingdom first.

Matt. 6:25-34 Observe birds and flowers. Can you add to your height?

To what is the worrier likened:

Flowers worrying about clothes, Matt. 6:28-29, Lk. 12:27-28
Watch a flower as it progresses from bud to blossom. How hard has it worked at clothing itself? What did it do?

Birds worrying about food, Matt. 6:26, Lk. 12:24
Do some bird watching! Do birds sit in their nest, rubbing their wings together as they worry about where their next meal will come from? What do they do?

Trying to "think" yourself taller, Matt. 6:27, Lk. 12:25
Measure your child's height. Then have him spend all day trying to think about making himself taller. Measure again at the end of the day. Did it work?

The blessings of trusting our Provider:

Ps. 37:3 Will be fed.
Take your child out to dinner with you and commend him for his growing trust in God.
Have a special "In God We Trust" family feast. Serve special foods and spend the meal reviewing God's faithfulness in your lives, how He has provided for you -- your home, your clothing, your food, your church family, your automobile, your income, your friends, etc.

Ps. 37:4-5 Will receive heart's desires.

Isa. 26:3 Trust in God leads to perfect peace.

Pr. 28:1 Righteous are bold as a lion.
*Cut out a photo or drawing of a lion. Write this verse below it and
post it in the child's room.*
Study lions together.

Pr. 15:15 Merry heart has a continual feast.
Try the "In God We Trust" feast previously explained.
*How about a week of feasts? Fix all your family's favorite meals,
served on special dishes, with background music, even candlelight!
Spend time each meal reading Scripture that discusses God's
faithful provision and protection, and the blessings of trusting
in Him.*

Phil. 4:6-7 Peace will guard your heart.
*This might be a help to a chronic "worry-wart:" Write out this
verse and illustrate it with a simple heart and a picture of a
guard standing watch over it. Let your child illustrate this
himself. Post it over his bed or in another prominent place.*

Matt. 6:33 Seek God first, and He will add all the material
blessings that we need.
*When a physical need arises stop and pray for it. We seem to
be continually in need of new rubber boots for someone in the
family, but we have never needed to go out and buy new ones in
the store. We pray for them. What a blessing to hear our boys
walking up to a garage sale wondering where their boots are!
God has always provided them! And our children's faith is
strengthened in these experiences.*

Ps. 4:8 Sleeps peacefully.
*If you have a child who has trouble sleeping, consider the
possibility of worry as a problem. Are you exposing your
child to information that might cause him to worry?*
*Pray with the child before bedtime, and commit his worries
and anxieties to the Lord.*

Ps. 55:22 Will be sustained. Righteous will not be moved.

Ps. 32:10 Will be surrounded by mercy.

Pr. 29:25 Will be safe.

Jer. 17:7,8 Like tree, roots by river, won't suffer in heat,
will stay green.
*Give the child a special little tree to plant. Let the tree
act as a reminder of God's blessing when we trust in Him.*

Have him go out and water his tree whenever he expresses worry about something.

Stories that illustrate the consequences of worrying:

10 Spies, Num. 13:28+ Evil, fearful report led to rebellion and defeat. Spies were killed by plague. (The 2 believing spies were spared and blessed.)

Martha, Lk. 10:38-42 Was reproved. Should focus on Jesus.

Elijah, I Kgs. 19:4-15 God provided his needs with ravens who fed him.

Israelites at Red Sea, Ex. 14:10-12 Panic. Preferred to serve Egyptians than to trust God to protect them. They were delivered by God.

Stories that illustrate the blessings of trusting in God:

Jacob, Gen. 32:6-12 Feared meeting with Esau. Prayed for God's protection. Recalled God's promises.

Asa, II Chr. 14:11 Against Ethiopians, "It is nothing with thee to help, whether with many, or with them that have no power..." Led to military victory.

Hezekiah, II Chr. 32:7-8 Advised people to not fear Sennacherib, "but with us is the Lord our God to help us, and to fight our battles." Assyrian armies left in shame without any battle.

Abraham, Gen. 22:1-19, Heb. 11:17-19 Unquestioning obedience and faith when asked to sacrifice Isaac. God provided a ram.

Abraham, Gen. 12:1-4, Heb. 11:8 Obeyed God and left his home in faith.

Daniel, Dan. 6:4-23; Heb. 11:32,33 Obeyed God and was delivered from the lions.

Shadrach, Meshach, and Abednego, Dan. 3:8-30, Heb. 11:32-34 Obeyed God and were delivered from the fiery furnace.

Verses to memorize:

Matt. 6:33 But seek ye first the kingdom of God, and his

righteousness; and all these things shall be added unto you.

Luke 12:34 For where your treasure is, there will your heart be also.

Luke 12:32 Fear not, little flock; for it is your Father's good pleasure to give you the kingdom.

Matt. 6:32 For your heavenly Father knoweth that ye have need of all these things.

Ps. 118:8 It is better to trust in the LORD than to put confidence in man.

Pr. 3:5-6 Trust in the LORD with all thine heart; and lean not unto thine own understanding. In all thy ways acknowledge him, and he shall direct thy paths.

Ex. 33:14 And he said, My presence shall go with thee, and I will give thee rest.

Phil. 4:6-7 Be careful for nothing; but in every thing by prayer and supplication with thanksgiving let your requests be made known unto God. And the peace of God, which passeth all understanding, shall keep your hearts and minds through Christ Jesus.

Phil. 4:19 But my God shall supply all your need according to his riches in glory by Christ Jesus.

Ps. 37:25-26 I have been young, and now am old; yet I have not seen the righteous forsaken, nor his descendants begging bread. He is ever merciful, and lends; and his descendants are blessed. (NKJV)

Ps. 4:8 I will both lie down in peace, and sleep; for You alone, O LORD, make me dwell in safety. (NKJV)

Ps. 55:22 Cast thy burden upon the LORD, and he shall sustain thee: he shall never suffer the righteous to be moved.

Rom. 8:28 And we know that all things work together for good to them that love God, to them who are the called according to his purpose.

Rom. 8:31 What shall we then say to these things? If God be for us, who can be against us?

Rom. 8:35 Who shall separate us from the love of Christ? shall tribulation, or distress, or persecution, or famine, or nakedness, or peril, or sword?

Rom. 8:37-39 Nay, in all these things we are more than conquerors through him that loved us. For I am persuaded, that neither death, nor life, nor angels, nor principalities, nor powers, nor things present, nor things to come, nor height, nor depth, nor any other creature, shall be able to separate us from the love of God, which is in Christ Jesus our Lord.

Ps. 37:5 Commit thy way unto the LORD; trust also in him; and he shall bring it to pass.

Lam. 3:23 They are new every morning: great is thy faithfulness.

Ps. 23:1 The LORD is my shepherd; I shall not want.

Ps. 116:7 Return unto thy rest, O my soul; for the LORD hath dealt bountifully with thee.

Acts 27:25 Therefore take heart, men, for I believe God that it will be just as it was told me.(NKJV)

Laziness

(See also Unfaithful Employee)

General information and commandments about this sin:

Ex. 23:12, Ex. 20:9, Ex. 34:21 6 days you shall work.
A commandment!

Deut. 22:1-4 Regarding others' belongings: should not ignore animals going astray from owner, but should return them to him. If owner is not nearby, or is unknown, you should keep it for him until he looks for it. Applies to any belongings one finds. Should not ignore an animal that has fallen, but should help it.
There are plenty of opportunities to apply this principle in our homes. A child needs to exercise the initiative and energy to pick up misplaced items and return them to their owners, rather than leaving them where he sees them -- on the floor, outside, in the hands of an unauthorized younger sibling, etc. A child who is unwilling to do this is usually motivated by laziness. It requires our effort and energy to be a help in this way. Enforce this policy in your home. (We're working on this one!)

I Tim. 5:8 One who doesn't provide for his family is worse than an infidel.

Pr. 26:16 A lazy man is wise in his own eyes.

Pr. 26:15 Won't bring hand to mouth out of bowl.
He's too lazy to even use what he has!

Pr. 20:4, 22:13 Makes excuses, has fearful imaginations.
Recognize excuse-making as a manifestation of laziness.
Fear can lead to inaction and laziness, and must be dealt with in a child's life. (See "Fear.")

Pr. 12:27 Doesn't roast his prey.
A lazy man is wasteful. He denies others of resources, and then does not use them himself.
Watch for this tendency in your child, and discipline for it.

Pr. 18:9 Is brother to him who destroys.
Laziness leads to waste and destruction. Leaving a shovel out in the rain instead of putting it away leads to the destruction of the shovel. Leaving socks all over the floor can lead to their loss.
Levy fines for these sorts of laziness. We charge one dollar each time the boys' shovel is left outside. (This hurts the lazy child, and also provides resources for replacing the shovel if it is ruined from neglect.) The son who leaves his socks all over the house buys his

own socks from the spending money that he works to earn.

Pr. 19:15 Casts one into a deep sleep.
Laziness seems to breed more laziness.
Laziness causes one to miss out on many opportunities.
Perhaps an appropriate discipline for a younger child who is lazy would be a nap (a "deep sleep") or earlier bedtime.

Pr. 31:27 Virtuous woman doesn't eat the bread of idleness.
To allow laziness in our daughters is to neglect the training that we need to provide so that they will be godly, virtuous women, who can serve God and their families well.

Pr. 21:25 Hands refuse to work.

Pr. 21:26 Covets greedily all day long.
Laziness often leads to the sin of covetousness. The lazy man wants what others may have, but does not want to work for it.

Pr. 14:23 Idle chatter leads only to poverty.
Beware of the child who always has something to tell you, when he should be doing his chores, helping clean up the living room floor, etc. Do not allow him to sneak out of his work in this way, but tell him to come and talk with you after his work is done.
Enforce a time limit for work that is done, to help the lazy talker stick to his job. If he is not done by the specified time, give him additional work, or deny pay if it was originally a paid job.
Observe, also, if a child is always talking about doing something, but never doing it. Encourage him to put his talk into action, or confront him about the dishonesty of always talking and never doing.

Pr. 15:19 A lazy man is contrasted with a righteous man.
This means laziness is sinful!

I Cor. 4:2 Steward must be faithful.
Require faithful service from a child who has be given a job, and faithful care from a child who has been entrusted with privileges or possessions. If he is not faithful, remove his privilege. "Fire" him, and reduce him to "slave labor," where he works for you without pay, or renders more work after the original job is completed properly.

Ec. 11:4 Observe wind, regard clouds, won't sow or reap.
A lazy child looks for any available excuse. Do not allow excuses.

Eph. 6:6 Serve not with eyeservice. Don't be men-pleasers but work as servants of Christ.
Discipline a child when he obviously has been dawdling on a job, and leaps into action when you come by.

Remind the man-pleaser that God is always watching him and his faithfulness in work, even though you and other people cannot always be monitoring him.
Ask him, "How would you work if Jesus were standing here watching you the whole time?" Remind him that He is!

Col. 3:22-23 Work with sincerity to God, not men.
A man-pleaser is a hypocrite. (See "Hypocrisy.")
Observe the video cameras set up in the corner of grocery stores and other shops. What a person does in that store is always visible on the video screen. What a child does, or doesn't do, when we are not with him is always visible to God.

Eph. 5:15-16 Walk as wise, redeeming the time.
Laziness is foolishness, and it wastes valuable time that we can never regain.

Pr. 6:6-9 The lazy person indulges in excessive sleep.
Do not permit a child to spend too much of his time sleeping. He needs enough sleep to maintain his health and energy, but should not be allowed to sleep away the day.

Titus 2:9-10 Please master, don't hold back, but be faithful. Adorns doctrine.

Rom. 12:11 Not lagging in diligence, fervent in spirit, serving the Lord.
Laziness hinders our service to God.

What happens, or should happen, to the lazy person:

Pr. 10:4 Becomes poor.
Do not pay a child for work that has been done in a lazy or incomplete fashion.
When one of our children is exceptionally slow and lazy in his work, we charge <u>him</u> for the job. If it is a job we normally would pay for, he pays us the same wage from his spending money.
Our basic procedure for a lazy worker is: 1. Half-pay for the job. 2. No pay for the job. 3. If he still persists, he pays us for the job.
Levy a fine (from spending money) to cover the costs that have resulted from the child's laziness, or have the child pay for an object that has been lost or destroyed due to neglect and laziness.

Pr. 13:4, 20:4 Has nothing.
Do not replace possessions lost to laziness.
Take away possessions if child is lazy in caring for them. We have

had problems with a sea of boots in our backroom. Boys come in from chores, kick off their boots, and leave them for the rest of us to wade through, and to jam up into doorways. Things neatened up pretty quickly when we started confiscating any neglected boots, and required payments of up to one dollar to purchase them back.

Pr. 10:5 Causes shame.

Pr. 12:24 Put to forced labor (bondage).
Give the lazy worker extra, unpaid work to do. If he is lazy in that work, give him more! He'll give in eventually!
Have the child rehearse a job over and over. Our lazy laundry folders refold, in my presence, any poorly folded items 10 times each.

Pr. 19:15 Suffers hunger.

II Thess. 3:10 No work, don't eat.
This works well for us. If morning chores are not complete by breakfast time, the child misses breakfast. If livestock is found without food, the child doesn't eat either.

Pr. 20:4 Beg during harvest.
The child should enjoy no benefit of labor that he should have done but did not. (i.e. If he was lazy in helping to care for the garden, perhaps he should miss out on the first watermelon feast of the season. ·If he allowed everyone else to do the work of cleaning up the living room floor before storytime, perhaps he should go to bed while everyone else enjoys stories with Daddy.)

Pr. 20:13 Love sleep, come to poverty.
Do not allow oversleeping.
Require child to adhere to a schedule. Fine him for not getting up in time, or do not pay him for chores which were unfinished due to not getting up when he should in the morning.

Pr. 21:17 Love pleasure, become poor man.
Too much pleasure tends to keep us from more productive uses of our time, and also consumes the resources we do have.

Pr. 21:25 Desire kills him.
Tends to indulge in coveting and envy.

Pr. 23:21 Drowsiness clothes a man in rags.
Have a lazy child buy his own clothes.

Pr. 24:32-34 Poverty comes upon him like a prowler or armed man.
Does a prowler announce his arrival? Does he call ahead to tell us he is coming?

Pr. 28:19 Following frivolity (as opposed to diligence) leads to poverty.

Ec. 10:18 Building decays. From idleness of hands the house leaks.
Results in damage and waste.

Pr. 24:30-31 Field and vineyard overgrow with thorns and nettles,
walls are broken down.
*"Receive instruction" from examples of this in life. Observe the
state of an old abandoned house, or an untended garden. What
happens to the berry vines when they are not pruned and tied
back?*
*Don't do the work for the child. Don't pick up his socks, don't help
him finish a job when he has dawdled. Let him experience the
consequences of his laziness.*

II Thess. 3:10-11, I Thess. 4:10-12 Become busybodies.

I Tim. 5:13 Wanders, gossips, is a busybody.
*If you are dealing with a meddling busybody, is there also a problem
with laziness? Keep the lazy meddler busy with work and
responsibility.*

Matt. 25:26-30 Loss of all.
Take away the lazy child's possessions, privileges, time. etc.

Pr. 18:9 Produces waste.
*Point out when this happens (i.e. Laziness in caring for toys or
clothing can produce loss or damage.) Have the child pay for the
damage, or replace lost or ruined items.*

Heb. 6:12 Be not slothful, but followers of faithful and patient.
*Read biographies of diligent men (i.e. Abraham Lincoln, J.C. Penney,
disciplined athletes, musicians, scientists, etc.)*
*Try to set up an apprenticeship or helping position with a person
who is disciplined, diligent, conscientious, and patient. (He may
have to be patient to be able to work with your lazy child!)*
*Encourage friendships with other children who are faithful and
patient, rather than with those who are foolish and slothful.*
*Study diligent people in the Bible -- Joseph, Noah, Proverbs 31
woman. (See "Stories" section in this chapter.)*

Ec. 4:5 Consumes own life strength.

Eph. 4:28 Should work instead of stealing.
*Laziness can lead to theft of those things which the lazy man desires
but is unwilling to work for.*

Pr. 6:6-11 Observe the ant.
Do a unit study on ants.
Find an anthill. Watch the ants. What can we learn from them?

Set up an ant farm to observe.

Compare the lazy man with the diligent man:

Study and take notes on these verses together with your child. (See "Comparison Worksheet" at back of book.)

Attitude toward work Pr. 19:24, 21:25, 14:23 / Pr. 31:13

Regarding wisdom Pr. 10:5, 26:16 / Pr. 10:5

Regarding the use of time I Tim. 5:13, II Thess. 3:11, I Thess. 4:10-12 / Pr. 31:27

Regarding provision and food II Thess. 3:10, Pr. 19:15, Pr. 20:4 / Pr. 28:19, Pr. 12:11, II Tim 2:6, Pr. 27:18

Regarding the opinion of others Pr. 10:5 / Pr. 22:29, 25:13, 31:28, 31:31, 27:18

Regarding status in life Pr. 12:24

Regarding their rewards Col. 3:23,24 / Matt. 25:26-30

Regarding contentment Eccles. 5:12 / Pr. 21:25-26

Regarding success Pr. 15:19 / Eccles. 4:5

Regarding wealth Pr. 10:4,5; 13:4,11; 27:23-27 / Pr. 10:4, 13:4, 14:23, 20:13, 21:17, 23:21, 24:3-4, 28:19

To what is the lazy man likened:

Lk. 13:6-9 A tree that doesn't bear fruit and is cut down.
Talk about this while cutting out dead branches in trees or berry vines.

Pr. 10:26 Vinegar to teeth, smoke to eyes.
Have the child swish some vinegar around in his mouth. How do his teeth feel afterwards?
Stand in the smoke of a campfire or brush fire. How does it make your eyes feel? Do you want to stay there? Is a lazy man the kind of person we seek after?

Pr. 15:19 Hedge of thorns.
Set up an obstacle course for your child. Run him through brambles and thorns and tangled vines. Set up another "obstacle course,"

which is simply a straight, unencumbered path across the yard.
Time him as he runs each course. Which one was faster? Which
one did he like best?

Pr. 26:14 Door on hinges. Turns on bed.
  The door moves, the person turns over, but there is no progress.
  Observe a door swinging on its hinges. Does it go anywhere?

Pr. 6:11 Poverty comes like a thief or armed man.
  Overtake the child "like a robber," or if he is not too easily
  frightened, wake him up in the morning, armed with a squirt gun.
  Discuss how poverty will overtake him without warning.

Pr. 25:19 Bad tooth or foot out of joint.
  Can't rely on them, they cause pain, affects what you can do.

Isa. 56:10 Dumb dogs, can't bark, love to sleep.
  How useful and effective is a watchdog that cannot bark, and that
  only sleeps?

Blessings of diligence:

Ec. 5:12 Sleep is sweet.
  Allow the child to have a friend spend the night.
  Give the child a special slumber party.
  Give the child a gift of new bedding, new special sheets, a new
    bedspread, etc.

Pr. 12:11 Till, will be satisfied with bread.

Pr. 28:19 Till land, will have plenty of bread.
  Have a special feast for the diligent child. Serve him first.
  Bake bread together and enjoy it warm out of the oven.
  Fix a special loaf of cinnamon bread to enjoy together.
  Have a special family "Harvest Party" when all the canning and
    gardening is done for the year, or when the garden is at its peak.
  Thank your diligent gardeners and canners with an extra yummy
    feast fresh from the garden.

Pr. 31:28 Husband and children will praise the diligent woman.

Pr. 31:31 Fruit of her hands, and her own works will praise her.
  Praise the diligent child. Draw attention to his work.

II Tim. 2:6 Will be first partakers of fruits.
  Serve the diligent child first.

Pr. 27:18 Tend the fig tree, eat the figs. Wait on master, will be honored.

Allow the diligent child to "eat" the "fruit" of his labor. This might be the literal enjoyment of the produce he has helped tend in the garden. Or it could be letting the "assistant cookie baker" lick the bowl, serving the table setter first at mealtime, or allowing the child who washed the car to sit in the front seat on an outing.

Pr. 13:4   Soul of the diligent will be made fat, rich.
Pay for work done.
Take the child out to dinner.
Fix the child's favorite foods.
Give the child an extra serving at mealtime.

Pr. 13:11   One who gathers by labor will increase.

Pr. 12:14   Recompense of man's hand will be rendered to him.

Pr. 15:19   Way will be a highway.
Compare travel on a winding gravel road in the country and on a straight and paved highway. Which is easiest to travel? Which is quickest?
Use string to mark two paths across the yard, one a twisting, winding path, and one a straight path. Which measures longest?
Try this with two roads to the same point on a road map.
Make the diligent child's way smooth when you can.

Pr. 22:29   Will stand before kings.
Honor the child with praise before grandparents, authorities.
Have a special award ceremony, presenting the child with special recognition or a special gift, trophy, homemade medal, certificate or cash, with Daddy making the formal presentation.
Have a special meal of recognition and gratitude in honor of the child. Invite grandparents, church family, friends. Make a special little speech of gratitude about the child.
Dad, commend him for his diligence.

Pr. 25:13   Refreshes master like cold of snow at harvest time.
Take the diligent child out for an ice cream cone after a hard day of work.
Take the family to the mountains for a snow trip in recognition for special diligence in completing a big task.
Take the child skiing or ice skating with you.

Pr. 27:23-27   Lambs for clothing, enough goat's milk and food.
Provide generously for the diligent child.
Give a gift of a wool sweater.
Perhaps a daughter would like to learn to spin or weave. Spinning or weaving lessons might make a good reward for a diligent

daughter. Or help her purchase a spinning wheel.
A diligent son might appreciate the gift of a dairy goat. With his
diligence, he might turn it into a profitable business venture!

Pr. 21:5 Plenteousness.
Give child first bid on optional paid household jobs.
For diligence in schoolwork, give him a gift certificate to a bookstore
or art supply store.
Reward him with a cash bonus for especially thorough work.

Pr. 12:24 Hand of the diligent will rule.
Proclaim the diligent child to be "Foreman-of-the-Day." He assigns
chores for the day, and is paid for inspecting and making sure jobs
are completed properly.
Assign the child to be "Teacher-of-the-Day" in school. Let him assign
work, check papers, handle science experiments, etc., or let him
teach you the lesson.
Make the diligent child "Master-of-the-Day." He chooses the menu
for dinner, books for storytime, games at playtime, seat in the car,
etc.
Play "Simon Says" with diligent child as "Simon."

Stories that illustrate the consequences of laziness:

Parable of the talents, Matt. 25:14-30 Lazy servant had to give his
one talent to the faithful servant who had 10 talents.

Spies, Num. 14:6-8 Made excuses, were cowardly. Were killed by
plague.

Jonah, Jon. 1:1-3 Did not obey God by going to Nineveh. Was
swallowed by the fish.

Stories that illustrate the blessings of diligence:

Jeroboam, I Kgs. 11:28 Industrious, made ruler.

Joseph's brothers, Gen. 47:6 "Men of activity," became rulers of
Pharaoh's cattle.

Joseph, Gen. 39:3-6, 39:21-23, 41:41-44 Made overseer over all
Potiphar's household, given responsibility in prison, then made ruler
over all Egypt.

Nehemiah, Neh. 1:11, 2:1 Given position of trust before king.

Daniel, Dan. 6:1-3, 6:28 Ruled over princes.
Joseph, Nehemiah, and Daniel all stood before kings because of their diligence and integrity.

Rebekah, Gen. 24:15-20 Demonstrated her diligence to Abraham's servant. Was honored, given jewels, made wife of Isaac.

Rachel, Gen. 29:9-10

Zipporah, Ex. 2:16-21
Both of the women above were busy working when their future husbands found them.

Ruth, Book of Ruth, Her diligence and integrity led to provision for her and Naomi, and then to marriage to Boaz.

Jacob, Gen. 29 Worked for 14 years to take Rachel as his wife.

Dorcas, Acts 9:36 Was loved and remembered for her kindnesses and good works.

Verses to memorize:

Eph 6:6-7 Not with eyeservice, as menpleasers; but as the servants of Christ, doing the will of God from the heart; with good will doing service, as to the Lord, and not to men:

Col 3:22-23 Servants, obey in all things your masters according to the flesh; not with eyeservice, as menpleasers; but in singleness of heart, fearing God: and whatsoever ye do, do it heartily, as to the Lord, and not unto men.

Gen. 3:19 In the sweat of your face you shall eat bread till you return to the ground, for out of it you were taken; for dust you are, and to dust you shall return. (NKJV)

Pr. 31:27 She watches over the ways of her household, and does not eat the bread of idleness. (NKJV)

Pr. 12:24 The hand of the diligent will rule, but the lazy man will be put to forced labor. (NKJV)

Pr. 19:15 Laziness casts one into a deep sleep, and an idle person will suffer hunger. (NKJV)

Pr. 22:29 Do you see a man who excels in his work? He will stand before kings; he will not stand before unknown men. (NKJV)

Unfaithful Employee

(See also Laziness)

A child is in the position of servanthood to his parent. He is subject to the parent. If we pay the child for certain household chores, we can set up a employer/employee relationship that gives us the opportunity to train him to be a good and faithful employee. Ideally, we want to train our children so that they will have the self-discipline, diligence, creativity, and resources to become self-employed. In preparation for this, however, working for his parents gives the child another type of experience that enables him to grow in diligence and faithfulness. He can learn greater self-discipline as he subjects himself to the discipline of an authority over him.

Note: We have published a little book entitled "Stewardship Street," in which we explain our system of hiring our children. People tend to be very opinionated about the issue of paying children for chores. We have seen tremendous benefit in doing so -- not with the purpose of bribing them to do their work, but with the goal of training them to earn, budget, and wisely handle money. (See ordering information at the back of this book.)

General information and commandments about this sin:

Matt. 20:1-15 Should fulfill "contract."

Lam. 3:27 Is good to bear yoke in youth.

I Tim. 6:1 When under yoke, count masters worthy of all honor.

Lk. 16:10 Faithful in little, will be faithful in much.
Unjust in little, will be unjust in much.
*Give the faithful "employee" more privilege, honor, and
responsibility.*
Give him a "raise."

I Pet. 2:18 Be subject to masters, to good and gentle, but also to froward.

Tit. 2:9-10 Obedient servants, good fidelity, not holding back. Adorns doctrine of God.

Eph. 6:5-7 Serve masters as unto God, not with eyeservice as manpleasers, but as servants of Christ.
*Ask the child, "How would you work if you were reporting to Jesus
as your boss?"*

I Tim. 5:18 Workman is worthy of his reward.

Lk. 10:7 Workman is worthy of his hire.

Mt. 10:10 Workman is worthy of his meat.

Rom. 4:4 Reward to worker is a debt, not grace.
These 4 verses above make it clear that a worker earns his pay. The employer owes it to him.

Gen. 3:19 Eat bread by sweat of the brow.
The government welfare system is unbiblical. I believe an allowance, without conditions, encourages the same type of mindset as welfare. We need to help our children understand that material blessing involves work. God is gracious, but He has also told us "6 days shalt thou work..." and, "if any would not work, neither should he eat."

Pr. 19:10 Not seemly for servant to rule over princes.

Mal. 1:6 Servant honors his master.

Matt. 8:9 Tell servant, "Do this," and he does it.
We should expect and require this type of obedience.

Jn. 13:16 Servant is not greater than his master.
A good employee must be humble. Do not tolerate pride against your authority.

I Cor. 4:2 Steward is required to be found faithful.

Col. 3:22-25 Serve not with eyeservice, but to God. Do heartily.

What happens, or should happen, to the unfaithful employee:

II Thess. 3:10 Doesn't work, shouldn't eat,
Don't pay for inadequate work.

Pr. 13:17 Wicked messenger falls into mischief.

Matt. 3:10 No fruit, hewn down and put in fire.
"Fire" the child you have hired, if he is not doing the work as specified. Replace him with a more willing and faithful worker.

Matt. 13:12 Take away what he does have.
Levy a fine of money, time or possessions, or take away his job.

Lk. 19:12-26, Matt. 25 Gave what unfaithful servant had to the faithful servant.
Give the job to the faithful worker.

If two children were working on a job together, but one child was
not being faithful in his work, give his share of the pay to the other
child.

To what is an unfaithful employee likened:

Pr. 26:6 Cutting off feet, drinking damage. This is what it is like to
send a message by the hand of a fool.
Feet cut off are useless. A message sent with a fool is useless.

Pr. 25:19 Bad tooth, foot out of joint.
Think about this truth when the child is trying to eat around a loose
tooth, or after having dental work done.
How useful and comfortable is a bad tooth, or a sprained ankle?

Pr. 10:26 Vinegar to teeth, smoke to eyes.
Rinse mouth with vinegar, and discuss its effect.
How comfortable is it when cigarette or campfire smoke blows into
your eyes?

Blessings of faithful employees:

(See also blessings in chapter on "Laziness.")

Pr. 17:2 Wise servant will rule over son that causes shame. Will have
part in inheritance among brothers.
Make a special contribution into the child's long-term savings.
Appoint the child as "Foreman-of-the-Day," having him oversee and
assign chores for rest of children. Pay him for this job.

Pr. 27:18 Keep fig tree, eat figs. Wait on master, leads to honor.
Set up a system of profit sharing for the child who is a faithful
employee in the family business.
Our children work hard helping me can when they know we will have
a "peach break" or a "pear break" after we finish a box of fruit.

Matt. 24:45 Faithful, wise servant will be ruler over household.
Give more responsibility and privilege.
Appoint him in charge of various tasks in the household.
Give him more planning responsibility.
This is what happened to Joseph!

Lk. 19:16 Ruler over many things.

Stories of faithful servants:

Joseph, Gen. 39 +   Brought blessing to his master, was made ruler, was honored and prosperous, resisted sin, ruled in prison, then ruled over Egypt. Was faithful in little, and then faithful in much. Blessing brought to family.

Midwives, Ex. 1:15-21   Obeyed God, blessed by God and given families.

Daniel, Dan. 1 and 6   Favored by prince of eunuchs. Rule was increased. The king "thought to set him over the whole realm."

Abraham's servant, Gen. 24   Trusted God, would not eat until he completed his errand. Did not want to tarry.

Jonathan's servants, I Sam. 14:7   Brave and loyal.

Abigail's servants, I Sam. 25:14-17   Told Abigail of Nabal's foolish response to David. Warned of David's anger.

David's servants, II Sam. 15:15,21   Loyal, ready to do his will.

Ziba, II Sam. 9   Told David of Mephibosheth. Served him.

Naaman's servants, II Kgs. 5:2,3,13   Captive Israelite girl told him about Elisha.   Servants encouraged him to follow Elisha's instructions.

Centurion's servant, Matt. 8:9   Does what he is told.

Cornelius' servants, Acts. 10:7-23   Fulfilled errand.

Parable of talents, Matt. 25:14-23, Lk. 19:12-19   Faithful over few, ruler over many.

Jacob, Gen. 30:27-31   Brought blessing to master. Prospered.

Stories of unfaithful servants:

Ziba, II Sam. 16:1-4, 19:17-30   Slandered his master, was disloyal.

Jeroboam, I Kgs. 11:26   Rebelled against Solomon.

Gehazi, II Kgs. 5:20-27   Took gift from Naaman by deceit. Leprosy.

Zimri, I Kgs. 16:9-10; II Kgs. 9:31   Killed Elah, master and king.

Servants of Abraham and Lot, Gen. 13:7   Strife among themselves.

Servants of Abimelech, Gen. 21:25   Violently stole Abraham's well.

Servants of Absalom, II Sam. 13:28-29, 14:30   Obeyed Absalom in

sinful actions. Conspired with him.
*Here is an example of subordinates sinning by obeying their master
in his sinful plans and actions.*

Servants of Shimei, I Kgs. 2:39 Ran away, led to Shimei's execution.

Servants of Joash, II Kgs. 12:19-21 Conspired against master,
murderered him.

Servants of Amon, II Kgs. 21:23 Conspired against master and
murdered him.

Unbelieving spies, Num. 13:32, 14:1-4 Put fear in people's hearts.

Parable of talents, Matt. 25:1-30 Gave what he had to faithful
servant. Was cast out.

Verses to memorize:

Col. 3:23 And whatsoever ye do, do it heartily, as to the Lord, and
not unto men.

Titus 2:9-10 Exhort bondservants to be obedient to their own
masters, to be well pleasing in all things, not answering back, not
pilfering, but showing all good fidelity, that they may adorn the
doctrine of God our Savior in all things. (NKJV)

1 Cor. 4:2 Moreover it is required in stewards, that a man be found
faithful.

Eph 6:5-7 Bondservants, be obedient to those who are your masters
according to the flesh, with fear and trembling, in sincerity of heart,
as to Christ; not with eyeservice, as men-pleasers, but as
bondservants of Christ, doing the will of God from the heart, with
goodwill doing service, as to the Lord, and not to men.

Haste

(See also Impatience)

The hasty person exercises his self-will and does not take the time to inquire before going into action. We parents need to beware of this tendency. It is easy to assume that we know all the facts, and to be hasty in our discipline. We need to pray for wisdom in each situation. We need to listen carefully to both sides of an argument. We need to take time to instruct the wrongdoer, rather than simply disciplining in haste.

General information and commandments about this sin:

Pr. 14:29 Exalts folly.

Pr. 19:2 Sins.

Pr. 29:20 More hope for a fool than for one hasty with words.

Ec. 5:2 Let words be few; remember your position.

Pr. 24:27 Prepare work in field, then build house.
Require the child to present a plan, to exhibit forethought.
Require necessary finances before child launches into business idea.

Pr. 25:8 Don't go hastily to court.

Ec. 7:9 Don't be hasty to be angry.

Pr. 29:11 Fool utters all his mind.
Train the child to weigh his words before he speaks. Encourage this
by not allowing him to immediately voice his opinion on an issue,
but requiring him to first take time to think out his response.
We should do this, too!

Pr. 28:22 One who hastens to be rich has an evil eye.

Pr. 24:6 There is safety in a multitude of counselors.
Train your child to seek counsel, to plan carefully before making any
major decision.
Set an example of this in your own life.

What happens, or should happen, to the hasty person:

Pr. 28:22, 21:5 Leads to poverty.
Do not spare your child from the natural consequences of his haste.
It is hard to do, but sometimes our children learn the most from their

*mistakes. (i.e. If your child is determined to purchase an item that
you know is inferior quality, or of short-lived interest, give him your
opinion and then let him make his own decision. After he has
hastily spent his money, takes the item home, and watches it break
after a couple hours of play, he will better understand the benefits
of heeding good counsel.)*

*Pray for God's providential working out of circumstances to
demonstrate this principle to your child. Graciously point out this
truth when poverty follows after haste.*

Pr. 20:21 Inheritance gained hastily will not be blessed in the end.

Pr. 25:8 Neighbors will put to shame.

Pr. 28:20 Hasten to be rich, will not go unpunished.

*Business ventures are good opportunities for children to learn the
dangers of haste. Give them the chance to put their money-making
ideas into action (using their own money), and observe what
happens if planning and forethought have not gone into the
venture.*

Pr. 15:28 Should study to answer.

Parents, set an example of this in your discipline!
Teach the child to wait and pray before answering.
Teach him to study the Bible for answers before hastening to action.
*What does the Bible say about this? Does it line up with Scriptural
principles, or does it violate them?*
*After a hasty mistake, examine the child's action with him. What
should he have done differently?*

Ex. 14:13 Stand still.

Teach the child to <u>stop</u>*, think, plan and consider before he acts.*

Js. 1:19 Swift to hear, slow to speak.

Stop talking and listen!
*A person who is determined to pursue his hasty "plan" is usually
spending a lot of energy talking about it, rather than listening to
advice.*

Matt. 12:36 Will give an account of every evil word.

*Tape record or write down a hasty conversation that you overhear.
Review it with the child. Have him give account to you for his
words.*
Teach the child from the consequences of a hasty conversation.

Pr. 29:18 No counsel, people perish.

*Teach child to seek counsel before major decisions or actions. Have
him write out a plan, study Scripture for guiding principles, and ask
the advice of good counselors.*

Ps. 119:24 God's testimonies are our counsel.
What does the Bible say we should do, or should have done? What principles are there to guide us in this decision or action?

To what is the sin of haste likened:

Matt. 13:20,21 Seed that comes up in haste and then withers.

Blessings of those who are not hasty:
(See also blessings in the chapter on "Foolishness.")

Pr. 21:5 Leads to plenteousness.

Pr. 22:3, 27:12 Foresees evil and hides.

Pr. 15:18 Appeases strife.

Stories that illustrate the consequences of haste:

Moses, Num. 20:10-12 Struck rock in anger and impatience. Was not allowed to enter Promised Land.

Jephtha's vow, Jg. 11:31-39 Led to the sacrifice of his daughter.

Rehoboam forsaking counsel, I Kgs. 12:8-15 Led to rebellion of Israel.

Josiah against Necho, II Chron. 35:20-24 Didn't take counsel or foresee evil. Led to his death.

James and John, Lk. 9:54 Swift to speak.

Esau, Gen. 25:29-34 Led to poverty (loss of blessing).

Peter, Jn. 18:10 Cut off ear of soldier.

Potiphar, Gen. 39:17-20 Did not give Joseph trial, but was swift to wrath.

Darius, Dan. 6 Sought no other counsel, did not study before he answered. Led to injustice.

David and Ziba, II Sam. 16:1-4, 19:24-30 David was not slow to speak, but answered and judged quickly without studying the matter or seeking the counsel of others. Led to injustice.

Saul, I Sam. 13:12-14 Acted against God's counsel and commandments. **Led** to loss of kingdom.

David and Nabal, I Sam. 25:13-21 Quick to anger and action.

Joshua and the Gibeonites, Josh. 9:14,15 Didn't seek counsel of God, and was deceived by their trickery.

Moses, slaying Egyptian, Ex. 2:11-12, Acts 7:24-25 Led to his flight to Midian.

Stories that illustrate the blessings of prudence:

Isaac and people of Gerar, Gen. 26:15-22 Appeased strife.

Moses, Ex. 16:7-8 Recognized that the people were complaining against God.

Job, Job 1:21, 2:9-10, 42:12-13 Was slow to speak. Ended in even greater
blessing to Job.

Jacob, when meeting Esau, Gen. 32:3-21 Foresaw potential evil, planned, appeased strife.

Joseph, Gen. 41:33-57 Foresaw evil and coming famine, planned ahead and country had plenty.

Jethro, in counseling Moses about judges, Ex. 18:17-23 Foresaw problems, planned a system for relief and justice, gave good counsel.

David's response to Saul, I Sam. 24:3-21 Stood still. God's commandment was his counsel, did not enter strife.

Israelites and the 2-1/2 tribes, Josh. 22:10-34 Initially assumed wrongly, but were swift to hear and slow to speak. Studied their answer.

Joseph responding to Mary's pregnancy, Matt. 1:19 Slow to speak, did not go to court hastily.

Abigail, I Sam. 25:23-31 Appeased strife, foresaw evil, appealed to David's conscience.

Hezekiah and Rabshekah, II Kgs. 18:36, 19:1-36 Counseled people to not answer him. Sought Isaiah's counsel, was slow to speak, appeased strife.

Verses to memorize:

Luke 21:19 By your patience possess your souls.

1 Thess. 5:14 Now we exhort you, brethren, warn those who are unruly, comfort the fainthearted, uphold the weak, be patient with all. (NKJV)

James 1:19 Wherefore, my beloved brethren, let every man be swift to hear, slow to speak, slow to wrath. (NKJV)

Prov 15:22 Without counsel, plans go awry, but in the multitude of counselors they are established. (NKJV)

Prov 21:5 The plans of the diligent lead surely to plenty, but those of everyone who is hasty, surely to poverty. (NKJV)

Ps. 119:24 Thy testimonies also are my delight and my counsellors.

Pr. 3:5-6 Trust in the LORD with all thine heart; and lean not unto thine own understanding. In all thy ways acknowledge him, and he shall direct thy paths.

Impatience/Irritability

(See also Haste, Arguing, Anger)

General information and commandments about this sin:

II Pet. 1:5-6 Add to faith, virtue, knowledge, temperance, patience, and godliness.
Build on the foundation of faith.

I Cor. 13:5 Love is not easily provoked.
Do a word study on "love" with your child.

Col. 1:9-11 Pray for knowledge, wisdom, understanding, fruitfulness. Increase in knowledge, strengthened with His power to patience and longsuffering with joyfulness.
Pray together for patience through Christ's strength.

Rom. 5:3 Tribulation works patience.

Js. 1:3 Trying of our faith works patience.
Be thankful for tribulation as a means of bringing maturity into one's life.
Don't try to protect your child from God-sent tribulation in his life. Guide him and encourage him, but view the testing as a lesson from God.

Lk. 21:19 In your patience, possess your souls.
Review this idea. How would we possess our souls? After an incident of impatience, discuss how the child could have possessed his soul. What could he have done differently?

Eph. 4:1-2 Walk worthy, with lowliness, meekness, longsuffering, forbearing with love.
Discuss how we can do this. What would it look like?

I Thess. 5:14 Be patient toward all men.

I Tim. 3:2 Impatience disqualifies a man for the office of elder.

What happens, or should happen, to the impatient person:

Col. 1:10-11 Strengthened with all might according to His power, to patience with joy.
Pray daily with the child for God's strength to be patient.

Js. 5:10 Look to prophets as examples of patience and suffering.

Study the lives of various prophets -- Elijah, Elisha, Hosea, Isaiah, Jeremiah, Ezekiel, Daniel, John the Baptist. etc.
How did they demonstrate patience? What were the tests in their lives?

Heb. 6:12 Be followers of those with faith and patience.
Look for models of patience in the child's life. (And be a model!)
Arrange opportunities for your child to spend time with these people, getting to know them in a deeper way, working with them.
Many of the older saints in a church are rich sources of lessons in faith and patience and resting in the Lord. My contact with godly older folks in my childhood has left a lasting mark on my memory and soul.
Read biographies and Bible stories that give a better acquaintance with believers who were examples of patience.

Pr. 17:9 Cover a transgression with love.

Pr. 19:11 Glory to pass over a transgression.
Teach your child that there is a place for overlooking personal offenses. We do not need to insist on our rights. Jesus didn't.
Beware of bitterness in the heart of a child who may appear to "overlook" offenses.

Js. 1:18-19 Be swift to hear, slow to speak, slow to wrath.
Teach child to "listen quickly and act slowly."
When you overhear a child growing impatient remind him to be "swift to hear."

I Tim. 6:11 Follow righteousness, godliness, faith, love, patience, meekness.
Teach the child to ask himself when he is tempted to be impatient, "What would be the godly thing to do? The loving thing? The meek thing? What would Jesus do in this situation?"

The blessings of patience:

Ps. 37:9 Wait on the Lord, will inherit the earth.
Encourage the patient child with a gift for her hope chest or his tool chest. Pass on an heirloom.
Make a special deposit into his long-term savings.

Ec. 7:8 Patient spirit is better than proud spirit.
Even if the person with a proud spirit appears to have all sorts of talents and possessions, a person with patience is better.

Rom. 2:7 Patient continuance in well-doing leads to glory, honor,

immortality.
Honor patience and perseverence. Draw attention to it. Reward it with privileges, monetary blessing, trust, a special homemade certificate or trophy.

Gal. 6:9 Will reap if we don't faint.
Work with your child on long-range projects that require patience. Gardening, animal husbandry, growing trees, establishing a business, all help develop perseverence and patience. Start with shorter range projects and work up to longer range ones.

Js. 5:11 Count them happy that endure. Lord is pitiful to them and full of mercy.
Show mercy to the child who has exercised patience in a disagreement or trial.

Stories that illustrate impatience:

Moses striking the rock, Num. 20:8-12 Was not allowed to enter Promised Land.

Israelites, Ex. 32:1 Led to worship of idols.

Esau, Gen. 25: 29-34 Lost birthright.

Stories that illustrate patience:

Isaac and herdsmen of Gerar, Gen. 26:15-22 Dug new wells instead of insisting on rights.

Moses, Ex. 16:7-8 Recognized that Israelites complained against God rather than against him.

Job, Job 1:21, Js. 5:11 God was merciful to him, blessed him doubly after his trial.

Verses to memorize:

Rom. 15:5 Now may the God of patience and comfort grant you to be like-minded toward one another, according to Christ Jesus. (NKJV)

1 Cor. 13:4-7 Love suffers long and is kind; love does not envy; love

does not parade itself, is not puffed up; does not behave rudely, does not seek its own, is not provoked, thinks no evil; does not rejoice in iniquity, but rejoices in the truth; bears all things, believes all things, hopes all things, endures all things. (NKJV)

Gal.5:22-23 But the fruit of the Spirit is love, joy, peace, longsuffering, gentleness, goodness, faith, meekness, temperance: against such there is no law.

Gal. 6:9 And let us not grow weary while doing good, for in due season we shall reap if we do not lose heart. (NKJV)

1 Thess. 5:14 Now we exhort you, brethren, warn those who are unruly, comfort the fainthearted, uphold the weak, be patient with all. (NKJV)

Eph. 4:1-2 I, therefore, the prisoner of the Lord, beseech you to walk worthy of the calling with which you were called, with all lowliness and gentleness, with longsuffering, bearing with one another in love. (NKJV)

Anger

(See also Arguing, Hatred, Bitterness, Hitting, etc.)

General information and commandments about this sin:

Pr. 22:24 Don't associate with an angry man or you will learn his ways.
Do not allow your child to develop friendships with children who are quick to anger.

Pr. 12:16 Fool's wrath is known.

Pr. 14:29 Exalts folly.
An angry man demonstrates his foolishness for all to see.

Ec. 7:9 Anger is in the bosom of fools.

Matt. 5:22 Anger leads to danger of judgment.

Rom. 12:19 Give place to wrath.

Eph. 4:26 Don't let sun go down on anger.
Make this a policy in your home. Settle disagreements before going to bed.
We have this verse calligraphed and up on our wall.

Eph. 4:31 Put away anger (along with bitterness, clamor, evil speaking, malice.)
Write out covenant that outlines blessings of controlling anger, and consequences of indulging in anger.

Pr. 14:17 Deals foolishly.

Pr. 14:16 Is a fool.

Pr. 19:11 A prudent man turns away from anger.

Pr. 29:22 Stirs up strife, abounds in transgression.

Ps. 37:8 Cease from anger, do not do evil.

Js. 1:20 Man's wrath doesn't work God's righteousness.
What does anger accomplish?
Note the consequences of the child's angry actions and discuss them together.

Pr. 17:19 Loves trangression.

Matt. 11:29 Learn of Jesus, meek and lowly of heart.
Study Jesus' example. How did He speak and act?

What happens, or should happen, to the angry person:

Pr. 25:8 Brought to shame.
Discipline an angry child. Stop him in the middle of his outburst, remove him from the situation. Require confession and asking of forgiveness.

Pr. 15:18 Stirs up strife.
Remove the angry person and discipline him. If he is allowed to continually express his anger without consequence, he will destroy the peace of the entire household (or church congregation, community, etc.)

Pr. 19:19 Will suffer punishment. Deliver, will do it again.
Be consistent in always disciplining an angry child. Start with the temper tantrums typical of the young toddler whose desires are thwarted. We can't overlook these outbursts, considering them simply a "stage" he is going through. He will just graduate to another "stage" of uncontrolled anger as he grows older, unless he is taught to control his anger and forfeit his "rights."
Increase discipline when dealing with an habitually angry child.

Pr. 22:24 Make no friendship with an angry man. Do not go with him.
LImit child's contact with children who are given to anger.

Js. 1:19 Be swift to hear.
Teach the child to listen carefully, and then act slowly.

Pr. 14:30 Affects body badly.
During a child's angry outburst, stop and take his pulse and blood pressure. Observe his body. How does it compare with a time when he is normal and calm?
Anger affects a person's sleep. It can affect his digestion.

Pr. 17:14 Leads to quarrels.
Remove the angry child to end a quarrel.

Pr. 29:11 Wise man keeps his mind to himself, but a fool says everything he thinks.
Does your child want to prove himself a fool, or does he want to be wise? Train him to control his tongue.

Matt. 5:21-22 Angry man in danger of the same judgment as the murderer.
Anger, in its advanced stages, often leads to murder. (Notice examples in the "stories" section.) In the same way, anger, in the child, often leads to striking and physically injuring another child.

To what is the angry man likened:

Pr. 30:33 Churning milk that becomes butter.
Sweet cream inevitably becomes butter when it is agitated.
Make butter together, and talk about this verse.

Pr. 30:33 Wringing the nose produces blood.
Forcing anger produces strife just as inevitably as nose-wringing
produces blood, and churning cream produces butter.

Pr. 17:14 Like letting out water.
With sand or mud, construct a network of rivers and dams. Flood
it with a hose or bucket of water. What happens when the first
dam breaks?
(See also listings for this verse in the chapter on "Arguing.")

Pr. 25:28 City without walls.
Unprotected, without resistance to enemy (temptation). A city
without walls is vulnerable to attack.

Pr. 27:3 Heavier than stone or sand.
Fill a bucket with sand or rocks, and have the child carry it around
for awhile. How does anger affect the angry fool? How does it
affect the victim of the anger?

Pr. 19:12 King's anger is like the roaring of a lion.
Research: Why does a lion roar?

Pr. 27:4 Torrent.
Torrent is uncontrollable. Others are caught in its current. Is
destructive.
Observe a rushing river. Is it peaceful? Does it steer around
objects or merely crash over them? What happens to a stick when
it is thrown into the current?
Create a river system in the mud or sandbox. Then create a
"torrent" with the hose. What happens?

Blessings of the man with self-control:

Pr. 16:32 Better than the mighty or one who takes a city.
For the child who is learning to control his temper, present him with
a special medal-of-honor, certificate, trophy, homemade patch to
sew on his coat, or print up a special T-shirt similar to those
presented to runners who complete marathons, etc.

Pr. 14:29 Has great understanding.

Pr. 15:18 One who is slow to anger allays contention.

Pr. 20:3 Is an honor to cease from strife.
To cease from strife requires humility. Matt. 23:12 says that the humble will be exalted. Exalt your child with some of the following ideas:
Have a special family party or feast in honor of the peacemaker.
Have a "Servant's Day" when the family performs services for the "exalted" person.
Fly a special "name flag" from the front porch.
Note: Doorposts sells a set of patterns which includes instructions for making a "name flag" for each of your children. It includes the child's name, the meaning of the name, and special symbols that represent interests and events in the child's life. We hang this up on birthdays, and on other occasions when we want to honor a certain child. See ordering information at back of book.)

Ps. 37:9 Will inherit the earth.
Make a special deposit into the child's long-term savings.
Pass on a special heirloom when the child shows progress in gaining control over his temper.
Make it clear to your child that his share of inheritance of the family wealth is contingent upon him demonstrating self-control and control of his anger.

Stories that illustrate the consequences of anger:

Stephen's killers, Acts 7:54-59 Led to murder.

Cain, Gen. 4:5 Led to murder.

Esau, Gen. 27:45 Planned to murder Jacob.

Moses, Num. 20:10 Struck rock, kept from Promised Land.

Balaam, Num. 22:29 Struck the ass, desired to kill.

Naaman, II Kgs. 5:11 Anger over Elisha's instructions almost prevented him from being healed of leprosy.

David, in response to Nabal, I Sam. 25:13,21-22 Planned to murder.

Moses, Ex. 2:11-12, Acts 7:24-25 Murdered Egyptian.

Asa, II Chron. 16:10 Angry at Hanani's prophecy. Put him in prison.

Jonah, Jon. 4:1-11 Angry with God for sparing Nineveh and for destroying the gourd plant.

Simeon and Levi, Gen. 34:5-27, Gen. 49:5-7 Murdered. Descendants were scattered.

Nebuchadnezzar with Shadrach, Meshach, and Abednego, Dan. 3:13-19 Attempted to murder them.

Saul and priests, I Sam 22:3-19 Murdered.

Nebuchadnezzar with Chaldeans and astrologers, Dan. 2:12-13 Ordered execution of all the wise men of Babylon.

Martha, Lk. 10:38-42 Led to reproof.

Stories that illustrate those who were slow to anger:

Isaac and herdsmen of Gerar, Gen. 26:15-22 Led to peace and prosperity.

Jacob, with Laban, Gen. 29:15-28, 31:36-55 Prosperity.

Joseph, with his brothers, Gen. 45 and 50:15-21 Lack of anger towards his brothers led to prosperity for him and entire nation, and to his rulership over Egypt.

Verses to memorize:

1 Cor. 13:4-5 Love suffers long and is kind; love does not envy; love does not parade itself, is not puffed up; does not behave rudely, does not seek its own, is not provoked, thinks no evil. (NKJV)

Phil. 4:8 Finally, brethren, whatever things are true, whatever things are noble, whatever things are just, whatever things are pure, whatever things are lovely, whatever things are of good report, if there is any virtue and if there is anything praiseworthy; meditate on these things. (NKJV)

Gal. 5:22 But the fruit of the Spirit is love, joy, peace, longsuffering, gentleness, goodness, faith.

Pr. 16:32 He that is slow to anger is better than the mighty; and he that ruleth his spirit than he that taketh a city.

Matt. 11:29 Take my yoke upon you, and learn of me; for I am meek and lowly in heart: and ye shall find rest unto your souls.

Pr. 17:27 He who has knowledge spares his words, and a man of understanding is of a calm spirit. (NKJV)

Pr. 19:11 The discretion of a man makes him slow to anger, and his glory is to overlook a transgression. (NKJV)

Pr. 21:23 Whoever guards his mouth and tongue keeps his soul from troubles. (NKJV)

Ps. 141:3 Set a guard, O LORD, over my mouth; keep watch over the door of my lips. (NKJV)

Pr. 14:17 A quick-tempered man acts foolishly, and a man of wicked intentions is hated. (NKJV)

John 13:35 By this shall all men know that ye are my disciples, if ye have love one to another.

gluttony/Pleasure-Seeking

(See also Covetousness, Selfishness)

General information and commandments about this sin:

I Tim. 5:6 Pleasure-lover is dead while living.

Pr. 25:27 Not good to eat too much honey.
Practice moderation in your home. Do not encourage overeating or eating for mere entertainment.

Pr. 30:22 Earth can't bear up under a fool filled with food.

Ec. 10:17 Eat in due season for strength, not for drunkenness.
Pay attention to the way you use food with a baby or toddler. Beware of using food to quiet and control a child, in place of proper discipline. Do not use food as entertainment for a bored child. Gradually work a young child into the family routine, so that he is not constantly begging for food, or eating whenever he feels like it.

Pr. 23:1-3 Gluttony is forbidden.
Teach the child (and model before him) self-control at the table. Do not allow him to overeat.

Deut. 21:20 Linked with stubborn and rebellious.
The glutton, the stubborn, and the rebel all serve another master other than God.

Ps. 104:15 Bread strengthens man's heart.

I Cor. 10:31 Should eat and drink to the glory of God.
Based on the above 2 verses, help the child learn to think about what he eats, and how the food strengthens or weakens him, and whether the food will enable him to better glorify God, or hinder him in doing that.

I Cor. 9:27 Keep body under subjection.
Train the child to exercise self-control in other physical disciplines -- sports, exercise, routine, physical labor.
Train the child to submit to physical limits -- regular bedtimes, mealtimes, etc.

Phil. 3:19 The glutton's god is his belly. Minds earthly things.
Overattention to eating can affect our other priorities.

I Pet. 4:2 Shouldn't live in the flesh but to the will of God.

Pr. 15:21 Folly is joy to him who is destitute of wisdom.

Ec. 2:1 Pleasure-seeking is vanity.

What happens, or should happen, to the glutton and pleasure-seeker:

Pr. 21:17 Love wine and oil and pleasure, will not be rich.

Pr. 23:21 Drunkard and glutton will end in poverty.
If child has been gluttonous, perhaps he should skip his next meal.
An older child could pay a portion of the grocery bill if he is overeating, especially if he is eating everything out of the refrigerator between meals.

Pr. 25:16 Eat too much honey, will vomit.
Notice illnesses and discomfort that are connected with overeating.

Pr. 28:7 Companion of glutton brings shame to his father.
Communicate this to your child.
Be careful to set a good example in this area.

Pr. 23:1-3 If you sit with ruler, put knife to throat if you are given to appetite.
Teach the child to be especially careful about his eating manners when he is a guest.
The child sits with a "ruler" everytime his <u>*parents*</u> *are present at the table. Teach him to heed this admonition.*

Amos 6:4-7 Captivity.
The glutton is a slave to himself and his appetites.
"Enslave" the child with cleanup duties and dishwashing if he has been especially gluttonous at a meal.

Phil. 3:19 God is belly, end is destruction. Minds earthly things.
Gluttony is a form of idolatry.

Isa. 47:8-9 Seeking pleasure leads to widowhood and loss of children.
Loss of heritage. Pleasure-seeking affects family and future generations.
Deny long-term savings deposit to the gluttonous, pleasure-seeking child.

Lk. 8:14 Doesn't bring fruit to perfection.
Eat some unripe fruit together. Is it satisfying?

Job 20:12-16 Vomit up riches. Vipers tongue will slay.
Children might relate to this verse in a new way if you discuss it during a spell of stomach flu in your family!

Job 21:13 Go down to grave in a moment.

To what is the glutton likened:

Js. 5:5 Pleasure-seekers nourish hearts like fattening up animal for slaughter.
Animal enjoys the "feast" without knowing its outcome.
Remember, in <u>Charlotte's Web</u>, *Wilbur's shock when he discovered that he was going to be dinner after he was fattened up enough!*

Stories that illustrate the consequences of gluttony and pleasure-seeking:

Esau, Gen. 25:29-34, Heb. 12:16-17 Couldn't change circumstances after
his poor decision, gave up his birthright.

Sons of Eli, I Sam. 2:12-17 Sinned in sacrifice, led to their deaths.

Belshazzar, Dan. 5:1 Led to sin and foolishness.

Israel, Ex. 16; Num. 11:4,33; Ps. 78:18 Quail and manna. Hoarded.
Ate too much quail, led to plague. Always wanting to return to
slavery where they had melons, leeks, garlic, etc.

Prodigal son, Lk. 15:11-16 Led to want, poverty and loneliness.

Verses to memorize:

Rom. 13:14 But put ye on the Lord Jesus Christ, and make not provision for the flesh, to fulfil the lusts thereof.

Gal. 5:24 And those who are Christ's have crucified the flesh with its passions and desires. (NKJV)

1 Cor. 10:13 No temptation has overtaken you except such as is common to man; but God is faithful, who will not allow you to be tempted beyond what you are able, but with the temptation will also make the way of escape, that you may be able to bear it. (NKJV)

1 Cor. 10:31 Therefore, whether you eat or drink, or whatever you do, do all to the glory of God. (NKJV)

Immorality/Sexual Sin

This information can be preventative in nature. Saturate your child with Scripture. Much of the Book of Proverbs is devoted to the training of sons regarding strange women. Warn him of the dangers. Prepare him for the temptations. Protect him with the tradition of courtship, rather than exposing him to the dangers and temptations of dating.

General information and commandments about this sin:

Job 24:15 Waits for night.
  Many of the temptations of youth can be eliminated by exercising greater control over our children's evening and nighttime activities.

Pr. 2:16 Wisdom will protect from strange woman.
  Study the Bible with your children. Train them in wisdom. Arm them with God's Word.

Pr. 5:6 A strange woman's ways are unstable.
  Help your son learn to discern a "strange woman." Mothers are usually most sensitive to this spirit in other women. Help him recognize her actions and attitudes. Our daughters need to recognize this type of girl, as well, so that they are not influenced by them.

Pr. 23:28 A strange woman increases the unfaithful among men.

Mk. 7:21 Comes from the heart.

Mk. 7:21-23 Comes from within.
  Fill your child's heart with Scripture, and train him to apply and obey it. ("Thy Word have I hid in my heart, that I might not sin against Thee.")

Matt. 5:28 Sexual sin is a mental attitude. (To lust after a woman is to already commit adultery in the heart.)

Pr. 7:6 + Young man was aimless and loitering.
  Keep young sons and daughters profitably employed with good works, service, jobs, training in skills within the home.

Job 24:15 Thinks no one will see.
  Take time to do a thorough study of the attributes of God with your children. Put special emphasis on His omniscience and omnipresence.

I Cor. 6:18 Sins against own body.

Pr. 5:11 Flesh and body are consumed.

Study the diseases, psychological effects, and guilt associated with sexual impurity.

Neh. 13:26 Even Solomon, with all his wisdom, succumbed to temptation in this area.
None of us is immune to temptation. Our children need to understand this.

Ec. 7:26 He who pleases God will escape from the strange woman.

I Thess. 5:22 Abstain from all appearance of evil.
Enforce this principle. Do not allow even the slightest <u>appearance</u> of sexual impurity in the child's life; this includes their manner of dress, their speech, their "body language", their music and reading material.

Pr. 30:20 Becomes spiritually calloused.
Poke calloused foot or hand with a pin. The warning message of pain cannot get through, until greater injury occurs to the area.
A calloused heart is insensitive to God's prompting and early disipline.

What happens, or should happen, to the immoral person:

Lev. 20:10 Mosaic law required execution of adulterers.

I Cor. 6:18 Flee.
A child needs to be trained to <u>run</u> as soon as he encounters a tempting situation.
Do not place your children into compromising situations of temptation.
Beware of TV, reading material, etc. that you may have in your home. Avoid all <u>appearance</u> of evil!

Pr. 23:26 Give God your heart, observe His ways.
Study the Bible, pray for God-given wisdom.

Pr. 7:4 Embrace wisdom.
Study the Bible together! Teach your child to apply Scriptural principles, and to search out principles to guide his decisions and actions.

Pr. 2:18-19 Leads to death, <u>none</u> return.
Read stories that illustrate this truth. No one escapes the consequences of sexual sin.

Pr. 5:5 Feet go towards death, steps lay hold of hell.

Pr. 5:9 Honor goes to others, years are given to the cruel one, strangers will be filled with your wealth, labor in the house of a stranger, flesh and body consumed.
Discuss the effects of sexual impurity -- shame, guilt, changes in plans, debt, etc.
Read about the victims of abortion, unwed mothers, those with AIDS and other venereal diseases. How are their lives affected by their sin?

Pr. 6:32-33 Wounds and dishonor. Destroys own soul.
Sexual sin leaves emotional scars that affect our future.

Pr. 29:3 Companion of harlots wastes money.
Control the amount of spendable income available to the young person.

Rom. 1:28+ Given over to a debased mind.

I Cor. 6:9-10 Will not inherit kingdom.
Deny deposits into long-term savings account.
Deny the child's portion of inheritance of the family wealth when he does not repent of sexual sin. Good stewardship of God's blessings requires that we not entrust them to children who are knowingly living in sin. A "debased mind" will not use material blessings in a godly way.

Pr. 5:10, Pr. 29:3, I Kgs 11:11 Waste of wealth, given to others.
Point out to the child where his money goes when he sins in this way.
Is he using his money in a way that furthers the kingdom of God?
Sexual sin wastes the "wealth" of a pure conscience, which affects a person's future happiness, marriage, and family.

I Cor. 5:11 Cast out of fellowship.
Make it clear to the child that his sin interferes with his fellowship with God and with your family.
Consult with your church leaders for assistance in disciplining an unrepentant child who is participating in sexual sin.

II Tim. 2:22 Flee. Pursue righteousness, faith, love, peace with other believers.
Make sure your child is fellowshipping with other believers in the context of a local church.
Encourage friendships with godly young people.
Set up some sort of system of accountability between the child and you or another adult.

Matt. 5:29-30 Pluck out the eye that sins. Cut off the hand that sins.

"Disable" the child: Put restraints on a his free time. Remove as many sources of temptation as possible. Do not allow friendships with those who would tempt him into sexual sin. Restrict use of the car. Do not allow him to spend unsupervised free time with friends. Do not allow dating. Limit the amount of spending money available to him.

Rom. 13:12 Cast off the works of darkness, put on armor of light.
Immerse the child in Scripture.
Memorize the Ephesians 6 passage about the "Armor of God."

Ps. 119:9-11 Hide God's Word in heart, pay attention to God's Word.
Memorize, meditate, study, saturate!

Pr. 31:3 Destroys kings.
Study examples of kings in the Bible and in other accounts of history.
What happened to even David and Solomon when they yielded to sexual temptation?

Jude 7 Eternal fire.

Pr. 2:10,11,16 Wisdom and knowledge will lead to discretion, understanding and deliverance from the strange woman.

Pr. 6:20-24 Keep commandments, pay attention to reproofs of life to keep you from the evil woman.

Pr. 7:1-5 Keep commandments. Bind them on fingers, write them on the table of your heart.
Give the child a visible reminder of God's commandments -- a locket with a picture or Bible reference inside, a ring with a verse inscribed inside it, a calligraphed verse for the wall or for inside a wallet, a key chain or money clip with an inscribed or symbolic medal on it, etc.
(Num. 15:38-39 tells about the fringe sewn onto the hems of Israelite garments as a reminder to "do all my commandments, and be holy unto your God.")
Study the Word! Be in constant prayer for your children -- for their response to God's Word in their lives, for wisdom and courage and commitment. Make the Word the very center of your home. Teach your children the consistent habit of Bible study and prayer. Lead them in family worship. Model a true commitment to God and his commandments before your family. All these things will build up a protective hedge around your children!

To what is the sin of immorality likened:

(Solomon gives us lots of pictures!)

Pr. 5:3-4   Strange woman: lips are like honeycomb, mouth smoother than oil. Her end is bitter as wormwood, sharp as a two-edged sword.
Tastes sweet, but is bitter and fatal.
Do some research about wormwood. What is its history? What is it used for? What does it taste like?

Pr. 6:27   Fire in bosom.
What will happen if you carry a burning object up against you?

Pr. 6:28   Walk on hot coals.
Can you walk on them without burning your feet?
Talk about this on a hot day when the children are barefoot, and are trying to walk across hot pavement or sand.

Pr. 7:22   Ox going to slaughter.
If you work with animals, and you do any slaughtering, that is a perfect opportunity to talk about this verse. The children are usually sympathizing with the "poor little animal" that has no idea of what is ahead of him. The fool who enters into sexual sin is ignorant of its outcome, as well.

Pr. 7:22   Fool on his way to the stocks.
Study the use of stocks for public punishment during early colonial days. The offender's wrongdoing was made public with this type of punishment. The immoral person may think that no one will know about his sin, but it will be exposed, now or in the judgment to come.

Pr. 7:23   Bird hastening to snare, bird shot with arrow.
Study the techniques of trapping. All are based on hidden traps, trickery, and luring the animal. The immoral person <u>rushes</u> into the snare.
The bird shot with the arrow probably didn't even know he was in danger until it was too late to escape.

Pr. 9:17   Stolen waters are sweet, bread eaten in secret is pleasant.
If your child has had any experience with trying to sneak cookies or other treats from the kitchen, discuss this idea with him. What tempted him to eat his "bread" in secret? Did he enjoy it as much as he would have, if he had eaten it openly, with permission?

Pr. 11:22   Beautiful woman without discretion is like a gold ring in a pig's snout.

The beauty is misused, and becomes an object of disgust.
*Give a young girl a stuffed pig with a real gold ring sewn onto its
snout. Set it up as a decoration in her room. When she reaches
her teen years, if she is demonstrating discretion in her
relationships, give her the ring to wear. If there are situations that
prove her to be indiscreet, take the ring and sew it back onto the
pig's snout, until she proves herself wiser and more trustworthy.*
*A young man could be reminded of this same truth with a simple
cartoon drawing of the ring in the pig's snout. Frame the picture
and hang it up in his room. (If you think you can't draw, cut out
some magazine pictures to paste together for this picture.)*

Pr. 22:14 Mouth of the strange woman is a deep pit.

Pr. 23:27 A harlot or seductress is a deep pit, a narrow well.
A deep pit is hard to get out of once you fall in.

Pr. 27:8 Man wandering from his place is like bird wandering from its
nest.
*What child reaches adulthood without discovering a little lost bird,
or a dead baby bird that has fallen from its nest? Use that
opportunity to help explain this truth. Leaving the home, and the
protection, that God has provided for us is always foolish and
dangerous, with inevitable results.*

Stories that illustrate the consequences of sexual sin:

David, II Sam. 11-23 David was idle, at home instead of out on the
battlefield when he sinned with Bathsheba. Led to lying, murder, loss
of honor, rebellion in his family. First committed adultery with his
eyes. His sin was not hidden.

Samson, Jg. 16 Years were given "to the cruel one" as he worked,
blind, at the grindstone. He didn't flee from temptation, and didn't
flee from the strange woman.
*Both David and Samson would have benefited from obeying the
command to avoid the* <u>*appearance*</u> *of evil.*

Lot, in Sodom and Gomorrah, Gen. 19 Lot fled the city. Cities were
destroyed by fire.

Potiphar's wife and Joseph, Gen. 39:7-20 Joseph's wisdom
protected him from temptation. He <u>fled</u> from Potiphar's wife.

Eli's sons, I Sam. 2:22 Not disciplined correctly. They, <u>and their
father</u> were killed.

Verses to memorize:

1 Cor. 6:19-20 What? know ye not that your body is the temple of the Holy Ghost which is in you, which ye have of God, and ye are not your own? For ye are bought with a price: therefore glorify God in your body, and in your spirit, which are God's.

1 Cor. 10:13 No temptation has overtaken you except such as is common to man; but God is faithful, who will not allow you to be tempted beyond what you are able, but with the temptation will also make the way of escape, that you may be able to bear it. (NKJV)

Gal. 5:24 And those who are Christ's have crucified the flesh with its passions and desires. (NKJV)

Rom. 6:14 For sin shall not have dominion over you: for ye are not under the law, but under grace.

Ps. 119:9 How can a young man cleanse his way? By taking heed according to Your word. (NKJV)

Ps. 119:11 Your word I have hidden in my heart, that I might not sin against You! (NKJV)

Job 31:1 I have made a covenant with my eyes; why then should I look upon a young woman? (NKJV)

Ec. 12:14 For God will bring every work into judgment, including every secret thing, whether good or evil. (NKJV)

1 Tim. 5:22 Keep thyself pure.

Sinful Desires and Thought Life

(See also Envy, Covetousness, Immorality, Foolish
Unclean Speech, Hatred, Bitterness)

General information and commandments about this sin:

Rom. 16:19 Be simple regarding evil. Be wise regarding good.
*Don't expose a child's mind to details of evil. Newspapers,
magazines, newscasts, overheard conversations, even well-meaning
relatives and friends, can fill a child's mind with sin-laden
information.*

Rom. 13:14 Make no provision for the flesh. Put on Christ.
*Don't give your child opportunities to fill his mind with sinful
information. Fill his mind with Scripture.*

Js. 1:14 Man is tempted when he is drawn by his own lusts and
enticed.
Sinful thoughts lead to sinful actions.

Pr. 6:16-19 God hates a heart that thinks up wicked imaginations.

Matt. 5:28 Lusting after a woman is adultery in the heart.

Mk. 7:21-23 Comes from within.
*Replace these sinful thoughts of the heart with Scripture. Memorize,
meditate, study the Word together.*

Pr. 23:7 As we think in our heart, so are we.
*Encourage your children to become godly men and women as you
train them in the habit of Bible study, memorizing and prayer.*

I Jn. 2:16 Lust of flesh, lust of eyes, pride of life are not of the
Father.

I Tim. 5:22 Keep pure.

What happens, or should happen, to this person:

Pr. 6:23-25 Commandments, law, reproofs of instruction keep one
from strange woman.
*Study the Bible together, and train the child in the habit of diligent
personal Bible study.*
*Be faithful and bold in instructing a child and in confronting him
when you suspect secret sin in his life.*

II Tim. 2:22 Flee youthful lusts.

Teach your child to run from evil. Help him understand that he is not invulnerable, and that the easiest way to resist temptation is to run away from it.

Eph. 4:22 Put off the old man.
Draw two simple pictures, one of a "new man" and one of an "old man." Set them up on a shelf in the child's room. Which one is in control from day to day? Set that picture over the top of the other one.
Or make a paper doll from a picture of the child. Then make "old man" and "new man" clothes to put on the paper doll. Put clothes on the doll that are appropriate for the way the child is acting that day.

Tit. 2:12 Live soberly, righteously, godly.

Eph. 6:10-17 Put on the armor of God.
This armor is all defensive and protective in nature. The only offensive weapon listed is the sword, God's Word. It is our weapon against sin and temptation.

I Pet. 2:11 Fleshly lusts war against the soul.
Study the "Armor of God" in Eph. 6. Help your child learn to use his "armor" against temptation.
Make a set of armor for playtimes. Talk about each piece's meaning and function.

II Cor. 10:4-5 Use mighty weapons of God to bring thoughts into captivity to obedience.

Js. 4:7 Submit to God, resist the devil.
We cannot resist Satan by ourselves; we must submit to God.

Phil. 4:8-9 Think on these things: whatever is true, honest, just, pure, lovely, of good report, of virtue, of praise.
Design projects for your child that will encourage him to think on these good things listed above. Outline Bible study projects, reading assignments, writing assignments, works of service for others, etc. that will help the child develop a wholesome and pure thought life.

Js. 1:14-15 Temptation is the result of being drawn away by own lusts. Lust results in sin, sin results in death.
Sinful actions begin with sinful thoughts. Be diligent in guarding your child's thought life as much as possible.

Ps. 101:3 Set no evil thing before eyes.
Protect your child by not exposing him to visual temptations. Be sensitive to what you allow into your home via reading material and media. Avoid all <u>appearance</u> of evil, even if you think something is

harmless.
Teach your child to look away from those things that he sees which are temptations to him.

Ps. 119:37 Turn away eyes from vanity.

Job 31:1 Make a covenant with the eyes.
For a child who is struggling with visual temptation, work together in writing out an actual covenant. List the consequences the child could suffer for entertaining sinful temptations that come to him through his eyes. List the blessings that could result from resisting these types of temptation. Have the child sign the covenant, and then hold him accountable to it.

Heb. 4:12 The Word of God discerns the thoughts and intents of the heart.
Pray for God's Word to do its work in the child's heart. Pray for his sensitive spirit and obedient will.

Ps. 119:11 Hide God's Word in heart.
Be faithful in leading your child in memorizing Scripture.

Ps. 119:59 Think on God's ways, turn feet to testimonies.
Train child to immediately replace sinful thoughts with portions of God's Word. This requires faithful memorizing, review, and meditation on Scripture, so that it is quickly available for the Holy Spirit's use in the child's heart.

Rom. 12:1-2 Present bodies living sacrifices to God. Be transformed by the renewing of your mind.
Help the child develop a daily habit of offering himself as a "sacrifice" to the Lord. Commit his thoughts daily to God.
Help him renew his mind through prayer and Bible reading.

The blessings of a pure thought life:

Matt. 5:8 The pure in heart will see God.

Ps. 24:3-4 The pure in heart will ascend the hill of the Lord and stand in the holy place.
Work out a goal for a child who is struggling with his thought life. When he begins to gain real control over it, take him out for a special time with one or both parents -- a dinner out, a basketball game, an evening of bowling together, a shopping trip -- whatever you both would enjoy as a time of special fellowship and fun together.

Stories that illustrate the consequences of sinful thoughts:

David, II Sam. 11:1-5 Led to adultery and murder.

Amnon, II Sam. 13:1-20 Led to rape, and then to his murder.

Potiphar's wife, Gen. 39:7-12 Did not flee from her lusts. Kept pursuing, which led to injustice in Joseph's life.

(See also stories listed in chapters on hatred, envy and covetousness.)

Verses to memorize:

Rom. 16:19b But I want you to be wise in what is good, and simple concerning evil. (NKJV)

I Thess. 5:22 Abstain from all appearance of evil.

Rom. 12:1-2 I beseech you therefore, brethren, by the mercies of God, that ye present your bodies a living sacrifice, holy, acceptable unto God, which is your reasonable service. And be not conformed to this world: but be ye transformed by the renewing of your mind, that ye may prove what is that good, and acceptable, and perfect, will of God.

Job 31:1 "I have made a covenant with my eyes; why then should I look upon a young woman? (NKJV)

James 1:14 But each one is tempted when he is drawn away by his own desires and enticed. (NKJV)

1 Th. 4:7 For God hath not called us unto uncleanness, but unto holiness.

James 4:7 Submit yourselves therefore to God. Resist the devil, and he will flee from you.

Ps. 51:10 Create in me a clean heart, O God, and renew a steadfast spirit within me. (NKJV)

Ps. 19:14 Let the words of my mouth, and the meditation of my heart, be acceptable in thy sight, O LORD, my strength, and my redeemer.

Ps. 119:11 Thy word have I hid in mine heart, that I might not sin against thee.

1 Tim. 5:22b Keep thyself pure.

1 Pet 2:11   Beloved, I beg you as sojourners and pilgrims, abstain

from fleshly lusts which war against the soul. (NKJV)

Ps. 139:23 Search me, O God, and know my heart: try me, and know my thoughts.

Immodesty

(See also Overconcern for Beauty, Immorality,
Sinful Desires)

General information and commandments about this sin:

Tit. 2:5 Should be discreet and chaste.
The father, guided by Scripture, should establish this standard, just as the husband will later in a daughter's life.

I Tim. 2:9 Adorn in modest apparel with propriety and moderation; not with braided hair, gold, pearls, costly clothing, but with good works.
Keep a child, especially a daughter, in this case, busy with <u>good works</u>. Devise projects of service to others, train her in domestic skills and duties.
Study Proverbs 31 together, and use the virtuous woman as a model of good works to pattern your daughter's activities after.

I Pet. 3:3-4 Beauty is not outward arranging of hair, wearing gold and fine apparel, but is the hidden person of the heart, a gentle and quiet spirit.
Train a daughter in Bible study and prayer. Occupy her time with activities that will help to build her character.
Be consistent, as parents, in expecting a gentle and quiet spirit of submission from your daughter. Cultivate this inner beauty in her so that she will not feel the need to draw attention to herself with immodest actions and clothing.
Teach your daughter to exercise a gentle and quiet spirit when relating to her siblings and friends.
Encourage (or require?) her to spend more time in Bible study and prayer than she does on her personal appearance.

Matt. 5:27-28 To cause man to look after her in lust is to cause him to commit adultery.
Teach daughters about man's tendency to be tempted by what he <u>sees</u>. Help her realize that she is causing a young man to fall by tempting him with her appearance.
Help your daughters develop the inner persons of their hearts. Direct them in good works.
Impose standards of dress for a daughter; it will protect her and will be good practice for her learning to submit to her husband later in life.
A standard of dress imposed on a young man can also teach him proper submission to God's authority, while protecting him from

temptation and sin.

I Cor. 11:15 Long hair is given to woman as a covering, her glory.
It seems that the least we can assume from this verse is that a woman's hair should be longer than the man's.

Isa. 3:16-24 Overdoing of bodily ornaments is associated with haughtiness.
Examine your child for indications of pride in his life. Deal with that sin as a way of getting to the root of a problem with immodesty.

Deut. 22:5 Levitical law forbade women to wear men's clothing.
Although this may not be law now, there certainly seems to be some wisdom in girls wearing clothes that are different than boys' clothes.

Ec. 7:26 A woman whose heart is snare and nets is more bitter than death.
Immodesty is often a manifestation of a heart that is desiring to snare others.

I Thess. 4:1-9 Be consecrated, abstain from sexual vice, manage own body in purity and honor. Do not use it in the passion of lust. We are called to holiness.
Teach your child to manage his body in purity and honor by covering it properly, and by controlling his body in a discreet manner.
Holiness and consecration can be demonstrated by our modest behavior and appearance.

I Thess. 5:22 Abstain from all <u>appearance</u> of evil.
Immodest behavior and appearance can lead others to believe we are different than we are, even if our intention is not sinful.
Help your child see the way he comes across to others. He may not be aware of his actions. Review your daughter's flirtacious conversation with her, and help her see the implications of her behavior. Help a son understand that what he says can deeply affect a young lady's response to him.
Lead your children to a place of resolve, where he commits himself to building others up with his actions and appearance, rather than becoming a stumblingblock and source of temptation to others.

Rom. 12:1-2 Should present our bodies as living sacrifices to God. Should not be conformed to the world's standards, but transformed by the renewing of our minds.
Encourage your child to daily offer his body as a sacrifice to the Lord.
Help him to examine his life, and to discern if he is being transformed by God and His Word, or if he is being conformed to

the world's sinful standard. Why does he dress the way he does? Why does she act the way she does? Is it because of a desire to please God, or a desire to please self and the world?

Pr. 6:25 Lust not after her beauty. Don't be taken by her eyelids.
Man is <u>commanded</u> to stay away from the immodest woman.

Rom. 14:12-13 Will give an account to God. Don't put a stumblingblock or occasion to fall in brothers' way.
Will your child be able to give an honest account to God for his actions and appearance?

Rom. 14:23 If a person doubts and still eats, he is damned because he doesn't eat of faith.
This principle can be applied to dress -- if there is any question about wearing a particular garment or type of clothing, then <u>don't</u>.

To what is the immodest person likened:

Pr. 11:22 Beautiful woman without discretion is like a gold ring in a pig's snout.
(See ideas for this verse in chapters on "Immorality" and "Brawling Woman.")

Stories that illustrate modesty and immodesty:

Vashti, Es. 1:11-22 Was removed from the throne.

Bathsheba, II Sam. 11:2-5,27; 12:9,10 Her immodesty was a temptation to David, and led to adultery, murder, and destruction within the king's household.

Verses to memorize:

Matt. 5:27-28 Ye have heard that it was said by them of old time, Thou shalt not commit adultery: but I say unto you, that whosoever looketh on a woman to lust after her hath committed adultery with her already in his heart.

1 Thess. 5:22 Abstain from all appearance of evil.

Titus 2:5 To be discreet, chaste, keepers at home, good, obedient to their own husbands, that the word of God be not blasphemed.

Rom. 12:1-2 I beseech you therefore, brethren, by the mercies of God, that ye present your bodies a living sacrifice, holy, acceptable unto God, which is your reasonable service. And be not conformd to this world: but be ye transformed by the renewing of your mind, that ye may prove what is that good, and acceptable, and perfect, will of God.

Wastefulness/Extravagance/Carelessness

(See also Haste, Poor Manners)

General information and commandments about this sin:

Pr. 12:27 Is lazy. Doesn't roast his prey.

Pr. 21:20 Fool squanders his belongings.
Pr. 19:10 also says that luxury is not fitting for a fool.
Take away possessions of a child who is wasteful and neglectful.
If he is not taking care of a particular toy or item of clothing,
  take it away.

Deut. 22:1-4 Regarding others' possessions when you find them out of place:
Don't ignore; return it.
Child should learn to exercise initiative in returning an item that he
  finds out of place, or that has been lost.
Don't know owner, or he is not with you; keep it for him until he looks for it.
"Finders keepers, losers weepers," is not the rule here. The child
  should take an item into safekeeping until he locates the owner, or
  until the owner finds him.
Don't hide yourself; help.
A child needs to learn to help when he sees another in need of help.
  (i.e. when another child spills all his crayons he can help pick them
  up.)

I Cor. 4:2 Steward must be faithful.

Pr. 18:9 One who is slack in in his work is brother to one who destroys.
Laziness and neglect lead to waste and destruction.
Fine a child, from his spending money, for carelessness. (i.e. If he
  leaves his socks all over the house, fine him a certain amount for
  each sock you find.)

Ex. 21:29-34 Regarding an animal with a past history of hurting others, which has again injured someone:
Destroy animal and fine owner.
Take away the item and levy a fine from the child's spending money.
  (i.e. If child leaves scissors out and baby gets ahold of them, take
  away the privilege of using the scissors, and collect a fine from the
  child.)
If person digs a hole and does not cover it, and animal falls in and dies, the person should pay for the animal.

This principle can be applied to areas of neglect that cause injury to others. (i.e. If a child leaves a toy on the step and someone falls on it and sprains his ankle, the child should help pay for the medical care from his spending money. If there are no medical costs, the child should perform the duties of the injured person -- his chores, etc.)
Punishments differ according to whether the incident is accidental, or if it has occurred in the past. These are punishments that deal with carelessness that causes injury to others.

Deut. 22:8 · Put battlement on roof to avoid blood to your house.
Take preventative measures to help avoid injuries to others. Teach this principle by example in your own household, and enforce it with your children. They need to learn to take precautions in order to protect others.

What happens, or should happen, to the careless person:

Pr. 21:17 Love pleasure, will be a poor man. Love wine and oil, will be poor.
Take away possessions from the wasteful, extravagant person.
Levy fines or require restitution to owner of ruined items.

Lk. 15:12-14 Wastefulness and extravagance lead to poverty.

Pr. 21:20 Foolish swallows up treasure and oil.

Pr. 13:22 Will prevent one from leaving an inheritance.
Deny deposit into long-term savings.
Levy fine from long-term savings.

Pr. 31:20 Will prevent one from helping the poor and needy.
This hinders us from serving others the way God wants us to.

Matt. 25:29 What little he has will be taken away.
Deny possessions, earnings, privileges.

The blessings of frugality:

Pr. 13:22 Leaves inheritance for children's children.
Make deposit into child's long term savings.
Establish a fund into which you can deposit money for your children's children.

Pr. 21:20 Treasure and oil is in the dwelling of the wise.

Give the child a "treasure," as a reward for his frugality -- an ounce of silver, a special gift, a gift certificate to a favorite store.
Give "oil" to the frugal child -- perfume, bath oil, a case of oil for the young driver, etc.

Pr. 31:20 Enables one to help the poor and needy.
Make a special deposit into the child's charity savings. Let him decide on a special project or family to give the money to, or a special purchase to make for a needy family or project.

Pr. 31:27 Doesn't eat the bread of idleness.

Matt. 25:29 Will be given more.
Entrust more privileges, possessions, and responsibilities to the child.

Stories that illustrate the consequences of wastefulness:

Prodigal son, Luke 15 Led to poverty, shame, loneliness, humility.

Foolish virgins, Matt. 25:1-13 Unprepared for bridegroom.

Foolish servant, Matt. 25: 14-30 Buried his talent, lost what he had.

Stories that illustrate the blessings of frugality:

Joseph in Egypt, Gen. 41:48-57 Prepared for famine to come, saved nation, and his own family, from starvation. Was made ruler over Egypt.

Jesus feeding crowds, Matt. 14:20, 15:37 Gathered leftovers.

Proverbs 31 woman

Verses to memorize:

Pr. 12:27 The lazy man does not roast what he took in hunting, but diligence is man's precious possession. (NKJV)

Matt. 25:29 For to everyone who has, more will be given, and he will have abundance; but from him who does not have, even what he has will be taken away. (NKJV)

Pr. 21:20 There is desirable treasure, and oil in the dwelling of the wise, but a foolish man squanders it. (NKJV)

Pr. 18:9 He who is slothful in his work Is a brother to him who is a great destroyer. (NKJV)

Drunkenness
(See also Gluttony)

(Most of this information will hopefully be for preventative instruction, not for actually dealing with children who are drunkards. These same principles could also apply to drug abuse problems.)

General information and commandments about this sin:

Pr. 20:1 Arouses brawling, not wise.

Pr. 31:4+ Not for kings and princes.

Pr. 23:20 Be not among winebibbers.
Do not allow friendships with young people who drink.

What happens, or should happen, to the drunkard:

Pr. 20:1 Arouses brawling.

Pr. 23:33 Leads to more sin.
The drunkard is controlled by something other than the Holy Spirit.

Gal. 5:19-21 Won't inherit kingdom of God.
Deny child's part in family inheritance.
Deny deposit into long-term savings.

Eph. 5:18 Dissipation. Be filled with the Holy Spirit.
Pray for the Holy Spirit's work in the child's life.

I Cor. 5:11 Do not eat with him.
Do not associate with other young people who drink.

Isa. 28:7 Err in vision, stumble in judgment.
Point out when this happens.
Do not protect a child from the consequences of his errors in judgment.

Isa. 5:22,23 Pervert justice.

Pr. 31:5 Forget law, pervert justice.
Drunkenness affects perception. A drunkard will not uphold God's law in his own life, or apply it in the society around him.

Pr. 21:17 Love wine and oil, will not be rich.
Take away spending privileges.

Pr. 23:21, 21:17 Comes to poverty.

Do not give the child money.
Limit what is available to him from his earnings.

Pr. 23:29 Has woe, sorrow, contentions, complaints, wounds without cause, red eyes, see strange things, utter perverse things.
Affected emotionally, mentally, and physically.

Pr. 23:35 Will seek wine again.

1 Cor. 5:11 Not to keep company with a Christian who is a drunkard.
Do not allow the child to associate with young people who are drunkards, especially those who profess to be believers.

Hosea 4:11 Enslaves the heart.
The drunkard serves a master other than the Lord Jesus Christ.
Discuss the child's actions when he is under the influence of alcohol. Do they demonstrate control over himself, or enslavement to a stronger influence?

Pr. 23:31 Look not on the cup.
Stay away; don't even <u>look</u> at it!

Deut. 21:20,21 Glutton and drunkard were stoned according to Mosaic judicial law.
Were made a public example.

Isa. 19:14 Err in works.
Perception is distorted; actions are wrong.

To what is overdrinking likened:

Pr. 23:32 At last wine bites like serpent, stings like viper.
Concealed, but fatal.

Pr. 23:34 Like one who lies down in the midst of the sea.
What will happen to him?

Pr. 23:34 Like one who lies on top of a mast.
A precarious place for a nap!

Stories that illustrate the consequences of drunkenness:

Lot, Gen. 19:33 Caused him to err in vision, participate in incest, and to generate offspring who would be enemies of the Israelites.

Nabal, I Sam. 25:36 Oblivious to the happenings in his own

household.

Amnon, II Sam. 13:28 Dulled senses, judgment, led to his death.

Elah, I Kgs. 16:9 Dulled senses, defenseless against his murderers.

Benhadad, I Kgs. 20:16-21 Error in judgment, led to defeat in battle.

Ahasuerus, Est. 1:9-22 Perverted justice, poor judgment.

Verses to memorize:

Pr. 20:1 Wine is a mocker, strong drink is a brawler, and whoever is led astray by it is not wise. (NKJV)

Eph. 5:18 And do not be drunk with wine, in which is dissipation; but be filled with the Spirit.

Pr. 23:21 For the drunkard and the glutton will come to poverty, and drowsiness will clothe a man with rags.

Lying/Deceit/Dishonesty

(See also False Witness, Gossip, Flattery)

General information and commandments about this sin:

Mk. 7:21-23 Comes from the heart.

Pr. 6:19, Pr. 12:22 Is an abomination to God.

Ps. 62:4 Bless with mouth, curse inwardly, is hypocritical.

Pr. 13:5 Righteous hate lying.
  Do not tolerate dishonesty in <u>any form</u> with your child.
  Do not live dishonestly in <u>any way</u>, as an example to your child.

Pr. 14:8 Folly of fools is deceit.

Pr. 17:7 Lying lips don't become a prince.
  Take away leadership responsibilities from a lying child, inside and
    outside the home.
  Do not grant the lying child leadership over his siblings in various
    tasks.

Pr. 19:22 Poor man is better than liar.

Isa. 57:11 Motivated by fear.
  Study fear together. How can fear be a motivation for lying?

Pr. 10:18 Hides hatred.

Jn. 8:44-45 Satan is the father of lies.
  Ask the child, "Who do you want as your Father? What does Satan
    give you as his child? What does God give you as His child?"

Pr. 26:28 Hates those it afflicts.

Pr. 17:4 Listens to spiteful tongue.

Pr. 21:6 Gaining treasure through lying is the fleeting fantasy of
  those who seek death.

Pr. 29:12 If a ruler pays no attention to liars, all his servants become
  wicked.
  We parents must discern when a child is being dishonest, and
    discipline him consistently, or dishonesty will infect the entire
    family.

Deut. 25:13-16 Unjust weights and measures are an abomination.
  Insist on complete honesty in all transactions. Set a flawless
    example of this.

Eph. 4:25 Put away lying.

Perhaps some sort of ceremony could symbolize this commitment. i.e. Draw a simple picture of lips that are speaking lies. Talk about the sin of lying. Read these verses. Pray for God's strength to overcome the temptation to lie, and then throw the drawing into a fire, or the garbage can.

What happens, or should happen, to the liar:

Pr. 3:3 Bind mercy and truth around neck. Write them on table of heart.
Make a necklace of beads of different colors. Have each color be a reminder of a particular verse the child has memorized to help arm him against the temptation to lie. Teach him to think through each of these verses when he is tempted to lie.
Give a locket to the child, with a Scripture reference of an appropriate verse written inside.
Inscribe the inside of a sterling silver ring with an appropriate Bible verse or reference.

Lev. 6:1-5 Lying about the possessions of others; should return item, plus one-fifth its value.
Examples:
Lying about object entrusted to him.
Lying about a lost object that he has found.
Gaining an item from someone through deceit and trickery.
The child needs to return the item, and pay a fine of 1/5 its value, or work an equivalent amount of time to pay that amount.

Rev. 21:8 Hell.

Rev. 21:27 Will not enter holy city.
Deny communion to a habitually lying child.
Deny the child's part in family inheritance until he overcomes the sin of lying.

Pr. 13:11 Wealth will be diminished.
Fine the child for lying.
Deny pay for work.

Pr. 26:26 Wicked revealed before congregation.
Conduct a formal "hearing" and issue a sentence. There are times where this might be appropriate to do with the entire family present.

Ps. 5:6 God destroys.

Pr. 12:19 Liars are but for a moment.

Ps. 55:23 Will not live out half their days.
Shorten a child's day by limiting free time, denying play time, giving extra chores and duties, going to bed early, taking an extra or longer nap.

Pr. 19:5 Won't escape.
Pray that God will help you discern when a child is lying, and that He will clearly discipline the child when you are unable to discern the truth.
Consistently discipline any form of dishonesty. Do not be tempted to overlook "white" lies. Anything less than the truth is a lie.

1 Pet. 3:10-12 God's face will be against the liar.
Communicate to the child that dishonesty affects the fellowship you have with him. It affects your trust in him, and requires you to discipline him over and over.
Cancel a special outing you may have planned with the child, when you discover him in a lie, and sense a lack of true repentance.

Ps. 101:7 Will not tarry in God's sight.
Send the child out of your presence when you know he is lying to you. Let him think for awhile, and then go in to instruct and discipline him.

Ps. 63:11 Mouth will be stopped.

Ps. 31:18 Put to silence.
Limit the child's speech. Don't allow him to offer excuses, argue with you, or debate his case while witnesses are speaking.
Cut the child off, challenge him in the midst of an obvious lie.

To what is the sin of lying likened:

Rom. 3:13 Open sepulchre.

Jer. 5:27 House full of deceit, cage full of birds.
Visit a pet store and watch a cage that is full of birds. How peaceful is it in that cage? What do the rest of the birds do if one becomes frightened and flies about? Can they escape?

Jer. 9:8 Like an arrow shot out.
Shoot arrows together. Aim at the target, pull back the arrow, let it go, and try to call the arrow back. Does it work? A lie cannot be recalled; its damage is already done as soon as it is uttered.

Ps. 52:2 Sharp razor.

Holds the potential for extreme pain, violence, and destruction.

Ps. 55:21 Words are smoother than butter, but are actually drawn swords.
Dishonest words may be pleasant, and may express what the listener wants to hear, but they are actually destructive weapons that harm those who hear.

Hosea 10:4 Judged like hemlock in furrows.
Weed the garden or flower bed together. Why can't you leave the weeds in? What happens when you do? What happens to the weeds after they are pulled up? Do you plant them in a new place?

Ps. 120:2-4 Sharp arrows, coals of juniper.
Have destructive potential.
Watch coals in a barbecue. How does one coal affect the next? Is the heat of a coal always visible?

Pr. 20:17 Bread of deceit is sweet. Turns to gravel.
(See ideas for this verse in chapter on "Theft.")

Jer. 9:3 Tongue bent like bow.
Ready to shoot arrows.

I Tim. 4:2 Conscience seared with hot iron.
No sensitivity to God's prompting.

Pr. 25:14 Clouds and wind without rain.
What happens to the crops that need watering when the clouds blow over without releasing any of their rain?
We parents need to remember this proverb. It is easy, with very honorable intentions, to tell a child that we're going to do things, or to say, "We'll see," without ever following through on our word. This sets an example of dishonesty before our children, and affects their trust in and attitude toward us.

Pr. 26:23 Earthenware covered with silver dross.
Compare sterling silver and worn silverplate.
Compare a silver ounce coin and a current coin with its "sandwich" of copper.
Paint a penny with silver paint. Is it a silver coin now?

Stories that illustrate the consequences of dishonesty:

Adam and Eve, Gen. 3:12,13 Blaming, making excuses
Cain, Gen. 4:9 Covering sin.

Satan, Gen. 3:1-5 Deceit, misled, contradicting God's Word.

Abraham, Gen. 12:11-19, 20:2 Lied regarding Sarah, God protected her.

Jacob, Gen. 25:29-33 Deceit, trickery.

Isaac, Gen. 26:7-10 Lied about wife.

Rebekah and Jacob, Gen. 27:6-24 Deceived Isaac, stole blessing, led to division of family.

Joseph's brothers, Gen. 37:29-35 Cruelly deceived father.
  Notice the pattern of dishonesty in these descendants of Abraham!

Laban, Gen. 29 Violated contract, deceived.

Gibeonites, Josh. 9:3-15 Trickery, spared but made slaves.

Delilah, Jg. 16:4-20 Conspiring, accepted bribe, led to Samson's ruin.

Ananias and Sapphira, Acts 5:1-10 Lied and were killed.

Saul, I Sam. 15:1-20 Blamed people, lost kingdom.

Peter, Matt. 26:69-75, Mk. 14:68-71, Lk. 22:56-62, Jn. 18:25-27 Denied Jesus out of fear of man.

The blessings of honesty:

I Pet. 3:10 Love life, see good days.
  Allow the child to have a friend over for the day.
  No homeschool for a day!
  Spend a special day out together.
  Declare a special day of honor at home for the honest child. Spend the day doing things that the child especially enjoys.

Ps. 15:1-2 Abide in God's holy tabernacle, holy hill.

Ps. 24:3-4 Will ascend hill of the Lord, stand in His holy place.
  Take the child for a special campout or ski trip.
  Arrange a special date with Mom or Dad to go shopping, fishing, to a baseball game, etc.

Pr. 12:19, 22 Truthful lip established forever, God's delight.
  Make a special deposit into child's long-term savings.
  Pass on a special heirloom to the child.

Pr. 29:14 The throne of the king who faithfully judges the poor will be established forever.

We, as parents, need to faithfully "judge the poor" in our household.

Pr. 16:13 Delight of kings.
Proclaim the child "Prince-for-a-Day." Let him wear a crown and robe (if he likes that sort of thing) and be his servants for the day!
Go to work with Daddy.
Have a family parade in honor of the truthful child.
Give a gift of special clothing.
Grant the child a special privilege or favor.

Pr. 3:3-4 Favor and high esteem in sight of God and man.
Award the child with a "Truthful Lips" certificate or trophy.
Fly the child's special name flag from the front porch.

Deut. 25:15 Days lengthened.
Later bedtime, no nap, allow to sleep later in morning, shorter school day.

Pr. 28:13 Will have mercy.
Reduce punishment if truth is initially confessed.

Pr. 16:13 King's love.
Write a special letter, commending the child for his honesty.
Take the child on a special outing or give a special gift.

Deut. 16:20 Inherit land God promised.
Deposit into long-term savings.
Grant a special portion of inheritance or a family heirloom.
Give child money toward the purchase of a parcel of land.

Stories that illustrate honesty:

Jacob returning money, Gen. 43:12

Overseers of temple repairs, II Kgs. 12:15, 22:4-7

Temple treasurer, Neh. 13:13

Verses to memorize:

Ps. 51:6 Behold, thou desirest truth in the inward parts: and in the hidden part thou shalt make me to know wisdom.

Pr. 12:22 Lying lips are abomination to the LORD: but they that deal truly are his delight.

Eph. 4:25 Wherefore putting away lying, speak every man truth with his neighbour: for we are members one of another.

Col. 3:9 Do not lie to one another, since you have put off the old man with his deeds. (NKJV)

Deut. 16:20 You shall follow what is altogether just, that you may live and inherit the land which the LORD your God is giving you. (NKJV)

Ps. 119:29 Remove from me the way of lying: and grant me thy law graciously.

Ps. 19:14 Let the words of my mouth, and the meditation of my heart, be acceptable in thy sight, O LORD, my strength, and my redeemer.

False Witness

(See also Lying, Gossip/Slander/Tattletale)

General information and commandments about this sin:

Pr. 6:19, 14:25, 14:5 God hates. Speaks lies.

Ex. 20:16 The 9th commandment, should not bear false witness against neighbor.

Matt. 15:19 Comes from the heart.

Pr. 19:28 Scorns justice.
A child who is a false witness scorns the system of justice within your family.

Lk. 16:10 Unfaithful in little, unfaithful in much.
Beware of <u>any</u> untruth.

Zech. 8:17 God hates.

I Kgs. 21:13 Sons of Satan.
What sort of inheritance do we get from Satan?

Ps. 52:3,4 Loves evil more than good, lying more than righteousness, devouring words.

Laws concerning witnesses:

Num. 35:30, Deut. 17:6, Deut. 19:15, Jn. 8:17, II Cor. 13:1, I Tim. 5:19, Heb. 10:28 Two witnesses are necessary for conviction.
Circumstantial evidence can function as one of these witnesses.

Deut. 13:19, Deut. 17:5-7, Acts 7:58 Witness was required to cast the first stone in execution.

What happens, or should happen, to the false witness:

Pr. 21:28 Will perish.

Deut. 19:15-20 Do to him what he thought would be done to the person he falsely witnessed against.
Give the same punishment to the false witness as you would have given to the child who was falsely accused, had you believed the witness. (i.e. If the false witness accuses another child of stealing a cookie from the cookie jar, the <u>false witness</u> should be disciplined

for the theft, as well as the real thief when discovered. If the false witness was the thief, then he would be doubly punished, once as the thief and once as the false witness.)

Zech. 5:4 Curse will enter house and consume it.
 Loss of inheritance.
 Deny deposit into long-term savings account.
 Take away possessions, privileges.

Pr. 19:5 Will not go unpunished.
 Be consistent in disciplining this sin. Do not overlook it.

Ps. 52:5 Destroy forever.

To what is the false witness likened:

Pr. 25:18 Maul, sword, sharp arrow.
 Destroys reputation, mangles character, leaves scars, wounds plans and interests.

Pr. 52:2 Sharp razor.
 Destructive.

Stories that illustrate the consequences of a false witness:

Doeg against Ahimelech, I Sam. 21:1,2 and I Sam. 22:8-18 Led to Ahimelech's execution by Saul. (See also Psalm 52.)

Against Naboth, I Kgs. 21:13, 21:19-29 "Men of Belial" conspired against him under Jezebel's direction. Led to injustice and Naboth's execution. Elijah prophesied that dogs would lick Ahab's blood, posterity would be taken away. Jezebel would be eaten by dogs. (See I Kgs. 22:38 and II Kgs. 9:30-37 for fulfillment of these prophecies.) Ahab repented and evil came in his sons' days instead of his.

Against Jesus, Matt. 26:59-61 Led to the injustice of His crucifixion.

Against Stephen, Acts. 6:8-13 Led to unjust execution.

Potiphar's wife against Joseph, Gen. 39:7-20 Led to unjust imprisonment.

Korah against Moses, Num. 16:1-3,13 Led to rebellion amongst people, and then to the death of all rebels.

Verses to memorize:

Pr. 19:5 A false witness shall not be unpunished, and he that speaketh lies shall not escape.

Ex. 20:16 Thou shalt not bear false witness against thy neighbour.

Pr. 19:28 An ungodly witness scorneth judgment: and the mouth of the wicked devoureth iniquity.

Gossip/Slander/Tattletale

(See also False Witness, Lying, Unkind Speech, Meddling/Busybody)

General information and commandments about this sin:

Lev. 19:16 Forbidden.

I Tim. 4:7 Reject wives' tales. Exercise to godliness.
Set example of this in your home. Do not gossip about others, slander your pastor, employer, etc.

Pr. 11:13, Pr. 20:19 Talebearer reveals secrets.
Teach your child to not entrust secrets and private information to another child who gossips.

Pr. 10:18 One who spreads slander is a fool.

Pr. 16:27 Digs up evil.
The gossip looks for evil. Teach the child to look for the good in a person.

Pr. 11:9 Hypocrite with mouth destroys neighbor.
Hypocrite has a destructive influence in church, friendships, etc.

Pr. 16:28, 17:9 Separates best of friends, sows strife.
Can ruin friendships.

Pr. 18:21 Death and life in power of tongue.
Draw a picture of this concept: draw a tongue with lines going to drawings of symbols of death and symbols of life. Write this verse under the drawing, and post it in a prominent place in your home.

Pr. 25:9 Debate case with neighbor himself, not to someone else.
Teach the child to <u>always</u> talk to the person he has a complaint against, and <u>not</u> to talk to other people about the problem.

Js. 1:26 Bridle not tongue, is deceitful and religion is in vain.

Rom. 1:28, 30 Is part of reprobate mind.
Gossip is listed right along with murder and fornication.

Js. 4:11 Speak evil of brother in judging, speak evil of law and judge law. Not a doer of the law. God is only lawgiver.
God is judge; we aren't.

Titus 2:3 Older women are not to be slanderers.
Call your daughter's attention to godly older women in the church. Develop friendships with them, and learn from them.

I Tim. 5:13 Result of idleness.
Keep the child who gossips <u>busy</u>. Give him extra work to do. Design

projects of service to others.

Pr. 11:9 Hypocrite slanders.
See chapter on "Hypocrisy."

II Pet. 2:10 One who speaks evil of dignities is presumptuous and self-willed.
Do not allow slander of authorities.
Set an example of this in your home.

Titus 3:2 Speak evil of no man.
Make this a policy in your home. Write the verse out and post it on the wall.

What happens, or should happen, to the gossip:

Pr. 25:10 One you gossip to may expose your shame.

Pr. 25:23 Brings angry countenance, like north wind brings rain.
Teach a child to consistently refuse to listen to gossip.
Set an example of this in your dealings with other adults, and in your dealings with your own children. Do not listen to their gossip and slander. Gently reprove them.

Pr. 26:20 Remove talebearer, removes strife.
Isolate the talebearer from the rest of the family until he is ready to confess and repent.
Do not allow association with another child who is a gossip. Explain this to the gossipping child and his parents.

Rom. 1:28+ Given over to a debased mind.

Ps. 101:5 Cut off.
Isolate the gossip, silence his tongue.

I Tim. 4:7 Exercise to godliness.
Write up a list of "exercises" for the gossip: portions of Scripture to study, verses to memorize, asking forgiveness of the victim of his gossip, going back to others he has gossipped to and confessing his sin, confessing his sin to God, confronting the person over an offense that he has gossipped over, praying, etc. Give him this list to go through each time he gossips.

Pr. 13:3 Open wide the mouth, leads to destruction.
Teach the child to keep his mouth closed when it doesn't need to be open.

Matt. 7:1-5 Remove plank from own eye.

Teach the child the habit of self-examination when he feels he has been wronged by another person. What part did he have in this problem?

Teach the child to pray before confronting another person about a wrong he feels has been committed against him.

Help the child see the "plank" in his eye when he comes to you with grievances against another. Do not listen to his report against another until he has examined his own part in the matter, and until he has talked to the person involved.

Matt. 18:15-17 Go to the person with whom you have a disagreement. If he refuses to repent, go back with witnesses. If he still refuses, go to the church.

Teach your child these steps. He should not come to you with most complaints against others (unless he has been physically injured and needs care) until he has directly talked to the person, and has returned again with witnesses. Then he should come to you, as the authority.

Note: Doorposts has a chart-and-book set which deals, in much more detail, with the problem of "tattletales" and children coming to parents with their offenses, instead of dealing with the people involved with the problem. Its title is "The Brother-Offended Checklist." (See ordering information at the back of this book.)

Ps. 15:1-3 Will not abide with God in tabernacle, holy hill.

Help the child understand that gossip breaks his fellowship with God.

Cancel plans you may have made with the child. Explain that this is to help him understand how his fellowship with God is affected by his sin of gossip and slander.

Pr. 20:19 Don't associate with flatterer, talebearer reveals secrets.

Teach your child about this type of person, and encourage him to not develop intimate friendships with gossips and flatterers.

Help your child see the truth of this verse when he is slandered by a "friend."

Matt. 12:36 Will give account of every idle word.

Take this seriously. Hold child responsible for what he says.

Tape record or write down a slanderous conversation you overhear the child participate in. Review it with him.

I Thess. 4:11 Be quiet, do own business, work with hands.

Give the child extra work when he gossips.

Design works of service they can perform for the victim of their gossip.

Phil. 4:8 Think on these things: whatever is true, honest, just, pure, lovely, of good report, or virtue and praise.

"This tongue wounds four at one stroke -- the backbiter himself, the object of his attack, the hearer, and the name of God."[1]

To what is gossip likened:

Pr. 12:18 Piercings of a sword.
Can't take back the stabbing of a sword. Leaves wounds and scars. We had a good chance to illustrate this proverb when Benjamin stabbed his thumb with a kitchen knife while cutting carrots. He has a good scar to help him remember this truth.

Pr. 16:27, Js. 3:5-6 Burning fire.
Fire destroys, spreads, causes permanent loss or damage. Watch a fire, or observe the aftereffects of a fire out of control. What does a fire do to its surroundings?

Pr. 18:8 Words inflict wounds to inmost parts of the body.
Gossip and slander affect the "vital organs" and deeply wound others.

Ec. 10:11, Ps. 140:3 Serpent biting, venom.
Strikes quickly, poisonous.

Pr. 26:20 Talebearer is to strife what wood is to a fire.
Try to keep a fire burning without adding any wood or other fuel. What happens?

Pr. 26:23 Potsherd covered with silver dross.
Is false. Paint a penny with silver paint. Is it a silver coin now? Compare sterling silver with worn silverplate. What do you see? Make a small pot out of clay. After it hardens, paint it silver. Now you have a silver pot, right?

Js. 3:4-5 Rudder on ship.
Steers the whole ship, determines its destination.

Ps. 52:2 Sharp razor.
Potential for destruction.

Blessings of resisting the temptation to gossip:

Ps. 15:1-3 Abide in God's tabernacle, holy hill, never moved.

Ps. 24:3-4 Ascend hill of the Lord, stand in holy place.

*Take the child out for a campout with Dad, or a weekend vacation
  with Mom.*
Go hiking or backpacking together.
Take a trip to the mountains together.
Go for a special ride together (bike, car, train, bus, etc.)
Give a young child a few trips around the backyard in the wagon.

I Pet.3:9-12 Love life, see good days.
*Grant the child a special day out; he chooses the location and
  activities.*
*Grant a special day of honor at home; he picks the menu, books to
  read, family activities, etc.*
Have a special friend over for the day.
No homeschool for the day.

Pr. 12:22 God's delight.

Pr. 22:11 King will be his friend.
*Appoint the child "Prince-for-a-Day." Give him a robe and crown to
  wear, and let the rest of the family serve him for the day.*
Have a family parade in honor of the child.
Have a special feast in honor of the child.
Give the child a gift of clothing or grant a special privilege.

Pr. 3:3-4 Favor and good understanding in sight of God and man.
Grant the child a special favor or privilege.
Take the child out for a special meal, dessert treat, sports event, etc.
Serve first at mealtime.
Give first choice in sharing situation.
Go along with parent when running errand.
*Write a special letter commending the child's righteous words and
  actions.*

Pr. 28:20 Will abound with blessings.
Bless the child with extra privileges, extra time with you, etc.

Stories that illustrate slander and responses to it:

Potiphar's wife, Gen. 39:14-18 Slandered Joseph, who was sent to
  prison. God still used it for good.

Sanballat and Tobiah with Nehemiah, Neh. 6 Tried to make
  Nehemiah fearful so that he would quit his work. Nehemiah prayed
  and trusted in God.

Zibah and Mephibosheth, II Sam. 16:3, 19:24-30 Slandered
  Mephibosheth to Daniel to gain his estate.

David's response to slander, Ps. 31:13-15, Ps. 35:21-28 Responded with prayer and rested in God's power and sovereignty.

Jesus' response to slander, Matt. 11:19, Mk. 14:64, Jn. 5:18, Jn. 8:48,52, Lk. 22:65, Lk. 23:5 Accused of gluttony, blasphemy and Sabbath-breaking. Didn't retaliate.

Verses to memorize:

Pr. 21:23 Whoever guards his mouth and tongue keeps his soul from troubles.(NKJV)

Pr. 11:13 A talebearer revealeth secrets: but he that is of a faithful spirit concealeth the matter.

Ps. 34:13 Keep your tongue from evil, and your lips from speaking deceit. (NKJV)

Eph. 4:31-32 Let all bitterness, wrath, anger, clamor, and evil speaking be put away from you, with all malice. And be kind to one another, tenderhearted, forgiving one another, just as God in Christ forgave you.

James 4:11 Speak not evil one of another, brethren. He that speaketh evil of his brother, and judgeth his brother, speaketh evil of the law, and judgeth the law: but if thou judge the law, thou art not a doer of the law, but a judge.

Ps. 141:3 Set a watch, O LORD, before my mouth; keep the door of my lips.

Job 27:6 My righteousness I hold fast, and will not let it go: my heart shall not reproach me so long as I live.

Acts 24:16 And herein do I exercise myself, to have always a conscience void of offence toward God, and toward men.

---

[1]Charles Bridges, <u>A Commentary on Proverbs</u> (Carlisle, Penn.: The Banner of Truth Trust, 1987), p. 478.

Meddling/Busybody

(See also Gossip, Arguing)

The meddler takes an undue interest in and wrongly reports of others' activities.

General information and commandments about this sin:

Lev. 19:16 Forbidden.

Pr. 6:19 God hates sowing discord among brothers.

Pr. 10:18 Is a fool.
A busybody proves himself a fool.

Pr. 10:19 Sin is not lacking in a multitude of words.
Enforce a time of silence upon the child.
Stop him when he begins to meddle in others' affairs. Do not listen.

I Pet 4:15 Should not be busybody; grouped with murderers, thieves, evildoers.

I Tim. 5:13 Idle, wandering from house to house.
Do not allow excessive socializing or too much time "gabbing" on the phone. Set an example of this in your own life.
Keep the meddler busy with household duties, schoolwork, service projects, etc.
Deal with laziness in the child's life. (See chapter on "laziness.")

II Thess 3:11,12 Not working.
Exercise more control over child's free time -- less playtime, less social time -- more chores, more training, more responsibility in the family, more time with you.

What happens, or should happen, to the busybody:

I Tim. 5:13 Give work to do.
Give the child more <u>work</u>! Give more responsibility, less free time, and less freedom.

I Thess. 4:11-12 Lead quiet life, work with hands, lack nothing.

II Thess. 3:11,12 Work in quietness, eat own bread.
Give the child more financial responsibility, which will require more time devoted to work, and leave less time for meddling.

Pr. 17:5 If glad at calamity, will not go unpunished.

*Let the meddler who is glad about someone else's wrongdoing,
receive the discipline that the wrongdoer would have received.*

Pr. 24:17-18 Rejoice not at enemy's fall or God will turn away His wrath from him.

Do not punish the offender when a meddler is obviously enjoying the situation. Explain this action to both the meddler and the original wrongdoer.

Pr. 25:17 Don't spend too much time in neighbor's house or he will weary of you and grow to hate you.

Teach this principle to your children. Don't allow them to overstay their welcome. Don't send them to other people's houses too often.

Set an example of this in your own social contacts.

Pr. 30:10 If you malign a servant to his master, he will curse you, and you will be found guilty.

Pr. 15:23 Speak in due season.

To what is the busybody likened:

Pr. 26:17 Someone pulling a dog's ears.
Will get bitten!
Notice a vicious, barking dog straining at the end of his leash. Would you go up and pull on his ears? What would happen?

Stories that illustrate the consequences of meddling in the affairs of others:

Jezebel, I Kgs. 21:9-14 Took up Ahab's offense against Naboth. Led to false witness, unjust execution, and later to Jezebel's death.

Verses to memorize:

1 Pet. 4:15 But let none of you suffer as a murderer, or as a thief, or as an evildoer, or as a busybody in other men's matters.

Pr. 15:23 A man hath joy by the answer of his mouth: and a word spoken in due season, how good is it!

Pr. 4:25 Let your eyes look straight ahead, and your eyelids look right before you. (NKJV)

Pr. 10:18 Whoever hides hatred has lying lips, and whoever spreads slander is a fool. (NKJV)

Ec. 3:1 To every thing there is a season, and a time to every purpose under the heaven:

Ec. 3:7 A time to rend, and a time to sew; a time to keep silence, and a time to speak.

Foolish, Unclean Speech

(See also Gossip, Lying, Sinful Thought Life)

General information and commandments about this sin:

Titus 2:7-8 Should demonstrate a pattern of good works, sound speech that cannot be condemned.
Teach your child to not say things that could be legitimately condemned.

Eph. 5:4 Not filthiness or foolish talk, but give thanks.

Js. 1:26 Bridle not tongue, religion is in vain.
Our tongue reflects our relationship to God.

II Tim. 2:16 Shun profane, vain babblings.
Do not associate with those who use their tongues for profane speech.
Do not allow a child to utter profanities and coarse speech.

Col. 3:8 Put off.
Do not allow or overlook unclean speech. Do not tolerate it.
Do not let uncleanness be a part of your conversation either.
Draw a picture of the child's face. (Don't worry about an exact likeness. A cartoon would be great. Or use an old photograph.) On a separate piece of paper draw a mouth, with filth coming out of it -- dirt, garbage, etc. Cut it out and tape it over the mouth on the original drawing. Then, remove the "dirty" mouth as a sort of symbolic picture of what the child is going to do with his speech. Tape the "dirty mouth" back on when the child indulges in unclean speech.

Ex. 20:7 Don't take the name of God in vain.

Lev. 19:12 Don't profane God's name.

Eph. 4:29 No corrupt communication, but edifying speech.
Teach the child to use his tongue for the building up of others. When he uses his tongue for unclean and coarse communication, have him think of something edifying -- building up -- that he can say to someone.
Have the child look up a specified verse from this section, and read it to you or memorize it.

I Thess. 4:7 God has not called us to uncleanness, but to holiness.
Jesus lived a holy life. " Would He say what I am about to say?"

Pr. 29:11 Fool utters all his mind.

Pr. 21:23 Keep mouth, keep soul from trouble.

What happens, or should happen, to one who indulges in unclean speech:

Pr. 10:31 Tongue cut out.
Remove the child from the rest of the family. Isolate.
Enforce a period of silence when the child cannot speak.

Pr. 15:4 Breaks the spirit.

Pr. 17:20 Falls into evil.
Leads to other evil, thought life and actions.

II Tim. 2:16 Leads to more ungodliness.
We must not overlook unclean speech.

Eph. 5:4 Give thanks.
Have child speak words of thanksgiving to God and to other people.

Phil. 4:8 Think on these things: whatever is true, honest, just, pure, lovely, of good report, virtue or praise.
Work on memorizing, Bible study, meditation.

I Tim. 4:7 Exercise to godliness.
Make a list of "spiritual calisthetics:" prayer, Bible reading, edifying others with our speech, performing good works of service, memorizing, etc. Assign the child a "workout" from this list when he is disciplined for unclean speech.

Js. 1:21 Lay aside filthiness, receive Word.
Stop to read the Bible with the child. Read verses about speech. Have him write out verses that teach about our speech.

Ps. 141:3 Set watch over mouth.
Appoint "guardian" over child's mouth. Who could work alongside him to encourage him to use his tongue in a godly way?
Write out this verse and post it on a wall in the child's room, or in another prominent place in the house.
Pray for God's conviction in this area.

To what is the sin of foolish, unclean speech likened:

Js. 3:5-10 Fire, unruly evil, full of deadly poison.
Study poisonous snakes and venom.

Observe the effects of fire, espcially an uncontrolled fire.
Observe forest or house after a fire.

Blessings of pure speech:

Pr. 20:15 Lips of knowledge are a precious jewel.
Give the child a ring or other jewelry with a precious jewel in it.
Give a young child an inexpensive ring or necklace, or a sword,
armor, etc. with imitation jewels in it. Take away when lips are
foolish or unclean.

Pr. 22:11 King will be his friend.
Crown the child "Prince-for-the-Day." Give him a crown and robe to
wear. Let other family members serve him throughout the day.
Go to work with Daddy.
Have a special family parade in honor of the child.
Give a gift of special clothing.
Grant a special privilege.

Verses to memorize:

Ps. 34:13 Keep your tongue from evil, and your lips from speaking deceit. (NKJV)

Pr. 4:24 Put away from you a deceitful mouth, and put perverse lips far from you. (NKJV)

Ps. 77:12 I will meditate also of all thy work, and talk of thy doings.

Ps. 141:3 Set a guard, O LORD, over my mouth; keep watch over the door of my lips. (NKJV)

Eph. 4:29 Let no corrupt communication proceed out of your mouth, but that which is good to the use of edifying, that it may minister grace unto the hearers.

Eph. 5:3-4 But fornication and all uncleanness or covetousness, let it not even be named among you, as is fitting for saints; neither filthiness, nor foolish talking, nor coarse jesting, which are not fitting, but rather giving of thanks. (NKJV)

Flattery

(See also Hypocrisy, Lying, Hatred)

General information and commandments about this sin:

Ps. 12:2 Flattering lips and double heart.

I Thess. 2:4-5 Flattery is pleasing men. We should please God.

Pr. 5:3, 7:5 Strange woman flatters.
Train young men to steer clear of girls who flatter them.

Gal. 1:10 If we strive to please men we are not servants of Christ.

Pr. 10:18 Hides hatred with lying lips. Is a fool.

Pr. 28:23 Finds less favor than one who rebukes.
Which person shows true love -- the flatterer or the loving reprover?

What happens, or should happen, to the flatterer:

Job 17:5 Speak flattery to friends, eyes of children will fail.
Deny inheritance.
Deny deposit into long-term savings.

Job 32:21-22 Lord takes flattering lips away.
Isolate the flatterer.

Ps. 12:3 Cut off flattering lips.
Advise the child to end friendship with a flatterer.
Impose a period of silence on the flattering child.
Quickly silence a flatterer. Do not allow him to continue.

Pr. 20:19 Shouldn't meddle with flatterer.
Do not develop a friendship with a flatterer.

Pr. 24:24 People curse, nations abhor.
In the end, people see through the flatterer's words.
A flatterer causes wise people to distrust him.
A flatterer ensnares foolish people.

Pr. 22:16 Give to the rich, come to poverty.
Levy a fine for bribery from spending money.

I Jn. 3:18 Should love in deed and truth.
*Help the child understand that love is demonstrated more through
 actions than through words.*
*Have the child write out specific actions that he can take to
 demonstrate love and respect for another person.*

Effects of flattery on the person who is flattered:

Pr. 7:5, 21 Causes foolish man to yield to adulterous woman.

Pr. 11:9 Destroys neighbor.

Pr. 29:5 Spreads net for neighbor's feet.

Pr. 26:28 Works ruin.

Pr. 27:21 Praise (genuine or false) is a test of man's true character.
The flatterer tests the person who is the object of his flattery. He tempts him to sin, pride, and foolishness.

Appropriate response to a flatterer:

Pr. 20:19 Meddle not with him.
Do not associate with him.

Pr. 27:21 Remember that character is being tested.
Read verses about pride.

Stories that illustrate the effects of flattery:

Adam and Eve, Gen. 3:5 Satan appealed to their intellect, led them to spiritual death and cursing.

Hushai and Absalom, II Sam. 16:16-19, 17:7-13 Spy. Gave bad advice cloaked in flattery, which led Absalom to reject better advice.

Woman of Tekoah, II Sam. 14:17-20 Led David to bring Absalom back.

Absalom, II Sam. 15:2-6 Flattered people at the gates of the city, stole their hearts, deceived them, led them to rebel against David.

Prophets, I Kgs. 22:13 Gave king what he wanted to hear. Micaiah did not flatter the king and was imprisoned. Ahab chose to believe the flattering prophets, which led to his death on the battlefield.

Darius's satraps, Dan. 6:6-9 Led him to err, which led to grave injustice. Satraps were later executed.

Tertullus flattering Felix, Acts 24:2-4 Trying to influence his thinking.

Herod, Acts 12:21-23 Accepted flattery. Did not give glory to God, and was killed.

Herodians with Jesus, Luke 20:21 Intended to snare him.

Blessings of the honest tongue:

Pr. 28:23 One who rebukes will find more favor than a flatterer.
Teach the child to deal honestly with other children.
Teach him to humbly and lovingly reprove a wrongdoer.

Heb. 3:13 Exhort to avoid hardness of heart.
We parents need to remember this. Our children will thank us later
for the reproof we have given more than for the words of flattery
we have spoken to them.

Ps. 141:5 Reproof is kindness and oil.
Make cookies or cake without any oil or butter in the batter. Does
it taste as good?

Pr. 25:12 Like an earring or ornament of gold is the wise reprover to
an obedient ear.
Give the child who has learned to speak honestly and to reprove
gently a gift of earrings, other jewelry, a medal-of-honor.
Pass on a piece of family heirloom jewelry to the child, to wear or to
put into his dowry savings.

Pr. 27:6 Wounds of a friend are faithful.
This is a good way to judge who are true friends.

Pr. 24:25 Rebuker receives delight and good blessing.

Pr. 12:22 Deal truly, will be Lord's delight.
Crown the child "Prince-for-the-Day." Give him a crown and robe to
wear and serve him throughout the day.
Go to work with Daddy.
Have a family parade in honor of the child.

Isa. 33:15-16 Speak uprightly, will dwell on high, defended, provided
for.
Go on a special ride with the child (bike, car, motorcyle, carnival
ride, etc.)
Ride to the mountains or to a scenic viewpoint.
Go to the mountains for a ski or sledding trip.

Stories that illustrate proper reproof:

Moses, Ex. 16:6,7; 32:19-30; Num. 14:41, 32:14 Reproving Israelites.
Realized the issue was rebellion against <u>God</u>. *One exception is found in Num. 20:10 where Moses speaks of "we" instead of God, and then strikes the rock instead of speaking to it.*

Moses, with Korah and associates, Num. 16:9-11 Recognized their rebellion against the Lord.

Nathan with David, II Sam. 12:1-9 Brought David to repentance and restoration.

Daniel with Nebuchadnezzar, Dan. 4:27 Warned him, encouraged repentance.

Daniel with Belshazzar, Dan. 5:17-24 Led to favor, and was made third ruler.

Verses to memorize:

Pr. 29:5 A man that flattereth his neighbour spreadeth a net for his feet.

Pr. 26:28 A lying tongue hateth those that are afflicted by it; and a flattering mouth worketh ruin.

Pr. 28:23 He that rebuketh a man afterwards shall find more favour than he that flattereth with the tongue.

Pr. 20:19 He who goes about as a talebearer reveals secrets; therefore do not associate with one who flatters with his lips. (NKJV)

John 3:18 My little children, let us not love in word, neither in tongue; but in deed and in truth.

Job 32:21-22 Let me not, I pray you, accept any man's person, neither let me give flattering titles unto man. For I know not to give flattering titles; in so doing my maker would soon take me away.

Hatred

(See also Anger, Sinful Thought Life, Flattery,
Gossip, Bitterness, Revenge, Cruelty)

General information and commandments about this sin:

I Thess. 3:12 Lord will cause you to increase and abound in love.
Set an example of love before your children.
Pray that God will increase love in the hearts of your children.

Lev. 19:17 Prohibited.

Pr. 10:12 Stirs up strife.

Pr. 10:18 Hide hatred with lying lips, is a fool.

Pr. 26:24-26 Dissembles with lips, lays up deceit within.
Hatred, unchecked within the family, causes great unrest in a home.

I Jn. 3:13-15 Is murderer, and does not have eternal life.

I Jn. 4:20 Can't love God.

Pr. 15:17 Is better to have a dinner of herbs where there is love, than
an ox with hatred.
*What about serving a dinner of vegetables only when contention and
hatred have been prevalent in the family?*

Heb. 10:24 Provoke each other to love and good works.
*Put the two hateful children together to perform some sort of joint
work of service for someone else.*
*Have the hateful child think of something loving he can do for the
object of his hatred. Then have him do it!*

I Pet. 2:17 Honor all men. Love the brotherhood.
How could the child honor the victim of his hatred? Have him do it!

I Jn. 2:9, 11 Hate brother, will be in darkness, blinded.
Turn out the lights at night and try to navigate through the house.
Blindfold the child and have him find his way through the house.

Matt. 19:19 Love neighbor as self.
*Teach the child to ask himself, "What would I want someone else to
do for me?"*

Rom. 13:10 Love works no ill to neighbor.

I Cor. 14:1 Follow after love.

I Cor. 16:14 Let all your things be done with love.

What happens, or should happen, to the hateful person:

Matt. 5:43-44 Love enemies, bless them, do good to them, pray for them.

Lk. 6:35 Love your enemies.
List ways to show love to an enemy. Try one!
Pray together for the child's enemy.

Gal. 5:19-21 Won't inherit kingdom of God.
Deny portion of family inheritance.
Deny deposit into long-term savings.

Pr. 26:26 Wickedness will be shown before congregation.

Matt. 6:15 Don't forgive brother, God won't forgive you.

I Jn. 2:9,11 Walks in darkness, blinded.

To what is the hateful person likened:

Ps. 57:4,6 Lions, set on fire, teeth are spears and arrows, tongue is sword.
Destructive.

Ps. 62:3 Bowing wall, tottering fence.
Dangerous, don't want to be too close.
Can you depend on a tottering wall?

Ps. 64:3 Tongue is sword. Bitter words are arrows.
Weapons.
Act out sword fight. What is the purpose of a sword?
Do some target practice with bows and arrows. What does the arrow do to the target?

The blessings of showing love to others:

Matt. 5:44-45 Love enemies. Bless those who curse you, do good to those who hurt you, pray for those who persecute and abuse you. Will be children of Father in heaven.

Lk. 6:35 Love enemies, do good, lend with no hope of return, reward

will be great, children of the highest.
*Crown the child "prince" or "princess," and allow him to choose
  activities, menu, etc. for the day.*
*Let the rest of the family serve the "prince" or "princess" for the
  day.*
No chores for the day.
Give a special gift of clothing.

I Jn. 2:10 Love brother, will abide in light, with no occasion of
stumbling.
Give the child a new flashlight, lantern, bedroom lamp.

I Jn. 4:12 Love one another, God dwells in us.

Jn. 13:35 Men will know we are His disciples.
*Make a special certificate that acknowledges the child's loving spirit,
  and hang it in a prominent place in your house.*

Col. 2:2 Knit together in love, hearts will be comforted.

Pr. 25:21-22 If enemy hungers, feed him. If he is thirsty, give him
drink. Heaping coals of fire on his head. God will reward you.
Help the child show kindness to an enemy. What happens?

Stories that illustrate the consequences of hatred:

*Study the outcomes of hatred. Study the source and motivations of
hatred.*

Cain and Abel, Gen. 4:8 Led to murder. Motivated by jealousy.

Sarah/Hagar, Gen. 21:10 Led to strife and cruelty. Motivated by
jealousy and pride.

Esau and Jacob, Gen. 27:41 Motivated by desire for revenge and
bitterness.

Joseph's brothers and Joseph, Gen. 37 and 42:21 Motivated by
jealousy, led to kidnapping and deceit.

Potiphar's wife and Joseph, Gen. 39:14-20 Desire for revenge led
to lying, injustice.

Saul and David, I Sam. 18:8-29 Motivated by jealousy and fear, led
to conspiracy and attempted murder.
I Sam. 19:11-17 Hatred for David led to strife with daughter.
I Sam. 20:30-33 Hatred for David led to anger with son and his
attempted murder.

I Sam. 22:6-18 Hatred for David led to unjust killing of Ahimelech.

Jezebel and Elijah, I Kgs. 19:1-2 Motivated by desire for revenge.

Haman and Mordecai, Est. 3:5-15; 5:9-14 Motivated by pride, revenge. Conspired to annihilate an entire race.

Daniel's enemies, Dan. 6:4-9 Motivated by jealousy, conspired against him and deceived king.

Amnon and Tamar, II Sam. 13:14-15 Hated Tamar after fulfilling his desire. Response to his sin.

Absalom and Amnon, II Sam. 13:22 Took up Tamar's offense, motivated by desire for revenge. Conspired and murdered.

Verses to memorize:

1 John 4:20 If a man say, I love God, and hateth his brother, he is a liar: for he that loveth not his brother whom he hath seen, how can he love God whom he hath not seen?

Col. 3:8 But now ye also put off all these; anger, wrath, malice, blasphemy, filthy communication out of your mouth.

Pr. 10:12 Hatred stirreth up strifes: but love covereth all sins.

1 Cor. 14:1a Follow after charity.

Matt. 19:19b Thou shalt love thy neighbour as thyself.

1 John 4:20 If a man say, I love God, and hateth his brother, he is a liar: for he that loveth not his brother whom he hath seen, how can he love God whom he hath not seen?

1 John 2:9 He that saith he is in the light, and hateth his brother, is in darkness even until now.

Matt. 6:15 But if ye forgive not men their trespasses, neither will your Father forgive your trespasses.

1 Pet. 2:17 Honour all men. Love the brotherhood. Fear God. Honour the king.

1 John 5:1 Whoever believes that Jesus is the Christ is born of God, and everyone who loves Him who begot also loves him who is begotten of Him. (NKJV)

1 John 4:11 Beloved, if God so loved us, we ought also to love one another.

Bitterness

(See also Hatred, Revenge, Anger, Sinful
Thought Life, Envy/Jealousy)

Hebrews 12:15 is a good reminder to us as parents, "Looking diligently lest any man fall of the grace of God; lest any root of bitterness springing up trouble you, and thereby many be defiled." We must not overlook any beginnings of bitterness in the hearts of our children, or it will grow and infect our entire family.

General information and commandments about this sin:

Pr. 10:12 Hatred stirs up strife.

Pr. 15:17 Dinner of herbs is better with love, than fatted calf with hatred.

Eph. 4:31-32 Put away bitterness. Be kind, tenderhearted, forgive as Christ forgave.
Work with the child to write out the things he is bitter about. Pray, confess the bitterness, give it up to God, reconcile with any people involved, forgive them, and then throw the list away.

Col. 3:13 Forgive as Christ forgave.

Lev. 19:17 Shall not hate brother. Rebuke, and not bear sin.
Teach the child to talk to the person who has offended him. Teach him to gently and humbly reprove when necessary.

Lev. 19:18 Not bear grudge, love neighbor as self.
Teach child to ask himself, "What would I want?"

Js. 5:9 Grudge not, lest you be condemned.

Lk. 17:3-4 Rebuke, forgive repentant.

Matt. 5:23-24 Be reconciled with brother before offering gift at altar.
Teach this principle. Reconcile differences before prayer, before family worship, before Sunday, before communion.

Mk. 11:25 Forgive, when praying, so that God can forgive you.

Lk. 6:36 Be merciful, as Father is merciful.

What happens, or should happen, to the bitter person:

Matt. 18:15-17 1. Go to brother and explain your grievance. 2. Return with two or three witnesses. 3. If still unrepentant, go to the church.
Teach this sequence to your children. If they learn to apply these instructions now, they will be much happier and less contentious as adults, too. In step 3, they should come to you as the authority in the home.
Note: Doorposts carries a chart-and-book set entitled "The Brother-Offended Checklist," which expands on these principles in much greater detail. See ordering information in the back of this book.

Matt. 18:21-22 Forgive 70 times 7.
True forgiveness involves forgetting the previous offense, so it will be impossible to keep "score" of how many times a person forgives another! We shouldn't remember the last time.

Rom. 12:14 Bless those who curse you.
Pray for perceived enemy, show kindness to him.
This is hard to do! Approach it as an experiment -- what might happen if we try this the way God says to?

Js. 2:13 If we show no mercy, we will be judged without mercy.

Matt. 6:14-15 God won't forgive you.
Discipline the bitter child without grace and mercy.

I Jn. 4:20 Can't love God.

I Cor. 4:12-13 If reviled, should bless. If persecuted, should suffer. If defamed, should intreat.
We should not be constantly striving for our "rights," but should graciously accept what God, in His providence, brings into our lives for our growth.

To what is the bitter person likened:

Matt. 18:23-35 Unmerciful servant.
Master did not show mercy in return.
How much has God forgiven us? We should forgive others in the same way.

Pr. 18:19 Offended brother is like the bars of a castle, harder to win than a strong city.
Build a model, fortified castle with a portcullis, or a fort. Act out an attack or siege.

Act out together an attack outside. Build up fortified walls out of sticks, logs, snow, etc. for one side, and let the other side attack. How hard is it for the attackers to penetrate the fortress?

Stories that illustrate the consequences of bitterness:

Joseph's brothers, Gen. 37:3-4 Bitter over Joseph's favor and future position. Led to strife, troubles, defilement, lying, kidnapping.

Esau, Gen. 27:41 Hated Jacob because of trickery and loss of birthright and blessing of firstborn. Planned murder of Jacob, led to trouble, strife, separation.

Absalom, II Sam. 13:22 + Bitterness against Amnon led to strife, murder, dishonesty, judged with no mercy. Murdered and later was killed.

Haman, Est. 3:1-6 Bitter toward Mordecai. Led to strife, conspiracy, then condemned to death.

The blessings of a forgiving spirit:

Matt. 6:14 Forgive, will be forgiven.
Show more mercy in discipline to a child who is willing to forgive others.

Lk. 6:35 Love enemies and do good, reward will be great, children of the Highest.
Commend the child when he returns good for evil.
Take him out to eat with you.
Enjoy a special date together.

Lk. 6:37 Don't judge, won't be judged; don't condemn, won't be condemned; forgive, will be forgiven.

I.Pet. 3:9 Not render evil for evil, railing for railing, but blessing. Will inherit blessing.
Make a special deposit into the child's long-term savings.
Pass on a special family heirloom, giving special recognition to the child for his forgiving attitude.

Stories that illustrate the blessings of forgiveness:

Prodigal son, Luke 15 Father forgave, rejoiced, honored after repentance, was waiting for the son. (Had probably been praying for him.)

Joseph, Gen. 45:4-8 Saw God's sovereignty. Forgave, was not angry.

David with Saul, I Sam. 24:10-12; 26:9,23; II Sam. 1:14-17 Recognized Saul as God's annointed and would not kill him, even when he had opportunity.

Solomon with Adonijah, I Kgs. 1:49-53 Showed grace and mercy (until
Adonijah later demonstrated that he was still proud and rebellious.)

Verses to memorize:

Eph. 4:31-32 Let all bitterness, and wrath, and anger, and clamour, and evil speaking, be put away from you, with all malice: and be ye kind one to another, tenderhearted, forgiving one another, even as God for Christ's sake hath forgiven you.

Matt. 18:15-17 Moreover if thy brother shall trespass against thee, go and tell him his fault between thee and him alone: if he shall hear thee, thou hast gained thy brother. But if he will not hear thee, then take with thee one or two more, that in the mouth of two or three witnesses every word may be established. And if he shall neglect to hear them, tell it unto the church: but if he neglect to hear the church, let him be unto thee as a heathen man and a publican.

1 John 4:20 If a man say, I love God, and hateth his brother, he is a liar: for he that loveth not his brother whom he hath seen, how can he love God whom he hath not seen?

Matt. 5:23-24 Therefore if thou bring thy gift to the altar, and there rememberest that thy brother hath ought against thee; leave there thy gift before the altar, and go thy way; first be reconciled to thy brother, and then come and offer thy gift.

Luke 6:37 Judge not, and ye shall not be judged: condemn not, and ye shall not be condemned: forgive, and ye shall be forgiven.

Hitting, Biting, Kicking, etc.

(See also Anger, Hatred, Revenge, Cruelty)

Physically harming another person is striking out at man, who is made in God's image, just as murdering another person is striking out at man who is made in God's image. Gen. 9:6 says, "Whoso sheddeth man's blood, by man shall his blood be shed: for in the image of God made he man." Based on this principle, we make parallels between the Bible's instructions for the punishment of murderers, and the discipline of our children when they strike out at another person. The same emotions and motivations are often involved in striking other people and in murder.

General information and commandments about this sin:

Gen. 9:5-6 Shed man's blood, by man his blood will be shed.
The parallel can be made for spanking a child after he has physically harmed another child.

Matt. 5:21-22 If angry with brother without a cause, are in danger of judgment, just as murderer is in danger of judgment.
Be consistent in firmly disciplining any physical harming of other people.

Pr. 6:17 God hates hands that shed innocent blood.

Matt. 15:19 Evil thoughts and murders come from the heart.

Num. 35:32-33 Show no mercy. Defiles the land.
Do not show mercy to the child who harms others. His uncontrolled anger and cruelty will "defile" the household.

Js. 4:1-3 Motivated by lust.
Deal with envy, covetousness, selfishness, and pride in the heart of the cruel and striking-out child.

What happens, or should happen, to the person who harms others:

Many of the following examples of punishment are Mosaic judicial laws concerning murder. Many of these principles, however, can be applied in the case of harming other people.

Lev. 24:20-21, Ex. 21:23-25 Murderer was punished life for life, *lex talionis.*

Spank the hitting, biting child.

Another principle that does not come out in these laws is the need to ask forgiveness of the victim. Obviously, in murder, this is impossible. When a child has injured another child, though, he should go back to the person, confess his wrong, and ask forgiveness.

Ex. 21:18-19 Injure. Pay for loss of time and doctor.

Do the mother's chores that she could not do while she was attending to the harmed child.

Serve the victim of the child's striking. Provide for their comfort.

Do the victim's chores.

Levy a fine from spending money.

Ex. 21:16 Kidnapping punished by death.

Holding a child against his will (locking him in his room, holding him under a blanket, etc.) is considered kidnapping in our household.

We discipline the offender with spankings.

Ex. 21:15 Hit parents, put to death.

Spank. Also deal with the problem of defiance.

Ex. 21:12,14 Strike man so that he dies, killer should die.

This is an example of premeditated murder, and is punishable by death.

Premeditated, intentional harming of others should be disciplined with spankings.

Num. 35:16-21 Strike with iron, stone, hand weapon, hurl at him, strike with hand so that victim dies, should be punished with death.

Spank for any intentional injury to another.

Num. 35:22-28 If another person is accidentally injured so that he dies, the person who injured him should be judged. If judged innocent, he should reside under the protection of the City of Refuge.

In the case of what appears to be accidental injury to another, the situation should be carefully judged. If the child is judged innocent, perhaps an appropriate parallel to the City of Refuge would be helpful in instructing a careless child who harmed the other child out of negligence. He could be temporarily confined to his room or a chair, or put under your surveillance for a period of time. If he ventured out of the designated area, he could be disciplined with a spanking, or with extra time in his "city of refuge."

Gen. 9:5-6 Blood for blood.

In extreme cases of continued problems with biting, we have braced ourselves and, in a controlled and unemotional way, bitten the biter. I know it sounds awful, but we take time to explain why we are doing this, and that we want the child to understand how much it hurts to be bitten. Communicate grief over the action, and pray together. This has broken a couple of biters in our family of their habit.

Num. 35:30, Deut. 17:6 Death penalty required the testimony of two or three witnesses.

This is a good policy before spanking a child for hitting, too. Circumstantial evidence can serve as one witness. Often, when the whole story comes out, the "victim" of the hitting has also been at fault -- teasing, hitting, etc. -- and should be disciplined for his wrongdoing as well.

I Jn. 3:15 Hating brother is murder, no murderer has eternal life.

Ps. 5:6 God hates bloody, deceitful man.

Pr. 28:17 Man who is burdened with bloodshed will flee to the pit. Don't stop him.

Pray for the child's conscience to convict him and make him miserable until he has confessed his wrong and asked forgiveness.
This would be another case for establishing a room ("pit") for the child to spend time in after injuring another child. This would allow him time to think over his action. (Use this in addition to talking with him and disciplining him. Don't just banish him to his room whenever he hits someone.)

Rom. 1:28+ Given over to a debased mind.

Stories that illustrate the consequences of murder:

Cain, Gen. 4:8-11 Motivated by envy. Was cursed.

David, II Sam. 11:14-17; 12:9 Murder, motivated by desire to cover earlier sin of adultery, and to enable him to take Uriah's wife for his own. Was disciplined with 4-fold death in his own family.

Ahab and Jezebel, I Kgs. 21:19 Conspired with false witnesses. Motivated by covetousness and desire to steal Naboth's vineyard. Led to their deaths.

Esau, Gen. 27:42 Planned to murder Jacob, motivated by desire for revenge.

Balaam, Num. 22:29 Struck ass, desired to kill him. Motivated by anger and impatience.

Amon, II Kgs. 21:23 Murdered by servants, who were motivated by hatred.

Absalom, II Sam. 13:22-29 Murdered Amnon. Motivated by revenge. Banished, and later killed.

Joab, I Kgs. 2:32-34 Solomon executed him for murder of Abner and Amasa. Joab was motivated by revenge. He usurped David's authority and took the law into his own hands.

Blessings of loving our brother:

(See blessings section in chapter on "hatred.")

Verses to memorize:

Rom. 12:10 Be kindly affectioned one to another with brotherly love; in honour preferring one another.

James 4:1-3 Where do wars and fights come from among you? Do they not come from your desires for pleasure that war in your members? You lust and do not have. You murder and covet and cannot obtain. You fight and war. Yet you do not have because you do not ask. You ask and do not receive, because you ask amiss, that you may spend it on your pleasures. (NKJV)

Revenge

(See also Judging Others, Anger, Sinful
Thought Life, Hatred, Bitterness)

General information and commandments about this sin:

Lev. 19:18 Not avenge, but love neighbor.

Pr. 20:22 Wait on the Lord.
*Pray with your revengeful child, that God will help him to wait on
Him to execute judgment.*

Pr. 24:29 Not render evil for evil.
*Do not allow child to return evil to one who has mistreated him. Help
him think of kindnesses he can show instead.*

Matt. 5:38-44 Love, bless, do good, pray.
*Pray for the person that the child wishes to avenge, that God will
work in his life, and that he will see the love of Christ in your child.*

Rom. 12:17,19 God will repay the evil man.
*Help your child remember this truth. It is not our place to execute
justice.   God is the final judge, and he has delegated the
responsibility of judgment to specific authorities here on earth. A
child who takes the law into his own hands will receive discipline.*

I Thess. 5:15 Follow what is good.

I Pet. 3:9 Not revenge, but blessing.
*Have your child pray and then write out a blessing for the person he
wishes to avenge.*
*Have your child write a letter of blessing and thanksgiving for the
good qualities he can see in the person.*

I Pet. 2:15 Silence foolish men with good doing.

I Pet. 2:23 Jesus did not threaten or retaliate but committed His soul
to a righteous judge.
*Teach the child to trust the outcome to God and to His appointed
authorities.*
Help him see when justice is executed without his revenge.

Titus 2:7-8 Live blamelessly so enemy can find no evil.

I Pet. 3:11 Pursue peace.
Ask the child, "Are you chasing after peace as fast as you can?"

What happens, or should happen, to the vengeful person:

Pr. 26:27 Will fall in own pit, stone will return upon him.
Pray for God's obvious judgment on the vengeful child.

Matt. 7:1-2 Judged by same standard he uses.
Judge the child by the same standard, and discipline him in the same way he punished the victim of his revenge.

Rom. 12:14 Bless those who curse you.

Rom. 12:21 Overcome evil with good.
Do something good for the person rather than returning evil for his actions.
Have the child write down a list of good things he could do for his enemy. Then have him choose at least one of them to do right away.

Rom. 12:17 Do good in sight of all men.

Rom. 12:19 Leave room for God's wrath.
Teach the child to wait for God to repay the one who has offended him.
Do not allow him to practice revenge.

Pr. 24:17-18 Rejoice when enemy falls, God will turn away His wrath.
When the child is obviously delighting in the discipline you are about to execute with another child, withhold that discipline. Explain this principle to both children.

Rom. 13:1-4 Authority is the avenger to execute wrath against evil.
The child is usurping authority and rebelling against God and His delegated authorities when he takes revenge into his own hands.

I Pet. 2:23 Jesus is our example. Commit to righteous judge.

Pr. 19:11 Glory to overlook transgression. (We are imitating God's character when we do this.)

Eph. 4:31-32, Gal 3:13 Forgive as Christ forgave us.
How much has God forgiven us?

I Pet. 4:19 Commit keeping of souls to faithful Creator.

The blessings of a forgiving spirit:

I Pet. 3:9 Will inherit blessing.
Make a special deposit into the child's long-term savings account.
Pass on a special family heirloom.

Pr. 20:22 God will save.
Help the child to see when God intervenes and executes judgment after the child has been tempted to avenge himself.

Pr. 25:21-22 Heap coals on enemy's head, God will reward.

I Pet. 3:10 See good days, love life.
Plan a special day out for the child. Let him choose the activities, location, etc.
Have a special day of honor at home.
Have a special friend over for the day.
No homeschool for a day, or a shorter day of schoolwork.

Lk. 6:35 Reward will be great.
There are times when a monetary reward might be an appropriate way to encourage a forgiving child.

Stories that illustrate the consequences of revenge:

James and John, Lk. 9:54 Wanted to destroy Samaritans. Jesus reproved them.

Haman, Est. 3:8-15; 7:5-10 Desired revenge against Mordecai. Conspired murder of an entire race, but "fell into his own pit."

Absalom, II Sam. 13:23-29 Revenge against Amnon. Led to murder, and then his own death. David should have punished Amnon after his rape of Tamar.

Simeon and Levi, Gen. 34:25 Murdered Shechemites in revenge for the rape of Dinah. Gen. 49:5-7 tell of Jacob's last words to Simeon and Levi when he is blessing his sons. Their tribes would be scattered.

Israelites and Amalekites, Deut. 25:17-19, I Sam. 15:1-9 God revenged.

Joab, II Sam. 3:27,30 Avenged his brother's death by murdering Abner. David should have punished Joab.

Stories that illustrate the blessings of forgiving and entrusting justice to God:

David, II Sam. 16:5-12 Trusted God, and reproved Abishai for his desire to kill Shimei, who was taunting David.

David, I Sam. 24:17; 26:7-25 Rewarded good in return for Saul's evil. Once again reproved eager Abishai for his desire to take Saul's life.

David, I Kgs. 2:5-6 Left instructions with Solomon to execute Joab to avenge the blood of Abner and Amasa. Justice was executed by God's proper delegated authorities.

Stephen, Acts. 7:60 Showed mercy to his murderers in his death.

Jesus, I Pet. 2:23 Committed his soul to the righteous Judge.

Joseph, Gen. 45:5-15 Recognized God's hand in his life. Didn't condemn brothers. God had used their actions to save them and their children. He blessed them with food, land, and provisions.

Verses to memorize:

Pr. 20:22 Say not thou, I will recompense evil; but wait on the LORD, and he shall save thee.

Rom. 12:21 Be not overcome of evil, but overcome evil with good.

1 Pet. 2:23 Who, when he was reviled, reviled not again; when he suffered, he threatened not; but committed himself to him that judgeth righteously.

1 Pet. 3:10-11 For he that will love life, and see good days, let him refrain his tongue from evil, and his lips that they speak no guile: let him eschew evil, and do good; let him seek peace, and ensue it.

Cruelty/Bullying

(See also Anger, Hatred, Bitterness, Hitting)

General information and commandments about this sin:

Rom. 13:10 Love does no harm.

I Jn. 4:21 If we love God, we will love our brother.

Js. 2:15-17 Faith without works is dead.

Zech. 7:9-10 Don't oppress, don't imagine evil.

Pr. 14:31, 17:5 Reproaches Maker.

Pr. 16:29 Entices neighbor, leads in way not good.
Guard other children from the influence of bullies.
Do not allow child to develop friendship with a cruel, oppressive child.

Pr. 29:14 King who judges the poor with truth, his throne will be established forever.
We parents need to judge each of our children with truth.

Isa. 1:17 Relieve oppressed.
A child should not simply stand by and watch if another child is being treated cruelly. He should stand up for him.

Ex. 23:2 Do not follow multitude in plotting against others.
A child should be disciplined when he joins in with a crowd in cruelty to another child.

Pr. 3:29 Don't devise evil against neighbor.

Matt. 25:34-46 When we do not provide and care for others, we are doing the same to Jesus.
Help the child learn to ask himself, "How would I treat Jesus? How would I treat a king? How would I treat even a friend who had risked his life for me? Am I treating this person in the same way?"

Ps. 10:2 Wicked in pride persecutes the poor.
Deal with the problem of pride in the child's life.

Lev. 19:14 Should not curse the deaf or place a stumblingblock before the blind. Should fear God.
The child should not be allowed to taunt the handicapped, or to make his way more difficult.

Pr. 12:10 Righteous man regards the life of an animal.
Teach the child how to properly treat animals, pets, livestock.

Pr. 3:3-4 Bind mercy and truth around neck, on table of heart.

Memorize verses that teach about kindness.
Make the child a necklace, pin, medal or "dog tags" with a verse about kindness inscribed on it.

What happens, or should happen, to the cruel person:

Amos 5:11 Will not profit from labor. Will build houses and not live in them. Will plant vineyard, but not drink the wine.
Do not pay the child for chores.
Confiscate his earnings from other sources.
Deny toy or possession.
Take away a project the child has long labored over.

Mic. 2:2-3 Take by violence, to disaster.
Design "disaster" for the child: deny planned activity, deny playtime or free time, levy fine from spending money.

Pr. 22:16 Come to want.
Remove toy or other possessions.
Levy fine from spending money.
Do not pay for work.

Zech. 7:11-14 Scattered. God will not hear. Desolate.
Isolate the child temporarily.
Withdraw your fellowship from the child.
Cancel plans for an activity the child may have been anticipating with you.

Ps. 57:6 Will fall into own pit.
Pray for God to direct circumstances in this way.
Discipline the child in a way that is similar to the way in which he was cruel to another child.

Pr. 17:13 Reward evil for good, evil will not depart from house.

Pr. 21:13 Will cry and not be heard.
Do not spare the child from the natural consequences of his cruelty.

Pr. 22:16 Oppress poor to increase riches, will come to poverty.
For example, if one boy is bullying his younger brother to obtain a toy, take the toy away from him, deny his playtime, levy a fine from his spending money, have him make double restitution.

Pr. 22:22-23 Will plunder soul of those who plunder.
Take away possessions, privileges, money.

Ps. 140:11 Evil will hunt him down and overthrow him.

Rom. 1:28+ Given over to a debased mind.

Matt. 25:46 Everlasting punishment.

Ps. 7:15-16 Fall into own pit, mischief will come on own head.
Return the same treatment as discipline for the cruel child.

Ps. 10:2 Taken in devices they have imagined.
Haman is a good example of this principle. He was hanged on the very gallows he had built for Mordecai.
When possible, use this punishment with your child. Use his planned cruelty against another as discipline for him.

Job 20:18 No enjoyment from proceeds of business. Will not swallow down what he labored for.
Deny pay.
Levy fine from spending money; pay into charity savings.
Take away a possession for which he labored long.

Isa. 14:2 Captivity, under rule.
Put child under your constant surveillance for a period of time.
Limit the child's freedom.
Give the child "slave labor" -- extra work without pay.
Enforce an earlier curfew.

Ex. 22:22-24 Afflict widow, orphan, God will kill with sword.
Spank the child.

Job 27:13-23 Destruction of offspring, hunger, heap up riches for the just and innocent.
Levy fine from the child's spending money, which he pays to the victim or to his charity savings.
Have the child skip a meal.

Ps. 12:5 God protects the oppressed.
We parents need to protect the victims of other children's cruelty. We cannot overlook the problem or brush it aside if we are going to obey God, and if we are going to give our children a true reflection of God's justice in our discipline.

Pr. 6:14-15 Sudden calamity without remedy.
Devise calamities for the child: changed plans, no free time, extra chores, etc.

Ps. 72:4 Break in pieces.
Use this as an object lesson when you break a dish.

Pr. 11:17 Troubles own flesh.

Js. 2:13 Judge without mercy.
Show no mercy in disciplining the cruel child.

Matt. 26:52 Take sword, perish by sword.

If cruel child strikes another child, he should be spanked.

To what is the cruel person likened:

Pr. 28:3 Poor man oppressing poor is like driving rain which leaves no food.
Observe the garden aften a heavy rain or hailstorm.

Ps. 10:9 Lion.
Study the lion together. How might a cruel person be like a lion?

Ps. 57:4,6 Teeth are spears and arrows. Tongue is a sword.

Pr. 30:14 Teeth are swords, jaw teeth are knives, to devour the poor and needy from the earth.
Have your child draw a picture of the mouth described in the two verses above. Does this mouth look like it is going to build another person up with its words?

Ps. 62:3 Bowing wall, tottering fence.
This sort of wall cannot be trusted. It is dangerous to even be near it. Unpredictable.

Job 27:18 Temporary. Builds house like a spider web or a booth.
Find a spider's web you can observe for a few days. How permanent is it? Does it change from day to day? Can it hold up to disturbances in its environment?
Build a "booth" or little shack together in your back yard. How sturdy is it? Does it hold up well in a wind storm? Does it offer adequate protection from the elements?

Pr. 26:27 Dig pit, fall in. Roll stone, return on him.
Act out this picture together.
Draw cartoon illustrations of this truth together.
Play a makeshift game where you set up a toy man (Lego, etc.) at the bottom of a slope. Roll a ball up the slope and see how many times the ball rolls back down and knocks the man over. The cruel man always gets "knocked over."

Blessings of the kind, compassionate person:

Ps. 37:26 Seed are blessed.
Establish a "Grandkid Fund" into which you make a special deposit when the child exhibits progress in kindness.

Pr. 11:17 Merciful does good to own soul.

Show the merciful child mercy in discipline situations.

Matt. 25:34+ Will inherit kingdom.
Pass on family heirloom.
Make a special deposit into the child's long-term savings.

Isa. 58:6-14 Health, glory of the Lord, light, guide, satisfy, like watered garden, spring.
Give the child a new flashlight, lamp, etc.
Give him a compass.
Take out to eat at an "All-You-Can-Eat" restaurant.
Contrast a portion of the garden that has been watered well, with another portion (maybe around the edges, if you water like me) that doesn't get watered as well. What differences do you see?
Find fresh spring water, and enjoy a cool drink!

Pr. 21:21 Life, righteousness, and honor.
Fly child's "Name Flag" from the front porch.
Write out a special certificate acknowledging the child's kindness, and hang it in a prominent place in your home.
Have a special family feast in honor of the merciful child. Commend him for his kindness in a little speech during the meal.

Matt. 5:7 Will obtain mercy.
Grant the child mercy in discipline.

Pr. 14:21 Show mercy to the poor, will be happy.
Make your child happy with a special privilege, activity, or honor.

Pr. 20:28 Mercy upholds king's throne.

Stories that illustrate the consequences of cruelty:

Look for motivations or root problems associated with the problem of cruelty in your child's life (pride, jealousy, covetousness, etc.) Deal with these discipline problems, too.

Penninah and Hannah, I Sam. 1:4-7; 2:3 Motivated by pride.

Story of the Good Samaritan, Lk. 10:29-37 Two men ignored him in his plight.

Ahab and Jezebel against Naboth, I Kgs. 21:2-16 Coveted and killed.

Joseph's brothers against Joseph, Gen. 37:18-20 Envy led to cruelty, which led to cursing, fear, and guilt.

David against Uriah, II Sam. 11:9-27 Motivated by covetousness, and desire to cover sin. Murdered Uriah. Led to judgment, deaths aud unrest in family.

Sarah against Hagar, Gen. 16:6; 21:9-14 Motivated by hatred and jealousy.

Egyptians against Israelites, Ex. 1:10-22 Motivated by selfishness.

Daniel's enemies, Dan. 6:4-17 Motivated by envy. Conspired for the unjust execution of Daniel, whom God protected.

Haman, Est. 3:5-15; 5:9-14 Motivated by envy and pride, attempted to have Mordecai killed. Was killed himself.

Potiphar's wife against Joseph, Gen. 39:14-20 Motivated by covetousness, lust, anger and revenge. Unjustly accused Joseph.

Herodias against John the Baptist, Matt. 14:3-10; Mk. 6:24-28 Motivated by desire for revenge.

Stories that illustrate mercy:

Prison keeper to Joseph, Gen. 39:21-23 Was blessed through Joseph.

Joshua to Rahab, Josh. 6:25 Led to fame and honor.

David to Saul, I Sam. 24:10-13,17; Ps. 20:1-6 Led to life, riches and honor.

Verses to memorize:

Micah 6:8 He hath showed thee, O man, what is good; and what doth the LORD require of thee, but to do justly, and to love mercy, and to walk humbly with thy God?

Col. 3:12 Put on therefore, as the elect of God, holy and beloved, bowels of mercies, kindness, humbleness of mind, meekness, longsuffering.

Pr. 11:17 The merciful man doeth good to his own soul: but he that is cruel troubleth his own flesh.

Pr. 21:21 He that followeth after righteousness and mercy findeth life, righteousness, and honour.

Pr. 22:16 He who oppresses the poor to increase his riches, and he who gives to the rich, will surely come to poverty. (NKJV)

Phil. 4:5a Let your gentleness be known to all men. (NKJV)

Pr. 3:31 Do not envy the oppressor, and choose none of his ways. (NKJV)

Titus 3:1-2 Remind them to be subject to rulers and authorities, to obey, to be ready for every good work, to speak evil of no one, to be peaceable, gentle, showing all humility to all men. (NKJV)

James 2:13 For he shall have judgment without mercy, that hath showed no mercy; and mercy rejoiceth against judgment.

1 Cor. 16:14 Let all that you do be done with love. (NKJV)

Pr. 26:27 Whoever digs a pit will fall into it, and he who rolls a stone will have it roll back on him. (NKJV)

Rom. 13:10 Love does no harm to a neighbor; therefore love is the fulfillment of the law. (NKJV)

Unkind Speech

(See also Cruelty & Scoffing)

General information and commandments about this sin:

Pr. 8:13 God hates.

Pr. 16:27 Digs up evil.

Matt. 12:34 Comes from abundance of heart.
Fill a pitcher with dirty water. Invite the children in for a glass of juice, and pour the dirty water into their glasses. Talk about this verse.

Rom. 1:29 Listed along with fornication, murder.

James 1:26 This person's religion is in vain.

James 3:10-13 Blessing & cursing should not come from same mouth.
Can you pour mud and hot chocolate out of the same pitcher at the same time?

Pr. 10:19 Multitude of words results in sin.
Limit the child's speech. Do not allow the child to talk for a specified amount of time.

Pr. 15:1 Stirs up anger.
Overlooking unkind speech amongst your children will only lead to other additional problems -- arguing, hitting, revenge, etc. Deal with the unkind tongue swiftly and consistently.

Pr. 16:28 Sows strife, separates friends.

Pr. 11:11 Leads to overthrow of city.
Unkind speech in your family will weaken it, and open it to all sorts of other temptation and sin.

What happens, or should happen, to the unkind person:

Rom. 1:28-32 Leads to debased mind.

Pr. 4:24 Put froward mouth far from you.
Remove offender from group, isolate him.

Pr. 10:19 Too many words leads to sin.
Limit the offender's conversation. Enforce a period of silence. Limit the child's time on the telephone.

Eph. 4:25,29,31 Put away. Only speak what is edifying.
Speak words that build.

Ps. 140:11 Not established on earth.
Fine from long-term savings.

Pr. 10:31 Tongue will be cut out.
Isolate the unkind child.
Do not allow the unkind child to speak for a specified time period.

Matt. 5:22 Judgment, hell.
Be consistent in disciplining for unkind words.

Matt. 12:34-36 Will give account for every idle word.
*Tape record or write down a conversation you overhear between two
children. Play it back, or read it for them, and discuss their words.*

Pr. 18:6 Mouth calls for blows.
*The child needs to understand that his unkind speech will lead to
strife with others.*
Spank him.

Eph. 5:4 Give thanks rather than jesting.
*Have the child sit down and write out a list of all the things he can
be thankful for about the person he has treated with unkindness.*
*Have the child go back to the victim of his unkindness, and say
some words of gratitude to him -- what can he thank the child for?*

Pr. 15:28 In contrast to the righteous, he doesn't study to answer.

Pr. 13:3 Destruction.

To what is the unkind tongue likened:

Ps. 64:2-3 Tongue is a sword, bitter words are like arrows shot from
bows.
*Unkind words cannot be recalled. Once they are "shot" they will do
their damage.*

Ps. 140:3 Sharpened tongues like serpent's, adder's poison under
lips.
*Study about snakes and venom. How can you compare the tongue
to the poisonous snake bite?*

Pr. 12:18 Piercings of sword.
A sword pierces deeply. Unkind words leave scars.

Pr. 16:27, Js. 3:5-6 Burning fire.

Fire is destructive. Fire spreads quickly.
Watch a fire. What does it do to everything it touches? What is left after a fire runs out of fuel?

Js. 3:8 Full of deadly poison.
Talk about poisons -- venom, poisonous plants, medicines, etc.
What does poison do to the body? Can anything be done once a person has eaten something poisonous? (What should we do after we have spoken unkind words to another person?)

Js. 3:11 Fountain that produces both sweet and bitter water.
An unpredictable fountain is not a good source of water.
Can the same fountain produce both kinds of water?

Js. 3:12 Fig tree bearing olives. Vine bearing figs.
Does this happen?

Js. 3:12 Fountain that produces salt water and fresh water.
Try a sip of ocean water. It's salty, and always is!

Js. 3:3 Bit in horse's mouth.
The tongue affects the whole body and its actions.
Go to a rodeo or a riding stable and observe how the horses are directed by the bit and bridle.

Js. 3:4 Ship's rudder.
A very large ship is controlled by a tiny rudder.
Study ships and their construction.

Rom. 3:13 Open sepulchre.
What is a grave designed for? The unkind tongue is waiting for its next victim.

Stories that illustrate the consequences of unkind speech:

Nabal, I Sam. 25:10+ Surliness, unkind words, and ingratitude led to strife, and to David's anger which almost cost Nabal his life.

Children mocking Elisha, II Kgs. 2:23-25 Mauled by bears.

Blessings of the righteous who resist this sin:

Pr. 15:23 Has joy.
Create a joyful occasion for your child: a family party, a special friend over for the day, an outing with you, etc.

Pr. 16:24 Like honeycomb, sweet, health.

Give honeycomb to eat.
Go out together for sweet treat.
Make cookies together.
Decorate a special cupcake or cake, and make a mealtime presentation in honor of the kind child.

Pr. 16:13, 22:11 Delight of kings, king will be his friend.
Crown the wise-tongued child "Prince-for-a-Day." Let him wear a crown and robe, and have the rest of the family serve him.
Have a special family parade in honor of the child.
Grant a special privilege.
Go to work with Daddy.
Give a gift of special clothing.

Pr. 25:11 Apples of gold in settings of silver.
Give the child a special handmade certificate. (i.e. "The Golden Apple Award")
Serve the child a small apple on a silver plate.
Serve the child's meal with special silverware, plate and cup.
Have a tea party, using silver service.
Serve breakfast-in-bed on a silver tray (or a shiny cookie sheet?). Include peaches or apricots or Golden Delicious apples ("apples of gold").
Buy the child a toy "silver" tea set.

Pr. 25:15 Breaks the bone.
Soak a chicken bone overnight in vinegar. Can you break it now?
Talk about experiences with broken arms, legs, etc. A broken bone hurts, and it disables a person.

Pr. 27:9 Ointment and perfume.
Give the child a gift of cologne, bubble bath, etc.
Ointment and perfume attract others, are pleasant, and heal.

Pr. 10:11 Well of life.
Talk about the importance of water to our lives. We would not be able to live without water.

Pr. 12:18 Health.
Good health is a blessing from God. Poor health hinders us in our work and play, and is uncomfortable.
Give the child a "doctor kit."
Buy an older child some herb plants for a start on a medicinal herb garden project.

Pr. 15:4 Tree of life.
Buy the child a special tree of his own. Let him care for it, and benefit from its produce.

Buy or select a tree in your yard (choose a <u>big</u> tree if you have a child who has a <u>big</u> problem with unkind speech.) Each time the child must be disciplined for unkind words, send him out to the tree to cut off a branch. What will happen to the tree if the child does not mend his ways?

I Pet. 3:9,10 Will see good days, love life.
Grant the child a special day out. Let him choose the location and activities.
Have a special day of honor at home.
Invite one of the child's special friends over for the day.
No homeschool for the day!

Pr. 20:15 Precious jewel.
Give the child a jeweled ring (genuine or fake) with this verse inscribed inside the band.
Give a locket with this verse inside.
Make the child a sword and decorate it with jewels.

Pr. 10:20 Choice silver.
Give the child an ounce of silver or a silver dollar.
Give a gift of silver jewelry.
Pass on an heirloom of silver.

Pr. 18:20 Stomach will be satisfied with fruit of his mouth.
Have the family fix a special meal in honor of the kind child.
Eat out together.
Serve favorite foods for a meal.

Story that illustrates the blessings of a kind tongue:

Abigail, I Sam. 25:23-32 Her soft answer turned away David's wrath. Prevented David from sinful action, and led to Abigail's marriage to David.

Verses to memorize:

Ps. 141:3 Set a guard, O LORD, over my mouth; keep watch over the door of my lips. (NKJV)

Pr. 16:23 The heart of the wise teacheth his mouth, and addeth learning to his lips.

Pr. 18:21 Death and life are in the power of the tongue: and they that love it shall eat the fruit thereof.

Pr. 15:26 The thoughts of the wicked are an abomination to the LORD: but the words of the pure are pleasant words.

Pr. 15:28 The heart of the righteous studies how to answer, but the mouth of the wicked pours forth evil. (NKJV)

Eph. 4:29 Let no corrupt communication proceed out of your mouth, but that which is good to the use of edifying, that it may minister grace unto the hearers.

Ps. 19:14 Let the words of my mouth, and the meditation of my heart, be acceptable in thy sight, O LORD, my strength, and my redeemer.

James 1:26 If anyone among you thinks he is religious, and does not bridle his tongue but deceives his own heart, this one's religion is useless. (NKJV)

Matt. 12:37 For by thy words thou shalt be justified, and by thy words thou shalt be condemned.

Insensitivity/Lack of Compassion

(See also Cruelty, Selfishness, Unkind Speech)

General information and commandments about this sin:

Pr. 27:14 Bless friend with loud voice in morning, will be counted a curse.
Teach the child to be considerate of others when he wakes up earlier than others in the morning. The same principle could apply to any time when others are resting or sleeping.

Rom. 12:15 Rejoice with those who rejoice, weep with those who weep.
Teach a child to put himself in another person's position. What would he like someone to do for him if he was sad, lonely, rejoicing over good news, etc.? Much of this can be· taught by example as we show sympathy to a hurting child, and happiness with a joyful child.

I Pet. 3:8 Be pitiful, have compassion for one another.

Job 6:14 Show kindness to afflicted ones.
Choose a family or individual in your church, neighborhood, or family that is in need of help. (This might be someone dealing with health problems, hospitalization, a new baby, financial hardship. death, pregnancy, a move, loneliness, a time of pressure or testing.) Work with your child to make a list of ways you could help them, and then work through the list together. Visit the person, fix meals together to take them, babysit together, send cards, draw pictures, write out verses, tape record Scripture reading, clean house, make gifts, do yardwork, shopping, etc.

I Thess. 5:14 Comfort the fainthearted, uphold the weak.
Younger siblings give older children a good opportunity to practice this skill.

Gal. 6:2 Bear one another's burdens.
Teach the child to ask himself, "How can I help to bear this person's burden?"

Deut. 22:1 See brother's ox or sheep astray, should return it. Don't hide self.
The child needs to learn to help take responsibility for others' belongings. He should not overlook others' possessions that are in danger of being lost, damaged, etc. He should return them to the owner, or put them away.

Ps. 112:5 Good man shows favor and lends.
Teach the child to be willing to lend to those who are truly in need.

Acts 20:35 Support the weak.

Rom. 15:1 Bear infirmities of the weak. Please neighbor to his edification.
Teach the child to be especially sensitive to the needs of the ill and elderly and disabled.

Pr. 31:9 Open mouth, plead the cause of the poor and needy.
Be an example of this as you work for the good of others -- unborn babies, elderly, orphans, etc.
Include your children in projects and acts of compassion.

Pr. 31:20 Virtuous woman extends her hands to the poor and needy.
Set an example in this. Train your daughter to use a portion of her time and energy in helping others in need. (Edith Schaeffer's book, The Hidden Art of Homemaking has some very inspiring and convicting accounts of extending the hand to the needy.)

Isa. 58:7 Give bread to the hungry, shelter to the homeless, clothes to the naked. Do not hide yourself.
Teach your child to show hospitality, and to give from the many blessings that God has given him.

Lk. 3:11 If you have two coats, give one to the person with none. Share your food with those who have none.
Set an example of this. Does your child really need all the clothes he has? Share some of them with someone who really does need them.
Do you really need to spend as much as you do on groceries? Perhaps you could cut back some, and use the extra money to help feed others.
Invite others to share your meals.

Rom. 12:13 Distribute to the necessity of the saints. Show hospitality.
Teach your child hospitality by your example as you open your home to others.

Rom. 12:20 Should even feed enemy when he is hungry, give him a drink when he is thirsty.
Help your child do this, and watch the results!

I Cor. 13:3 Have love with your acts of "charity" or there is no profit.
Teach the child to do this out of love, not seeking glory for himself.

Gal. 6:10 Do good to all men, especially those of the household of

faith.
Help the child understand his obligation to his brothers in Christ, as you minister to other believers in need.

Js. 1:27 Visit orphans and widows in affliction. Is pure religion.
Visit orphans and widows together. Do things that can help them.

Heb. 13:3 Remember those in bonds and adversity.
Write to persecuted believers in other countries.
Write to and visit prisoners.

Js. 2:15-16 No profit if you see brother or sister in need, and say, "Be warmed and filled," but don't provide his needs.

Ec. 7:2 Better to go to house of mourning than feasting. Living will lay it to heart.
We learn from our own grief and from the grief of others. It helps put our lives in better perspective, and teaches us compassion.
Do not try to protect your children from grief. Let him learn from it.

Job 16:5 Strengthen with mouth, comfort of lips will relieve grief.
Set an example of comforting with gentle words and with the words of Scripture.

II Cor. 1:3-5 God comforts us in our affliction so that we will be able to comfort others in trouble.
Help your child see this as a purpose in his own suffering.
Pray for circumstances that will soften the insensitive child's heart, and will give him greater empathy for the sufferings of others.

Job 31:16-23 Job prayed that his arm would be removed and fall out if he did not show compassion to others.
"Remove" the child's arm by temporarily disabling him. Tie his hand behind his back, tie a splint on it, etc.

Ps. 82:3-4 Defend the poor, fatherless; bring justice to the afflicted and needy, free from hand of the wicked.
Work as a family against abortion, euthanasia, government interference in the family. Volunteer in Crisis Pregnancy Centers, give shelter to an unwed mother, aid in an orphanage, do volunteer work for a political action group that is working to protect the rights of families, help a family with the financial expenses of adopting a child.
Teach a child to defend a child who is being wronged, rather than joining in with the wrongdoers.

What happens, or should happen, to the insensitive person:

Matt. 25:34-46 Goes to everlasting darkness. When we do not feed the hungry, take in the stranger, provide clothing, and visit the prisoner, we are showing neglect to Jesus and treating him in the same way.
Teach the child to ask himself, "What would I do for <u>Jesus</u> in this situation?"
Write out a list of ways to show compassion to this person in need. Pick one way, and <u>do</u> it.

I Jn. 3:17-18 Love in deed and truth. How does love of God dwell in him who doesn't show compassion to brother in need?
If we love God, we will follow His example of compassion, and we will want to show love for others, because of our love for Him.

II Cor. 9:6 Sow sparingly, reap sparingly.
Plant two rows of seeds in the garden. In one row, plant the seeds thickly. In the other row, sow the seeds thinly. What happens when the seeds sprout?

Pr. 17:5 One who is glad at another's calamities will not go unpunished.
Disipline the child who shows obvious pleasure in another child's discipline or disappointments. Disipline the child in the way you were about to discipline the other child.

To what is the lack of compassion likened:

Pr. 25:20 Singing songs to a heavy heart is like taking away a person's garment in cold weather.
Go outside on a cold snowy day, and take away the child's coat, hat, and mittens. Explain this verse to him.

Pr. 25:20 Vinegar on soda.
Try this experiment! What happens?

Blessings that come to the compassionate person:

Matt. 25:46 Eternal life.

Isa. 58:10 Light will rise in obscurity, and darkness will be as noonday.
Give the child the gift of a special candle, lantern, lamp, etc.

Lk. 12:33 Give alms, will provide bags that won't get old, eternal treasure.
Give the child a special leather pouch or beaded purse, etc.
Give the child a handful of change and a bag full of holes. Tell him he can keep all the money that will stay in the bag when he pours the money in it. Try it again with a bag without holes.

Lk. 14:12-14 Provide feast for those who can't repay, will be recompensed at resurrection.
Remind the child of the heavenly rewards for the good he does on earth.
Plan a party with your child; invite others who will not be able to repay -- poor or ill children, orphans, elderly people.

II Cor. 9:6 Sow bountifully, reap bountifully.
Try the same experiment that is suggested with this verse in the "What Happens" section.
How much grows in a garden without seeds planted in it?

Ps. 41:1 Consider the poor, will be delivered in time of trouble.
Show mercy, give aid to the child.

Ps. 112:4,5,9 Light in darkness, horn exalted with honor.

Stories that illustrate the consequences of insensitivity:

Nabal, I Sam. 25:4-12 Refused David's request for food. Eventually cost him his life.

Unforgiving servant and creditor, Matt. 18:32-35 Was delivered to "tormentors" after he was unwilling to forgive the small debt that was owed to him.

Stories that illustrate the blessings of compassion:

Good Samaritan, Lk. 10:30 Did not ignore the man in his need.

Pharaoh's daughter adopting Moses, Ex. 2:6-10

David to Mephibosheth, II Sam. 9:1-13 Gave him land, and fed him at his table.

Elisha to the widow and her son, II Kgs. 8:1 Warned her of the coming famine.

Elisha and widow, II Kgs. 4:1-7 Provided means for her to pay her debt and save her sons.

Woman who provided room and board for Elisha, II Kgs. 4:8-37 Gave birth to child in old age after years of barrenness, and son was later raised from the dead by Elisha.

Ruth to Naomi, Ruth 1:16-17, 4:13 Loyal to Naomi, and worked to care for her. Led to marriage to Boaz.

Boaz to Ruth, Ruth 2:14-16,23 Allowed gleaning, protected her and gave her food. Took her as his wife.

Jesus, Study His perfect example of compassion: Matt. 8:16-17, Isa. 53:4, Matt. 9:36, Mk 14:14, Matt. 15:32, Matt. 20:34, Mk. 6:34, Lk. 7:13, Jn. 11:34-38, II Cor. 8:9, Heb. 4:15

Verses to memorize:

2 Cor. 8:9 For ye know the grace of our Lord Jesus Christ, that, though he was rich, yet for your sakes he became poor, that ye through his poverty might be rich.

Heb. 4:15 For we do not have a High Priest who cannot sympathize with our weaknesses, but was in all points tempted as we are, yet without sin. (NKJV)

Gal. 6:2 Bear ye one another's burdens, and so fulfil the law of Christ.

1 John 3:17 But whoever has this world's goods, and sees his brother in need, and shuts up his heart from him, how does the love of God abide in him? (NKJV)

Pr. 17:17 A friend loveth at all times, and a brother is born for adversity.

Rom. 12:15 Rejoice with them that do rejoice, and weep with them that weep.

Rom. 15:2 Let every one of us please his neighbour for his good to edification.

Bad Friendships

General information and commandments about this sin:

II Cor. 6:14-17 Not unequally yoked. Be separate.
Read about yoking oxen. They need to be matched in size, strength or they will struggle against each other. They must work together.

Jn. 15:19 We are not of the world, God chose us.
We are set apart, chosen out.

Pr. 16:19 Better to be humble with the lowly than to divide the spoil with the proud.

Pr. 22:24-25 Make no friendship with an angry man or will learn his ways.
Do not allow your children to develop good friendships with children who are given to anger.

Pr. 23:20-21 Don't mix with winebibbers and gluttons.

Pr. 24:21-22 Don't associate with those given to change (pursuing imaginary improvements, change for the sake of change, railing, despising authority) Calamity will suddenly arise.
Help the child see when this happens in his life.
Do not allow your children to develop friendships with others who are continually discontented.

Pr. 24:1-2 Don't desire to be with evil men or envy them.

Pr. 29:24 Partner with thief hates his own life.
An "accomplice" or consenting bystander should be disciplined in the same way the thief is disciplined.

I Tim. 6:4-5 Withdraw from the proud arguer.
Exercise control over the friendships your child develops.
Talk to the other child when you come to the decision that you no longer want your child to be his close friend.
Talk to the child's parents, too, if you believe that it would be in the best interest of the child and the parents. They may need the gentle reproof of a loving friend or acquaintance.

Pr. 1:10 Don't consent when sinners entice.
Teach your child to discern and judge by the Bible's standards.
Teach him to stand up against wrong.
Protect your children as much as possible from this temptation, until he is older, with more wisdom, and less easily swayed.

Ex. 23:2 Don't follow crowd to do evil.

Follow Jesus.
Pray for a strong, godly friend for your child.
*Work with a "buddy" system, similar to the practice used when
   children swim. No one swims alone; they have a partner they are
   with, and each watches out for the other one. Don't send your
   child into a peer pressure situation without a dependable "buddy."*

I Cor. 5:11 Don't even eat with a Christian who is a fornicator,
   covetous, idolatrous, reviling, drunkard, extortioner.
   *Scripture is clear about this. We are not to fellowship closely with
   the unrepentant, sinning Christian. Enforce this with your child.*

II Thess. 3:14 Withdraw from the disorderly.
   Do not allow friendship with the disorderly.

Pr. 27:17 Friend sharpens countenance of another.
   *Help the child choose friends who will strengthen and build him up,
   and that he can build up in the same way.*

Js. 4:4 Friendship of world is enmity with God.

Eph. 5:11 No fellowship with darkness, but rather expose it.
   Teach the child to go away from wrongdoing.
   *As he matures teach him the proper way to reprove a wrongdoer,
   and how to tell authorities of another's wrongdoing.*

Amos 3:3 Can two walk together unless they agree?
   *Go for a walk with your child but keep insisting on going the
   opposite direction your child is going. How far do you get?*

Ps. 101:5 Cut off him who slanders neighbor, don't suffer the proud.

Ps. 101:7 Don't allow liars and deceitful to tarry in your sight.

Pr. 1:15 Don't walk with sinners, don't even stay in their path.
   *This is why we need to exercise control over our children's
   friendships. We need to help them stay out of the path of sinners.*

Pr. 4:14-15 Don't enter path of wicked, don't go in way of evil men.
   Avoid it, pass not by it, turn from it, pass away.
   Don't get near it!

Pr. 20:19 Don't meddle with flatterer.

Pr. 12:26 Way of wicked seduces the righteous.
   A righteous child will be seduced by the wicked.

Pr. 28:19 Follow vain persons, leads to poverty.
   Help child notice when this happens in his life.

Ps. 26:4-5 Don't sit with vain persons, don't go with wicked
   dissemblers, hate congregation of evildoers, don't sit with wicked.

I Cor. 15:33 Evil company corrupts good morals.
Our old sin natures make us much more prone to be corrupted by the sin of others, than for sinners to be influenced by our righteousness, especially in the case of young children.

II Pet. 2:18-19 Speak swelling words in vain, allure those who live in error. Brought under bondage of one who overcomes you.

II Pet. 3:17 Don't fall from steadfastness by being led away with the error of the wicked.
A bad friendship can counteract much of the good training a child is receiving at home.

Num. 16:26 Depart from the tents of wicked men. Touch nothing of theirs, lest you be consumed in their sins.

Ps. 1:1 Don't <u>walk</u> in counsel of ungodly. Don't <u>stand</u> in way of sinners, don't <u>sit</u> in seat of scornful.
Stay away!

Pr. 9:6 Forsake foolish and live.

Pr. 14:7 Go from presence of foolish man when you don't perceive lips of knowledge in him.
Teach your child to leave the company of another child when his conversation demonstrates that he is foolish and rebellious.

Rom. 16:17 Mark those who cause divisions and offenses contrary to doctrine learned and <u>avoid them</u>!

II Thess. 3:14-15 Note man that doesn't obey the Word. Have no company with him, to his shame. Don't count as enemy, but admonish him as a brother.
Breaking off fellowship with a disobedient believer can be useful in bringing him to repentance.

Pr. 27:6 Wounds of friend are faithful. Kisses of enemy are deceitful.
One way to recognize a true friend is by his loving, gentle reproofs.

Pr. 23:6 Don't eat bread of him with evil eye.

What happens, or should happen, to the person who keeps company with bad friends:

Pr. 12:26 Way of wicked leads astray.

Pr. 13:20 Companion of fools will be destroyed.

Pr. 16:29 Led in a way that is not good.

Pr. 22:24-25 Snare for soul, will learn his ways.
All these verses remind us that friendship with sinners costs too much. Do not allow these friendships. (This is part of many good reasons for homeschooling.)

Pr. 28:7 Companion of gluttons brings shame to father.

Pr. 29:9 Wise man contending with fool leads to no peace. He either rages or laughs.

Pr. 29:25 Fear of man brings a snare.
Man does not have an unchanging standard. We can never please all men all the time. God's standards are always the same.

Titus 1:10-11 Stop mouth of subversive talker.
Do not allow your children, or a child who is visiting in your home, to speak subversively without reprimand.

I Cor. 5:11 Do not eat with professing believer who is a drunkard, fornicator, railer, idolater, covetous or extortioner.

II Tim. 2:22 Flee youthful lusts, pursue righteousness, faith, love, peace with other believers.
Encourage and nurture friendships and fellowship with other believers.

Isa. 1:23 Companion of thieves will be punished by God.

Ps. 50:18-20 Consent with thieves, will be punished.
A child who consents with a thief should be disciplined in the same way as the thief.

Rom. 12:16 Associate with the humble.
Help your child choose good friends.

Ps. 106:41 Will be ruled by heathen.
The person that compromises his beliefs and adopts the practices of the ungodly will end up being ruled by the ungodly. (i.e. the U.S.A.)

Josh. 23:13, Jg. 2:3 Bad relationships become snares.

Ezra 9:7 Will be delivered into captivity, confusion and the sword.

Num. 33:56 God will punish the disobedient believer instead of the ungodly.

Pr. 2:10-12 Wisdom and knowledge in soul will give discretion that will preserve, and understanding that will keep and deliver from the evil man and froward talker.
A solid knowledge of Scripture is the main weapon we can give our children as they learn to stand against evil.
Teach your child good, consistent Bible study habits.

Be consistent in family worship.

Develop a program of Scripture memory and review and be faithful with it.

Apply Scripture and read verses to the child whenever questions come up regarding the activities of friends.

Pr. 14:7 Go from the presence of a foolish man.

To what are bad friendships likened:

Pr. 6:27-28 Fire in bosom burning clothes, walking on coals will burn feet. This is what friendship with an evil woman is like.
The consequences are guaranteed!

Pr. 25:26 Troubled fountain, corrupt spring, the righteous falling before wicked.
Would you drink dirty water out of a drinking fountain?

Pr. 25:19 Confidence in unfaithful man is like broken tooth or foot out of joint.
How easy is it for your child to eat with a loose tooth?
Is it harder to eat an apple with your two front teeth missing?
Is it easy to walk on a sprained ankle?
Both the loose tooth and the foot out joint hurt and hinder us.

Num. 33:55 Irritants in eyes, thorns in flesh.
Can't ignore pain. There will be infection if the foreign body is not removed.

Hosea 7:8 Cake not turned.
Serve pancakes for breakfast that have only been cooked on one side.

Stories that illustrate the consequences of bad friendships:

Elisha and youths, II Kgs. 2:23-25 Companion of fools. Entire group was destroyed.

Korah and associates, Num. 16:1-33 Rebellion against authority, all were destroyed.

Solomon, I Kgs. 11:1-8 Wives turned heart away to other gods and evil. Kingdom taken away.

Rehoboam, I Kgs. 12:8-16 Departed from wisdom of elders' counsel, and took the advice of the younger counselors. Led to rebellion.

Jehoshaphat, II Chr. 18:3, 19:2, 20:35-37 Made alliance with Ahab, and with Ahaziah. Threatened in battle, ships were destroyed.

Judas Iscariot, Matt. 26:14-16 Allied himself with the enemies of Jesus. Led to his eventual suicide.

David with Uriah, II Sam. 11 False friendship.

The blessings of good friendships:

We need to teach our children about what to look for in good friends, and we need to teach them how to be a good friend. "A man that hath friends must show himself friendly." (Pr. 18:24a)

Pr. 13:20 Walk with the wise, will be wise.
A wise friend will help a child grow in wisdom.

Pr. 27:17 Good friend is like iron sharpening iron.

Pr. 11:13 Faithful spirit conceals a matter. He can be trusted.

Pr. 17:17 Friend loves at all times. He is loyal.

Pr. 27:6 Wounds of a friend are faithful. He is faithful to reprove.

Pr. 27:9 Friend's hearty counsel rejoices the heart like ointment and perfume.
Give your child a gift of perfume, bubble bath, etc. in recognition of his faithfulness as a friend.

Stories that illustrate the blessings of good friendships:

David and Jonathan, I Sam. 18:1 Jonathan was not jealous of or threatened by David. He recognized God's working through David.

David and Hushai, II Sam. 15:37 "Spy" for David, did what he asked of him.

Elijah and Elisha, II Kgs. 2:1-14 Did not forsake.

Naomi and Ruth, Ruth 1:16,17 A loyal servant to her mother-in-law.

Daniel and his three friends, Dan. 2:49 Daniel was faithful to ask favor for friends.

Jesus, Mary, Martha, and Lazarus, Jn. 11:33-36 Jesus wept with them, raised Lazarus from the dead.

David, II Sam. 9:1-13 Honored his friendship with Jonathan by protecting and caring for Mephibosheth.

David and Abiathar, I Sam. 22, esp. vs. 20-23 Honored Ahimelech's loyalty with loyalty and protection.

David, II Sam. 10:2 Wanted to befriend Hanun because of the kindness that Nahash had shown to him. Was disdained.

David, Solomon, and Hiram, I Kgs. 5 Mutually blessed in building the temple.
David, in his integrity, was blessed with many loyal friends. He was himself a faithful friend.

Shadrach, Meshach, and Abednego, Dan. 1 Loyal together in obeying God.

Verses to memorize:

2 Tim. 2:22 Flee also youthful lusts: but follow righteousness, faith, charity, peace, with them that call on the Lord out of a pure heart.

Pr. 16:29 A violent man enticeth his neighbour, and leadeth him into the way that is not good.

Ps. 1:1-2 Blessed is the man that walketh not in the counsel of the ungodly, nor standeth in the way of sinners, nor sitteth in the seat of the scornful. But his delight is in the law of the LORD; and in his law doth he meditate day and night.

1 Cor. 15:33 Do not be deceived: "Evil company corrupts good habits." (NKJV)

Rom. 12:21 Be not overcome of evil, but overcome evil with good.

Pr. 4:14-15 Do not enter the path of the wicked, and do not walk in the way of evil. Avoid it, do not travel on it; turn away from it and pass on. (NKJV)

Eph. 5:11 And have no fellowship with the unfruitful works of darkness, but rather reprove them.

Ps. 141:4 Incline not my heart to any evil thing, to practice wicked works with men that work iniquity: and let me not eat of their dainties.

Pr. 24:1 Be not thou envious against evil men, neither desire to be with them.

Ps. 119:63 I am a companion of all them that fear thee, and of them that keep thy precepts.

Pr. 1:10 My son, if sinners entice thee, consent thou not.

2 Cor. 6:14 Be ye not unequally yoked together with unbelievers: for what fellowship hath righteousness with unrighteousness? and what communion hath light with darkness?

Amos 3:3 Can two walk together, except they be agreed?

Poor Manners

(See Selfishness, Wastefulness/Carelessness,
Unkind Speech, Insensitivity, Pride)

Some of these principles have become real foreign to us. Our society has abandoned the practice of honoring others, especially elders. Our children are naturally somewhat reserved (or anti-social?), and some of these practices have really challenged their willingness to obey and humble themselves.

General information and commandments about this sin:

Pr. 25:17 Don't be in neighbor's house too often or he will grow weary of you and hate you.
Enforce this principle.
Make your home interesting and fun so that your children will not be tempted to spend too much time in someone else's house.

Pr. 27:14 Call loudly early in the morning, will be counted a curse.
Set an example of this by waking your children gently, and by being considerate of others if they are sleeping while you are up.
Send the child to bed when he is being too loud when others are resting or sleeping.

Lev. 19:32 Rise before elder, honor old man, fear God.
Teach child to stand before elders, give chair, serve.

Rom. 12:13 Distribute to needs of saints, hospitality.
Set an example of hospitality and openness in your home.
Teach your children the fundamentals of hospitality.

Rom. 12:10 In honor, prefer one another.
Teach your child to ask himself, "What can I do that will show that I prefer this person over myself?"

Gal. 6:10 Do good unto all, especially the household of faith.

Eph. 4:32 Be kind, tenderhearted.

Col. 3:12,14 Mercy, kindness, humility, meekness, longsuffering, charity.
Study a basic manners book, and make a list of manners that you want to practice in your family. Find verses that give a reason for following each of these rules (i.e. Lev. 19:32 tells us to stand before our elders.)

I Pet. 3:8 Compassion, courteous, pity.
Study Jesus' example of these qualities.

II Pet. 1:7 Faith + knowledge + virtue + godliness + brotherly kindness + charity.
Faith and knowledge are the foundation for these other traits.

Lk. 14:8-11 Take lower place.
Teach child to do this and commend him when he does.
Call the child to the front occasionally.

Phil 2:3 Let each esteem other better than self.
Teach the child to make the desires of others more important than his own.

Lk. 6:31 Do what you would like to have done to you.
Always ask the question, "What would I like someone to do for me in this situation?" Then do it!

I Pet. 4:9 Use hospitality without grudging.

Matt. 25:34-46 What we do unto man, we are doing unto Jesus.
Ask, "What do we want to do for Jesus?"

Heb. 13:2 Sometimes entertain angels when we entertain strangers.

Deut. 23:23a Keep promises.

Pr. 23:1-3 Knife to throat if given to appetite in front of ruler.
Practice good manners and self control in front of "ruler" (father) at home, and then practice the same in restaurants and when you are guests in the home of another.

Pr. 25:6-7 Don't advance yourself before the king, don't stand in place of great men. Will be put lower.
Humble a child by sending him to a lower spot when he advances himself instead of thinking of others.

Lk. 10:5-8 Instruction to disciples. Say, "Peace be to this house." Not go from house to house. Eat what is set before you.
Practice eating what is set before you at home and at the homes of others.

I Cor. 10:27-28 Show deference to others.
Teach to consider the feelings of others.

Matt. 5:7 Merciful will obtain mercy.

Matt. 5:42 Give to him that asketh, lend to the poor.

Rom. 15:1 Bear infirmities of weak, not please ourselves.
Child needs to learn to consider the weaknesses of others.

Rom. 15:2 Please neighbor for his good to edification.
"What will build this person up?"

I Cor. 13:4+ Love is kind, not unseemly, seeks not her own.

Gen. 31:35 Stand in presence of superiors.

Pr. 31:26 Law of kindness in the tongue of the virtuous woman.

I Cor. 9:19 Servant to all.

I Cor. 10:33 Seek profit of others that they may be saved.

I Thess. 5:18 Be thankful.
If child fails to express thanks for a gift or favor, remove the gift from him.

Phil 2:4 Look on the things of others.

I Sam. 16:7 Man looks on the outside.
Man judges other men by outward appearances. Good manners present a good outer appearance to man. (God, however, still sees our heart.)

Js. 1:19 Be swift to hear, slow to speak.
Teach the child to be a good and patient listener.

What happens, or should happen, to the inconsiderate person:

I Cor. 15:33 Evil company corrupts good habits.
Limit the child's friendships.
Teach the child from the poor habits of others.
Isolate the poor-mannered child temporarily. (i.e. send from the meal table, out of the game, etc.)

Titus 3:1 Be ready for every good work.
Be ready to serve and help others.
Give a "Servant's Award" to a serving child -- a certificate, a special privilege, honor, etc.

I Tim. 6:18 Do good, ready to give, willing to share.
Practice this in your home.

Blessings of the considerate person:

I Tim. 6:18-19 Store up good foundation for time to come.
Give a daughter a hope chest, and periodically give an item to put in it, based on her consideration of others.
Give dishes, clothes, etc. for the future.
Give a son a tool chest, and periodically add a tool, based on his

consideration of others.
*Give other various tools for the future (automotive, household,
  carpentry, etc.).*
Deposit money into long-term savings account.
Pass on special heirlooms (jewelry, letters, photographs, etc.).

Lk. 14:8-11 Humble will be exalted.
Have a special family party or feast in honor of the polite child.
Exalt the child with no chores for the day.
"Servant's Day," when family performs services for polite child.
Fly child's special "name flag" from the front porch.

Matt. 5:7 Merciful will obtain mercy.

Stories that illustrate the consequences of poor manners:

Elisha and youths, II Kgs. 2:23-25 Disrespect. Were mauled by bears.

Nabal, I Sam. 25:10,11 Ingratitude and lack of hospitality. Led to his
death.

Michal, II Sam. 6:16 Contempt for husband led to barrenness.

Hanun, II Sam. 10:1-5 Shunning David's sympathy. Led to battle,
shame, defeat.

Ammonites and Moabites, Deut. 23:3-4 Did not show hospitality to
Israelites. Would not enter congregation of the Lord, through the
tenth generation.

Stories that illustrate good manners and consideration:

Melchizedek to Abraham, Gen. 14:18

Abraham to angels, Gen. 18:1-8

Lot to angels, Gen. 19:1-11 Lot and family were delivered from city.

Laban to Abraham's servant, Gen. 24:31

Laban to Jacob, Gen. 29:13-14

Joseph to brothers, Gen. 43:31-34

Pharaoh to Jacob, Gen. 45:16-20, 47:7-12

Jethro to Moses, Ex. 2:20

Rahab to spies, Josh. 2:1-16 She and family were spared in conquest of Jericho.

Widow to Elijah, I Kgs. 17:10-24 Food was provided for her and her son.

Tanner to Peter, Acts 10:6,23

Lydia to Paul and Silas, Acts 16:15

Phebe to Paul, Rom. 16:2

David to Mephibosheth, II Sam. 9:1-10

Kenites, I Sam. 15:6 Spared by Saul because of their kindness to the Israelites when they came out of Egypt.

Verses to memorize:

Phil. 4:5 Let your gentleness be known to all men. The Lord is at hand. (NKJV)

1 Pet. 3:8 Finally, be ye all of one mind, having compassion one of another, love as brethren, be pitiful, be courteous.

1 Tim. 6:18 Let them do good, that they be rich in good works, ready to give, willing to share. (NKJV)

Rom. 12:10 Be kindly affectioned one to another with brotherly love; in honour preferring one another.

1 Pet. 2:17 Honour all men. Love the brotherhood. Fear God. Honour the king.

Teasing / Troublemaking

(See also Scornful, Unkind Speech, Lack of Compassion)

General information and commandments about this sin:

Pr. 11:27 Seek mischief, will come to him.
Take away the child's privilege of playing.
Remove from the situation in which he was teasing.
Give him extra work to do.

Pr. 15:21 Folly is joy to him who is destitute of wisdom.

Pr. 24:8 One who devises to do evil is a mischievous person.

Pr. 3:30 Strive not without cause, if man has done you no harm.

Pr. 10:23 Does mischief as sport.
A child should not be allowed to entertain himself by antagonizing others.
Do not allow a child to make sport of that which calls for sympathy and tenderness.

Pr. 10:10 Wink with eye causes trouble and sorrow.

Eph. 5:4 Not convenient. Give thanks.
Have the teasing child say something thankful to the victim of his teasing.

Pr. 21:23 Keep mouth, keep soul from trouble.
Enforce a period of silence upon the teasing child.

Ps. 34:14 Depart from evil and do good.
Do something good for the victim of teasing.
Give the teasing child work and projects of service to perform.

To what is the teaser likened:

Pr. 26:18-19 Madman throwing firebrands and arrows.
Doesn't know where they will hit or how much danger he will do.

Stories that illustrate troublemaking and taunting:

Goliath to David, I Sam. 17:43-44 Led to defeat.
Notice David's godly response.

Rabshekah, II Kgs. 18:28-35 Led to defeat.

Notice Hezekiah's response.

Soldiers to Jesus, Matt. 27:28-41
Notice Jesus' godly response to taunting.

Hannah and adversary, I Sam. 1:5-7 Taunted about her barrenness.

Youths and Elisha, II Kgs. 2:23-25 Teasing and disrespect led to their destruction.

Verses to memorize:

Phil. 4:8 Finally, brethren, whatever things are true, whatever things are noble, whatever things are just, whatever things are pure, whatever things are lovely, whatever things are of good report, if there is any virtue and if there is anything praiseworthy; meditate on these things. (NKJV)

Matt. 19:19a Thou shalt love thy neighbour as thyself.

Ps. 34:14 Depart from evil, and do good; seek peace, and pursue it.

Foolishness vs. Wisdom

Compare a fool and a wise, prudent man. Use the worksheet provided at the back of this book to go through the following Scriptures together as a family. Make as many copies of this sheet as you need to to help you in organizing these categories.

Compare the fool and the wise man in the following categories: knowledge, mouth, relationship to mother and father, view of self, view of God, response to reproof, relationship to others, future, discipline, blessings and cursings, what they are likened to.

The verses listed are just to get you started. Get out your concordance and topical Bible and start digging!

General information and commandments about this sin:

Pr. 1:22	Pr. 10:14	Pr. 10:23
Pr. 14:3	Pr. 14:7	Pr. 14:15
Pr. 14:6	Pr. 15:7	Pr. 15:14
Pr. 15:20	Pr. 17:7	Pr. 15:5
Pr. 17:24	Pr. 12:11	Pr. 12:16
Pr. 12:23	Pr. 13:16	Pr. 14:8
Pr. 14:33	Pr. 14:35	Pr. 17:10
Pr. 17:21	Pr. 19:1	Pr. 19:3
Pr. 19:10	Pr. 21:20	Pr. 22:3
Pr. 12:15	Pr. 18:7	Lk. 11:39,40
Pr. 27:22	Pr. 29:11	Pr. 30:22
Pr. 28:26	Pr. 20:3	Pr. 13:19
Ec. 7:9	Ec. 10:14	Ec. 5:3
Pr. 3:35	Ps. 14:1	Pr. 18:2
Pr. 18:6		

The effect a fool has on his environment:

Pr. 10:8,10	Pr. 21:20	Pr. 20:3
Pr. 17:21	Pr. 17:25	Pr. 10:1
Pr. 18:6	Pr. 14:1	

What happens, or should happen, to the fool:

Pr. 10:8,10	Pr. 10:13	Pr. 10:21
Pr. 14:18	Pr. 10:17	Pr. 12:8

Pr. 14:7   Pr. 17:10   Pr. 14:35
Pr. 19:3   Pr. 19:29   Pr. 22:3
Pr. 24:7   Ps. 5:5   Js. 1:5
Ps. 107:17   Ec. 10:12

To what is the fool likened:

Pr. 11:22   Pr. 17:12   Pr. 26:1
Pr. 26:3   Pr. 26:9   Pr. 26:11
Ps. 49:13-14   Ec. 2:13   Ec. 7:6
Ec. 10:1

Stories about fools and foolishness:

Matt. 25:1-13   Lk. 12:16-20   I Sam. 25
I Kgs. 12:4-16   Matt. 7:24-27   Gen. 6:5-7
Ex. 5-14   II Chr. 28

General information and commandments about the wise man:

Pr. 8:12   Pr. 14:15
Pr. 15:5   Pr. 14:18   Amos 5:13
Pr. 22:3   Pr. 15:5   Pr. 12:23
Pr. 10:14   Pr. 15:7   Pr. 12:15
Pr. 14:6   Pr. 15:14   Pr. 15:20
Pr. 17:24   Pr. 12:16   Pr. 13:16
Pr. 14:33   Pr. 17:10   Pr. 21:20
Pr. 12:15

Blessings of the prudent:

Pr. 2:11-15   Pr. 2:16   Pr. 3:5-6
Pr. 3:7-8   Pr. 3:16-17   Pr. 3:14-15
Pr. 3:1-2   Pr. 3:23   Pr. 3:24
Pr. 4:8   Pr. 4:10   Pr. 4:12
Pr. 9:11   Pr. 10:8   Pr. 8:21
Pr. 16:16   Ec. 7:12   Ec. 7:19
Ec. 9:18   Pr. 15:20   Pr. 14:35
Pr. 15:24   Pr. 23:24-25   Pr. 23:25
Pr. 29:3

To what is the wise man likened:

Pr. 8:11	Pr. 16:16	Ec. 2:13
Ec. 7:12	Ec. 7:19	Ec. 9:18

Stories about wise men:

I Sam. 16:18	II Chr. 2:12	Gen. 32:3-23
Gen. 41:39-47	Jg. 8:1-3	

Wickedness vs. Righteousness

Compare the wicked man and the righteous man. Use the comparison worksheet provided at the back of this book. Go through the verses and categorize them under the following topics: what they are likened to, knowledge, mouth, view of God, cursings and blessings, view of self, response to reproof, relationship to parents, relationship to others, future, discipline, etc.

Make as many copies as you need of the worksheet to organize your studies.

The verses listed are just a sampling. A concordance and a topical Bible will give you lots more to work with!

General information and commandments about wickedness:

Pr. 11:20	Pr. 12:10	Pr. 12:12
Pr. 16:4	Pr. 17:11	Pr. 19:28
Pr. 21:7	Pr. 21:10	Pr. 12:5
Pr. 4:16-17	Pr. 21:29	Pr. 29:6
Ps. 10:2-11	Rom. 8:7-9	

What happens, or should happen, to the wicked:

Ec. 2:24-26	Pr. 20:26	Pr. 21:12
Pr. 21:18	Pr. 21:27	Pr. 22:5
Pr. 22:8	Pr. 28:1-5	Ps. 9:15-16
Pr. 28:12	Pr. 28:18	Ps. 37:17
Pr. 28:28	Pr. 29:2	Pr. 29:16
Pr. 10:27	Pr. 13:21-22	Ps. 11:6
Ps. 1:4-6	Pr. 10:24	Pr. 15:29
Pr. 15:6	Pr. 15:8	Rom. 2:7-10
Pr. 13:25	Job 20:5-29	Ps. 49:14
Ps. 7:15	Ps. 21:9-10	Rom. 8:6
Gal. 6:8	II Th. 3:6	Isa. 59:8
Job 24:20	Job 24:24	Ps. 73:3-4
Ps. 73:17-20	Pr. 2:22	Pr. 5:22-23
Ps. 37:10	Pr. 10:27-28	Pr. 11:5-6
Pr. 11:8	Pr. 11:10	Isa. 57:21
Pr. 14:19	Pr. 10:2-3	Pr. 11:3
Pr. 11:19	Pr. 12:13	Pr. 17:11
Jn. 8:34	Jer. 16:3-4	Ps. 32:10

To what is the wicked likened:

Pr. 25:4-5	Ps. 1	Hos. 8:7
Ps. 17:11-12	Isa. 56:10-11	Ps. 37:2
Ps. 49:14	Job 21:18	Isa. 57:20-21
Job 24:20, 24	Mal. 4:3	Matt. 13:48
Zeph. 1:17	Matt. 15:14	Jer. 6:28
Ezek. 2:6	Isa. 14:19	Isa. 57:20
Matt. 3:12	Jude 12-13	Lk. 6:43
Pr. 28:15	Pr. 26:11	II Pet. 2:17
II Pet. 2:22	Ps. 119:119	Ezek. 22:18-19
Hos. 13:3	Ps. 118:12	Isa. 1:30
Ps. 21:9	Hos. 7:4	Matt. 7:26
Isa. 9:18	Ps. 92:7	Ps. 37:35
Jer. 8:6	Ps. 83:13	Ps. 68:2
Hos. 13:3	Isa. 50:9	Pr. 10:25
Pr. 26:23	Jer. 6:30	Matt. 13:5
Ps. 58:4	Matt. 23:33	Matt. 13:38
Mal. 4:1	Matt. 7:6	

Blessings of the righteous:

Pr. 16:7	Pr. 15:29	Pr. 15:6
Pr. 11:3	Pr. 11:4-6	Pr. 11:8
Pr. 11:11	Pr. 11:18	Pr. 11:19
Pr. 11:21	Pr. 12:12	Pr. 13:21
Pr. 10:24	Pr. 10:30	Pr. 14:22
Pr. 14:26	Isa. 32:17	Pr. 19:23
Pr. 29:6	Ps. 32:10	II Tim. 4:8
Rom. 2:7-10	Ps. 37:26	Ps. 37:31
Ps. 112:1-10	Isa. 54:13	Jn. 15:14
Job 36:7	Gal. 6:8	Ps. 84:11
Ps. 121:3-8	Ps. 128:1-6	Ps. 145:18-21
Pr. 3:1-10	Isa. 54:14,17	Pr. 21:21
Pr. 29:25	Isa. 51:11	

To what is the righteous likened:

Isa. 58:11	Isa. 44:4	Ps. 1:3
Jer. 17:7-8	Ps. 92:12	Matt. 5:13
Matt. 3:12	Matt. 13:29-30	Ps. 103:5

Ps. 52:8
Hos. 14:6-7
Zech. 9:16
Matt. 7:24
Dan. 12:3
Mal. 3:17
II Tim. 2:3-4
II Tim. 2:5
Isa. 40:11

Ps. 68:13
Ex. 19:5
Jer. 24:2-7
Jg. 5:31
Matt. 5:14
Job 23:10
I Cor. 9:24
Ps. 78:52
Pr. 28:1

Mic. 5:7
Ps. 42:1
Matt. 13:47-50
Matt. 13:43
Phil. 2:15
Lam. 4:2
Heb. 12:1
Matt. 25:1-13

The law of the Lord is perfect, converting the soul: the testimony of the Lord is sure making wise the simple.

The statues of the Lord are right, rejoicing the heart: the commandment of the Lord is pure, enlightening the eyes.

The fear of the Lord is clean, enduring for ever: the judgments of the Lord are true and righteous altogether.

More to be desired are they than gold yea, than much fine gold: sweeter also than honey and the honeycomb.

Moreover by them is thy servant warned: and in keeping of them there is great reward. Ps. 19:7-11

Comparison Worksheet

Comparing : _____

Reference		Reference	

Sample

Comparison Worksheet

Comparing : <u>What the Wicked and Righteous are Likened to :</u>

Reference	Righteous	Reference	Wicked
Pr. 28:1	Bold as lion	Ps. 17:11-12	Lurking lion
Matt. 3:12 13:29,30	Wheat	Ps. 1	Chaff
Hos. 14:7	Corn		Tares
		Job 21:18	Stubble
Mal. 3:17	Jewels	Mal. 4:3	Ashes
Job 23:10	Gold	Jer. 6:30	Reprobate silver
Ps. 42:1	Thirsty deer	Mt. 7:6	Swine
S.S. 2:2	Lily among thorns	Ps. 118:12	Fire of thorns
Isa. 58:11	Unfailing spring	2 Pet. 2:17	Well without water

Resources

We offer here a brief list of resources our family has enjoyed most as we strive to bring Scripture into our home. These have helped us in applying some of the ideas we have mentioned in this book: telling stories from history and personal life, teaching Bible study methods to our children, having consistent family worship time, enjoying good quality children's music that teaches Biblical truths, memorizing Scripture.

Bible Study Materials:

The New Life Version Bible

Christian Literature International, PO Box 777, Canby, OR, 97013
(800) 324-9734, www.newlifebible.org

This is a very readable translation, not a paraphrase. It has a limited vocabulary. Difficult words are broken down into simple, meaningful phrases. For example, "the righteous" is translated "the man who does what is right." We have used this Bible quite a bit for family Bible reading times and for our younger children's Bible reading.

The Picture Bible

Christian Book Distributors, P.O. Box 7000, Peabody, MA 01961-7000, (800) 247-4784, www.christianbook.com

We have worn out our first copy of this! We read it a lot together. 266 stories from creation through Revelation. Comic-strip style illustrations, easy dialogue, and good coverage of Old Testament history stories. 766 pages.

Reading and Understanding the Bible
The Catechism for Young Children, 2 volumes

Vic Lockman, 233 Rogue River Hwy, #360, Grants Pass, OR 97527, (541) 479-1779, www.viclockman.com
Catechism for Young Children also available from **Doorposts**.

Great cartoon-illustrated books from Vic Lockman! *Reading and Understanding the Bible* discusses rules for literal language, figures of speech, parables, allegories, symbols and types, etc. *The Catechism for Young Children* books have been great for teaching basic doctrine. Our children love all Mr. Lockman's books.

Seven Steps to Bible Skills in Youth

Virgil W. Hensley, Inc., 6116 E. 32nd St., Tulsa, OK 74135
(800) 288-8520, www.hensleypublishing.com

How to *use* the Bible. History of how we got our Bible; overview of the Bible's organization; and instruction on reading Bible references and using concordances, marginal notes, and summaries.

MEMLOK Bible Memory System

MEMLOK Sales, 420 Montwood, La Habra, CA 90631-7411
(800) 373-1947, Canada (714) 738-0949, www.memlock.com
Available in NAS, NIV or KJV.

A topical memory program that uses flashcards with visual clues to help memory. Memorize one new verse a week, five minutes a day with extensive review, so that verses are retained. Over 700 verses to keep you memorizing for over 10 years.

Music:

Why Can't I See God?
Go to the Ant
Guard Your Heart

Available from **Doorposts** or Judy Rogers, 4865 Highway 138, Stockbridge, GA 30281, (678) 210-0272, www.judyrogers.com

These albums by Judy Rogers contain good music with solid Bible truths. *Why Can't I See God?* is catechism set to music! *Go to the Ant* and *Guard Your Heart* bring out themes from Proverbs.

Patch the Pirate

Majesty Music, (800) 334-1071, 733 Wade Hampton Blvd., Greenville, SC 29609, www.majestymusic.com
Available on cassettes and CD's.

We *like* Patch the Pirate! Each entertaining story centers on a theme (i.e. choosing friends and servanthood). Fun songs, good humor, great lessons to learn.

Just-for-Kids/Donut Man Tapes

Integrity Music Just-for-Kids, 1000 Cody Rd, Mobile, AL 36695
(800) 533-6912, www.integritymusic.com

Fun, lively music tapes that each focus on a central theme (i.e. love, helping, praise).

Stories:

Tiger and Tom and Other Stories for Boys
The King's Daughter and Other Stories for Girls

Grace & Truth, 3406 Summit Blvd., Sand Springs, OK 74063
(918) 245-1500, www.graceandtruthbooks.com

We have enjoyed these turn-of-the-century stories. Both books contain character-building stories that illustrate biblical values and principles.

Little House Series

Christian Book Distributors, P.O. Box 7000, Peabody, MA 01961-7000, (800) 247-4784, www.christianbook.com

The classic pioneer stories. We're enjoying these a second time since we have more little ones to read to. Full of good lessons on character.

Janette Oke's Classic Collection

Christian Book Distributors, P.O. Box 7000, Peabody, MA 01961-7000, (800) 247-4784, www.christianbook.com

There are 12 books in this series. While enjoying the adventures of different animals, we also learn about character and the consequences of sin.

Object Lessons from Nature:

Character Sketches

Institute in Basic Life Principles, Box 1, Oak Brook, IL 60522-3001, (630)-323-9800 www.iblp.org

There are 3 volumes in this set of beautifully illustrated books that combine history, nature, and science to teach us character lessons. We have really enjoyed these. IBLP also carries smaller character booklets and posters.

History:

"Little Bear" Wheeler Tapes

Mantle Ministries, 228 Still Ridge, Bulverde, TX 78163
(830) 438-3777, www.MantleMinistries.com

   12 volumes of dramatic historical accounts with Biblical application. Covering American history from the 1300's to the 1800's, each volume includes twenty stories with music and sound effects. "Little Bear" helps us see God's providence, and the many lessons we can learn from history. Our boys love these! Video storytelling tapes also available.

Games:

The Richest Christian

Ornament Publications, 2301 S. Country Club Road, Garland, TX 75041-2125, www.ornament-pub.com

   Learn Biblical principles of how to earn and use money with a fun game that also encourages the memorization of many Proverbs. Our children are especially impressed with the big shiney gold "Eternal Treasures" cards!

History:

"Little Bear" Wheeler Tapes

(Mantle Ministries, 140 Grand Oak Drive, San Antonio, TX 78232)
   12 volumes of dramatic historical accounts with Biblical application. Taken from the 1300's to the 1800's, each volume includes twenty stories with music and sound effects. "Little Bear" help us see God's providence, and the many lessons we can learn from history. Our boys love these! Video storytelling tapes also available.

Games:

The Richest Christian

(Ornament Publications, 2301 Country Club Road, Garland, TX 75041, $23.00 postpaid.)
   Learn Biblical principles of how to earn and use money with a fun game that also encourages the memorization of many Proverbs. Our children are especially impressed with the big shiney gold "Eternal Treasures" cards!

DOORPOSTS ORDERING INFORMATION

Plants Grown Up

A notebook full of goals and projects especially designed for sons on their way to manhood. Choose from hundreds of activities and Bible study ideas to help your sons prepare for their future roles as employees, employers, husbands, fathers, church and community leaders.

Designed to use throughout the years as your son matures, activities are appropriate for a very young boy and on until he is ready to launch into career, marriage, and raising your grandchildren! **$43**, *535 pages, spiral-bound. Includes chapters on:*

Family Worship	*Seeking Counsel*	*Manners*
Planning & Organizing	*Providing for Others*	*Serving Others*
Taking Initiative	*Godly Friendships*	*Bible Study & Prayer*
Overseeing Others	*Community Leadership*	*Protecting*
Household Repairs	*Persevering in Trials*	*Courtship*
Discipline of Children	*Hospitality*	*Sharing the Gospel*
Conquering Laziness	*Benevolence*	*Finances*
Fleeing Temptation	*Communication Skills*	*& much more!*

Polished Cornerstones

A 600-page book full of goals and projects especially designed for parents and their daughters. Choose from hundreds of activities and Bible study ideas to help your daughters prepare for their future roles as friends, homemakers, wives, mothers, church and community members. One copy works for all daughters of all ages! **$43**, *spiral-bound. 51 chapters on:*

Loyalty	*Listening*	*Contentment*
Thrift	*Prudence*	*Submission*
Goals	*Diligence*	*Stewardship*
Speech	*Single Life*	*Hospitality*
Purity	*Manners*	*Encouragement*
Mercy	*Teaching*	*Home Skills*
Justice	*Courtship*	*Peacemaking*
Respect	*Mothering*	*& much more!*

If-Then Chart

This is a chart designed to help you be more consistent in disciplining your children. The chart is divided into 3 columns. The left-hand column lists common areas of misbehavior (arguing, complaining, etc.), each illustrated with a simple cartoon. The center column gives a Scripture verse related to each sin. The third column is blank, for you to write in the agreed-upon consequences for each misbehavior. Instruction sheet offers suggestions for discipline. This chart has made discipline much easier in our home! **$5.00**

The Blessing Chart

This chart is designed to help you acknowledge and reward godly attitudes and behavior, in a way that is patterned after Scripture. Based on the ideas listed in **For Instruction in Righteousness,** *this chart comes with a booklet of ideas for rewards that relate to God's rewards in our lives. Left-hand column lists good character qualities, with cartoon drawings. Center column quotes Scripture verses that tell how God blesses us when these qualities are present in our lives. This chart offers a good balance for Moms like me who specialize in seeing what the kids are doing wrong!* **$5.50**

Blessing Chart Patterns

Step-by-step instructions and patterns for crowns, medals-of-honor, flags, and award certificates to photocopy for your own use. Easy, quick ideas for busy Moms with kids who like fun, glittery, make-you-feel-important stuff! **$4.00**

The Brother-Offended Checklist

A chart-and-book set that helps teach your children to follow Scriptural instructions when responding to those who have wronged or offended them. Instructs the offender regarding confession and repentance of sin. Chart is illustrated in cartoon-strip style, with steps for the offended and the offender to follow when they have a disagreement. Book expands on each step and refers to illustrative Bible stories, and gives Scriptural principles to help parents act as righteous judges when dealing with disagreements among family members and friends. Also includes memory verses to arm your child against temptation. **$8.50**

Service Opportunities Chart

A chart to simplify chore assignments in your household. Divided into 20 sections, you can list up to 40 of your most frequent chores. We provide 56 cartoon illustrations that you can color, cut, and glue next to each chore listing. The right-hand side of the chart can be left blank, or you can write in wages if you choose to pay for chores. Movable name stickers allow you to assign different chores each day to each child. A simple, flexible, inexpensive system. **$5.00**

Family Circles

This little kit could change the whole atmosphere of your home. It is designed to help you set aside time each day for each of your children and for your spouse.

It is simply two circles mounted on a piece of paper. The large circle is divided into sections for each child in your family. The smaller circle is divided into sections listing activities to share with your spouse.

Around the outside of the large circle different activities are written. As you **turn the circle each day,** *it will tell you what special thing to do with each person that day.*

This kit gives you **circles** *already drawn and marked for dividing into the desired number of sections, suggestions for profitable* **activities** *to rotate,* **drawings** *to paste onto each section so that eager non-readers will know what they "get to do with Daddy today,"* **instructions** *for assembly. All you need is scissors, ruler, pen, paste, and a brad fastener!* **$4.50**

Checklist for Parents

A series of 25 questions designed to **help parents examine themselves in light of God's Word.** *Organized under 6 areas of responsibility (love, prayer, instruction, protection, provision, and example), each question is followed by Scripture verses which explain what God requires of us as parents. Use as a tool for prayer times, Scripture memorization, preparing your children for parenthood.* **$3.50**

Stewardship Street

Discusses 7 different suggested budget categories for children, gives patterns and instructions for making a "street" of savings boxes out of milk cartons. Each box looks like a different house, store, or business along a street. Also includes patterns for making a memory visual that will help your children memorize verses that tell about God's plan for our money, and a record-keeping form for figuring percentages of earnings for each budget category. We've seen wonderful results with our children, using this system. **$5.50**

A Day of Delight

Dozens of creative ideas to help make Sunday a unique and joyous day of rest and celebration for the whole family (even Mom!) Ideas for preparing for Sunday throughout the week, making mealtimes special but easy, creating a treasure chest of special Sunday-only toys and books, and lots of ideas for toys, games, activities, and projects that focus on Scripture, fellowship, and meditation. Good source of ideas for family worship times, too! Our children count the days until Sunday now, since we started putting these ideas into action. **$5.00**

The Mighty Acts of God

A collection of ideas to inspire some **simple** *drama times in your family. Ideas for easy costumes (including patterns for almost-instant tunic and cape), simple props, fun meals to go with some Bible stories, and Scripture references and suggestions for acting out over 50 different Bible stories. These are* **simple** *ideas -- no scripts, no rehearsals -- just quick, spontaneous family play times that help teach Scripture's truths. Also includes ideas for acting out Bible stories with Legos, Playmobil, Fisher-Price, building blocks, stuffed animals, dolls, and other toys.* **$5.50**.

The Armor of God Patterns

Simple patterns and instructions for making a cloth "Breastplate of Righteousness," "Helmet of Salvation," "Belt of Truth," and "Shoes of the Gospel of Peace." Also a wooden "Sword of the Spirit" and "Shield of Faith." A durable alternative to plastic armor. **$3.50**

Watchwords

12 verses written in beautiful hand calligraphy to help you remember, discuss, and apply Scripture in your family's everyday activities. Frame and hang these verses throughout your house; we tried to include ones that would be appropriate in all different areas of the house. Verses include: Gal. 6:9, Ps. 101:3, Ps. 90:12, Ps. 141:3, Pr. 31:25-27, Ps. 121:3, Eph. 4:26, I Cor. 14:40, Ps. 127:4, Pr. 17:1, Lk. 6:31, Pr. 20:3. Off-white parchment. **$8.00** *per set*

Go-to-the-Ant Chart

This chart arms parents with Scripture for working with any child that needs training in diligence and faithfulness. Verses for easy reference on every area of laziness we could think of. Take your child to the chart, identify his slothful action or attitude, read what God says about it, and pray for His strength to obey. **$4.50**

Ruby Doll Kit

Make a delightful family of pocket-size dolls for your daughter while you teach her basic hand-sewing skills, study portions of Proverbs 31, and enjoy times of good fellowship together. Kit includes all fabrics and materials to make "Ruby," the Proverbs 31 woman in her purple silk and tapestry, and her husband "Victor" and their family of children, all clothed in scarlet. Bible studies deal with an overview of Proverbs 31, kind speech, diligence, and reaching out to the needy. Lots of fun and learning! **$27** *for complete kit* **$14** *for additional materials packets*

Order Form

Qty		Price	Total
	For Instruction in Righteousness (Spiral Bound)	28.00	
	Plants Grown Up	43.00	
	Polished Cornerstones	43.00	
	As Unto The Lord	15.00	
	If-Then Chart	5.00	
	Blessing Chart	5.50	
	Blessing Chart Patterns	4.00	
	Brother Offended Checklist	8.50	
	Go-To-The-Ant	4.50	
	Checklist For Parents	3.50	
	Family Circles	4.50	
	Day of Delight	5.00	
	Mighty Acts of God	5.50	
	Armor of God Patterns	3.50	
	Service Opportunities	5.00	
	Stewardship Street	5.50	
	Ruby Doll Kit	27.00	
	Virtuous Woman (Prov. 31 Study Guide)	5.00	
	Catalogs	FREE	
	Total amount of order		
	Postage and handling (see box below)		
	TOTAL AMOUNT ENCLOSED (U.S. Funds)		

Shipping	
$5.00 & under	$2
$5.01 - 15	$3
$15.01 - 30	$4
$30.01 - 50	$5
$50.01 & over	$6
Foreign Add	$3

Overseas - sent surface or write for airmail rates

Name: _____
Address: _____
Telephone: _____

Mail payment and order to: **Doorposts**
5905 SW Lookingglass Dr., Gaston, OR 97119
(503) 357-4749   www.Doorposts.net

Order Form

Qty		Price	Total
	For Instruction in Righteousness (Spiral Bound)	28.00	
	Plants Grown Up	43.00	
	Polished Cornerstones	43.00	
	As Unto The Lord	15.00	
	If-Then Chart	5.00	
	Blessing Chart	5.50	
	Blessing Chart Patterns	4.00	
	Brother Offended Checklist	8.50	
	Go-To-The-Ant	4.50	
	Checklist For Parents	3.50	
	Family Circles	4.50	
	Day of Delight	5.00	
	Mighty Acts of God	5.50	
	Armor of God Patterns	3.50	
	Service Opportunities	5.00	
	Stewardship Street	5.50	
	Ruby Doll Kit	27.00	
	Virtuous Woman (Prov. 31 Study Guide)	5.00	
	Catalogs	FREE	
	Total amount of order		
	Postage and handling (see box below)		
	TOTAL AMOUNT ENCLOSED (U.S. Funds)		

Shipping	
$5.00 & under	$2
$5.01 - 15	$3
$15.01 - 30	$4
$30.01 - 50	$5
$50.01 & over	$6
Foreign Add	$3

Overseas - sent surface or write for airmail rates

Name: _____
Address: _____
Telephone: _____

Mail payment and order to: **Doorposts**
5905 SW Lookingglass Dr., Gaston, OR 97119
(503) 357-4749   www.Doorposts.net